THE THRESHOLD CONCEPTS OF LEGAL WRITING

THE THRESHOLD CONCEPTS OF LEGAL WRITING

Kristen K. Tiscione &
Melissa H. Weresh

with contributing editors

Linda L. Berger, Kirsten K. Davis,
Ruth Anne Robbins, and David I.C. Thomson

CAROLINA ACADEMIC PRESS
Durham, North Carolina

Library of Congress Cataloging-in-Publication Data

Names: Tiscione, Kristen Konrad, 1959- author | Weresh, Melissa H. author
Title: The threshold concepts of legal writing / Kristen K. Tiscione, Melissa H. Weresh.
Description: Durham : Carolina Academic Press, 2026. | Includes bibliographical references and index.
Identifiers: LCCN 2026006858 | ISBN 9781531031572 paperback | ISBN 9781531031589 ebook
Subjects: LCSH: Legal composition | Law—Study and teaching | Law—Study and teaching | Writing—Study and teaching | LCGFT: Law materials
Classification: LCC K100 .T57 2026
LC record available at https://lccn.loc.gov/2026006858

Carolina Academic Press
700 Kent Street
Durham, North Carolina 27701
(919) 489-7486
www.cap-press.com

Printed in the United States of America

To our core group and contributing editors,
Linda, Kirsten, Ruth Anne, and David,
and our legal writing colleagues both far and near

—Kristen Tiscione & Melissa Weresh

Contents

About the Authors

Linda Berger is a Professor of Law Emerita at UNLV. Her scholarship and teaching center on legal rhetoric. She is a series editor of the U.S. Feminist Judgments Series; co-editor of *U.S. Feminist Judgments: Rewritten Opinions of the United States Supreme Court* (Cambridge 2016); and co-author *of Law & Rhetoric: A Primer* (Carolina 2024), *Legal Persuasion: A Rhetorical Approach to the Science* (Routledge 2018), and *Legal Research: Examples and Explanations* (Wolters Kluwer 2016).

A leader in discipline building and professional development initiatives, Prof. Berger received the inaugural ALWD Linda Berger Lifetime Achievement Award. She served as President of the Legal Writing Institute (LWI) and was a founder and editor-in-chief of *Legal Communication & Rhetoric: JALWD.*

Leslie P. Culver is a Professor (Clinical) of Law at University of Utah S.J. Quinney College of Law. Her work focuses on legal reasoning and conscious identity performance. She has taught legal writing and analysis for over fifteen years. Within legal writing, she uses contemporary argumentation theories and rhetoric to explore the overlap between identity performance and legal reasoning. Within the broader profession, she relies on communication theories to examine identity performance in the legal profession.

She has co-authored *I Wish I Read This Book Before Law School: Advice from Top Professors on How to Adjust, Succeed, and Thrive*, and is the editor of *Identity, Power & Professional Responsibility: Selected Readings and Materials* (forthcoming 2026). She is also a national presenter on identity performance and cultural awareness, recipient of a Fulbright Specialist Award, and a Research Fellow (2025–2028) with University of Free State (Bloemfontein, South Africa) where her collaborative work focuses on identity performance as a human dignity philosophy.

Kirsten K. Davis is a Professor of Law at Stetson University College of Law in Gulfport, Florida. She holds a J.D. from The Ohio State University Moritz College of Law and Ph.D. in Human Communication from the Hugh Downs School of Human Communication at Arizona State University. She has taught and studied legal communication and rhetoric for twenty-five years, authoring numerous articles and essays in the field. Currently, she is exploring the intersection of generative AI and legal writing practice and pedagogy.

Dr. Davis founded the Institute for the Advancement of Legal Communication at Stetson University College of Law and served as its director for a decade. She has served on the Boards of Directors for both the Legal Writing Institute and the Association of Legal Writing Directors. She is an editor and co-author *of Classical Rhetoric and Contemporary Law*, published in 2024 by the University of Alabama Press. Dr. Davis received the 2026 AALS Section Award for the Section on Legal Writing, Reasoning and Research, as well as Stetson's Excellence in Teaching Award in 2017, its Homer and Dolly Hand Award for Faculty Research in 2022, and its Dickerson-Brown Award for Faculty Excellence in Faculty Scholarship in 2024.

Sherri L. Keene is a Professor of Law, Legal Practice at Georgetown University Law Center and previously directed the legal writing program at University of Maryland Carey School of Law. Prior to teaching, Professor Keene represented clients in criminal appeals at the Federal Public Defender's Office for the District of Maryland. Professor Keene writes at the intersection of advocacy, psychology, and criminal law and considers how implicit biases can influence perceptions of legal actors in the criminal justice system. Her work often considers the role of storytelling in legal decision-making. Professor Keene was an inaugural recipient of the Association of Legal Writing Directors Diversity Award in 2021 and elected to the Board of Directors of the Legal Writing Institute in 2026.

Derek Kiernan-Johnson is a Teaching Professor of Law at the University of Colorado. He studies, among other things, the power and ethics of typography and design in legal persuasion. He is the author of *Telling Through Type: Typography and Narrative in Legal Briefs* (J. ALWD 2010) and regularly consults and lectures on matters typographical. He has also been instrumental in the founding of the applied legal storytelling movement through biennial conferences and scholarly contributions.

Kristen Murray is the Interim Dean and a Professor of Law at Temple University, Beasley School of Law. Her research interests include legal education, education law and policy, legal writing and persuasion, and alternative dispute resolution. She is the Managing Editor of *Legal Communication & Rhetoric: JALWD* and a member of the Board of Directors of the Legal Writing Institute, for which she also serves as Secretary. She earned her J.D. from Georgetown Law and her M.A. in Education and Human Development from George Washington University.

Julie Oseid is a Professor of Law at the University of St. Thomas School of Law in Minneapolis, Minnesota. She teaches Lawyering Skills courses and (In)Famous American Criminal Trials. She is the author of *Communicators-in-Chief: Lessons in Persuasion from Five Eloquent American Presidents* (Carolina Academic Press 2017). Her scholarship explores what lawyers can learn from great fiction and non-fiction writers. She is the recipient of the 2007 Warren E. Burger Prize. She loves teaching; she was delighted to be selected by students as the 2018 Professor of the Year.

Ruth Anne Robbins is a Professor of Law at Rutgers Law School, in Camden, New Jersey. She has taught legal communication and rhetoric in the first-year and upper-division curricula. She also teaches a Legislative & Policy Advocacy Clinic, focusing primarily on gender-based and domestic violence issues. She has received national, regional, statewide, campus-based, and student-voted awards for her teaching and service. These include the Thomas F. Blackwell Memorial Award for Outstanding Achievement in the Field of Legal Writing, an award co-presented by two national organizations; and the Lindback Foundation Award for Distinguished Teaching, an award presented at universities across the Philadelphia region.

Much of Professor Robbins' scholarship explores "applied legal storytelling," a field she helped found. She also writes about legal-document design, and one of her articles appeared by invitation on the website of the Seventh Circuit Court of Appeals. She has served as the president of the Legal Writing Institute and was a longtime editor-in-chief of *Legal Communication & Legal Rhetoric: JALWD*. She still serves as an emerita editor-in-chief.

JoAnne Sweeny is a Professor of Law at the University of Louisville, Louis D. Brandeis School of Law where she teaches, among other things, Lawyering Skills and Professional Identity Formation. Her scholarship focuses on feminist jurisprudence, freedom of expression, and legal storytelling.

David I. C. Thomson is a Professor of Practice and the John C. Dwan Professor of Online Learning at the University of Denver's Sturm College of Law, where he has taught legal writing and civil discovery law for twenty-two years. Professor Thomson has written and presented extensively on the intersections of technology, pedagogy, assessment, and legal education—in the U.S. and internationally. David is the author of *The Way Forward for Legal Education* (Carolina Academic Press, 2023) and *Law School 2.0: Legal Education for a Digital Age* (LexisNexis/Matthew Bender 2009). He is also Series Editor of the Skills & Values hybrid law school textbooks published by Carolina Academic Press. David was the recipient of the University of Denver's Distinguished Teaching Award in 2012.

Kristen K. Tiscione is a Professor of Law, Legal Practice, at Georgetown University Law Center, where she has been teaching legal writing, upper-level writing seminars, and public speaking in the J.D. and LL.M. programs for thirty years. Prior to joining the faculty at Georgetown, she specialized in commercial litigation at Kirkland & Ellis in Washington, D.C. Her scholarly interests include legal writing at the intersection of law, rhetoric, and composition and the role of legal writing in legal education. She is the author *of Legal Writing: From Advice to Advocacy* (West 2021), an editor and co-author of *Classical Rhetoric and Contemporary Law* (Alabama 2024), and two books translated into Italian, *Using Classical Rhetoric to Write Clearly* (Maggioli 2023) and *Principles of Logical Reasoning* (Maggioli 2024). She has served as the President of the Legal Writing Institute, the Secretary of the Association of Legal Writing Directors, and a member of the editorial board of the Legal Writing Journal. In 2024, she received the Thomas F. Blackwell Memorial Award for Outstanding Achievement in the Field of Legal Writing. Professor Tiscione earned her J.D. from Georgetown Law and her B.A. from Wellesley College.

Melissa H. Weresh is the Dwight D. Opperman Distinguished Professor of Law and former Herb and Karen Baum Chair of Ethics in the Professions at Drake University Law School. She is the 2017 recipient of the Thomas F. Blackwell Memorial Award for Outstanding Achievement in the Field of Legal Writing, the 2023 recipient of the Linda Berger Lifetime Achievement Award for Excellence in Legal Writing Scholarship, and the 2009 recipient of the American Inns of Court Warren E. Burger Prize. Professor Weresh is a Past President of the Legal Writing Institute, Past Chair of the AALS Section on Teaching Methods, and Past Chair of the Professionalism Section of the Iowa Bar Association. She is also past editor of both the *Journal of Legal Education* and *Legal Communication and Rhetoric: JALWD*. Her scholarly interests range from politics to professionalism, and from persuasion to pedagogy. Prior to joining the Drake law faculty, she practiced law in Ohio, specializing in environmental law. Professor Weresh received her J.D. from the University of Iowa and her B.A. from Wake Forest University.

THE THRESHOLD CONCEPTS OF LEGAL WRITING

ONE

Understanding Legal Writing Expertise as Threshold Concepts

Writing is at the heart of the legal profession. It is the primary form of communication for judges, legislators, lawyers, law professors, and legal scholars alike, often engaged in conversation with each other. Whether they write in the form of judicial decisions, proposed legislation, briefs, treatises, casebooks, or law review articles, to name just a few genres of legal writing, each writer contributes to our understanding of what law means and the functioning of our legal system. Despite the different roles these writers play, they share the same essential expertise—at the intersection of law, rhetoric, and composition—that distinguishes legal writing from other writing practices.

Like experts in any field or discipline, experienced legal writers often think intuitively.[1] In practice, they tend to "think fast,"[2] relying on accumulated knowledge and experience to make decisions efficiently.[3] Veteran litigators can dictate powerful briefs without outlines; corporate lawyers have hunches

1. *See, e.g.*, Martin M. Broadwell, *Teaching for Learning*, 20 The Gospel Guardian 1 (1969) (an early article on the four stages of competence, including unconscious competence); Daniel Kahneman, Thinking, Fast and Slow (2011) (exploring the differences between fast, intuitive thinking and slow, deliberate thinking); Gary A. Klein, Sources of Power: How People Make Decisions (1999) (exploring the relationship between expertise and intuitive knowledge); W. L. Robinson, *Conscious Competency—The Mark of a Competent Instructor*, 53 The Personnel Journal—Baltimore 538 (1974) (exploring the process of learning a new skill as progressing from unconscious incompetence to unconscious competence); Joseph Williams, *On the Maturing of Legal Writers*, 1 Legal Writing: J. Legal Writing Inst. 1 (1991) (exploring the acculturation of novice legal writers into the legal discourse community).

2. *See, e.g.*, Kahneman, *supra* note 1, at 20.

3. *See* Daniel Kahneman & Gary Klein, *Conditions for Intuitive Expertise: A Failure to Disagree*, 64 Am. Psychologist 515, 515–16 (2009).

about the pitfalls of a proposed deal, and legal scholars effortlessly grasp the weaknesses in competing legal theories. Yet these experts are often unable to articulate how they know what they know because much of their decision-making process operates "outside [their] consciousness."[4]

In psychologist Gary Klein's well-known study of firefighters, he discovered that experts make quick decisions based on intuition rather than on analytical reasoning.[5] As Klein explains, experts develop the ability to diagnose problems quickly and unconsciously by matching them to similar experiences from the past and running a sort of mental simulation to determine appropriate solutions.[6] In Klein's study, a fire-department commander in the midst of putting out a kitchen fire suddenly, and without apparent reason, ordered his team to evacuate the building, which collapsed soon thereafter.[7] When asked why he ordered everyone out, the commander struggled to explain his reasoning.[8] According to Klein, the commander had unconsciously identified the signs that the fire had occurred not in the kitchen but in the basement below.[9]

---

4. ANTONIO R. DAMASIO, DESCARTES' ERROR: EMOTION, REASON, AND THE HUMAN BRAIN 187 (1994) (describing intuition as covert cognitive emotion); *see also, e.g.*, Gary L. Blasi, *What Lawyers Know: Lawyering Expertise, Cognitive Science, and the Functions of Theory*, 45 J. LEGAL EDUC. 313, 344 (1995) (explaining that "[w]hat once required conscious thought becomes for the expert automatic, routine, and consequently much faster."); Eric Kandel, *The New Science of Mind and the Future of Knowledge*, 80 NEURON 546, 548–49 (2013) (explaining that our "adaptive unconscious" helps us think fast and make decisions while our conscious processes allow us to focus on what is happening in the moment).

5. *See* KLEIN, *supra* note 1, at 1–3.

6. *Id; see also* Linda L. Berger, *Applying New Rhetoric to Legal Discourse: The Ebb and Flow of Reader and Writer, Text and Context*, 49 J. LEGAL EDUC. 155, 163–65 (1999) (explaining legal writing expertise as the ability to use stored schemas of knowledge to solve legal problems); Blasi, *supra* note 4, at 318 (1995) (explaining that experts organize knowledge in ways that permit them to recognize patterns invisible to novices in complex situations); Leah M. Christensen, *The Paradox of Legal Expertise: A Study of Experts and Novices Reading the Law*, 2008 B.Y.U. EDUC. & L.J. 53 (exploring lawyering expertise in terms of the ways in which experts differ from novices in their approach to reading law).

7. KLEIN, *supra* note 1, at 32.

8. *Id.* at 31.

9. *Id.* at 31–32.

A. Using Threshold Concepts Theory to Uncover Legal Writing Expertise

Like Klein and others, we are interested in exploring the nature of expertise but in the context of legal writers. Thus, the goal of this project has been to identify as best we can the knowledge and experience that often unconsciously guide the decisions of expert legal writers. What specific body of knowledge do legal writers possess? How do they organize and rely on that knowledge to diagnose and solve legal problems? How does that expertise translate to effective legal writing in a variety of contexts? In short, what do expert legal writers know that makes them expert legal writers? And even more important, how might a deeper understanding of legal writing expertise improve the teaching and learning of legal writing in law school?

To accomplish our goal, we turned to threshold concepts theory, first developed by Jan H.F. Meyer and Ray Land in the early 2000s,[10] as the method of choice for articulating disciplinary expertise. The theory posits that the transition from novice to expert in any discipline involves the incorporation of troubling, transformative, integrative, and irreversible knowledge that is sometimes, but not always, bounded or unique to that discipline.[11] Meyer and Land describe this transition as akin to passing through various portals that transform understanding.[12] To identify the nature of the knowledge acquired is to articulate the threshold concepts of that discipline. In a sense, once a threshold concept is "seen," it cannot be unseen.

Threshold concepts theory explains that over time, as legal writers gain experience, their understanding of discipline-specific concepts and their

---

10. *See, e.g.*, Jan H.F. Meyer & Ray Land, *Threshold Concepts and Troublesome Knowledge: Linkages to Ways of Thinking and Practising Within the Disciplines*, *in* Improving Student Learning: Theory and Practice Ten Years On 412–24 (Chris Rust ed., Oxford Centre for Staff & Learning Dev. 2003) [hereinafter Meyer & Land, *Linkages*]; Ray Land, Glynis Cousin, Jan H.F. Meyer & Peter Davies, *Threshold Concepts and Troublesome Knowledge (3): Implications for Course Design and Evaluation*, *in* Improving Student Learning: Diversity and Inclusivity 53–64 (Chris Rust, ed., Oxford Centre for Staff & Learning Dev. 2005) [hereinafter Land et al., *Implications*].

11. Meyer & Land, *Linkages*, *supra* note 10, at 415–16; Land et al., *Implications*, *supra* note 10, at 53–54.

12. Meyer & Land, *Linkages*, *supra* note 10, at 412; Land et al., *Implications*, *supra* note 10, at 53.

application to different situations can become internalized or tacit.[13] Although much of that knowledge "remains mainly personal and implicit," it is "often shared within a specific community of practice."[14] The unspoken nature of disciplinary expertise helps explain why skilled legal writers often have difficulty articulating the substance of their expertise. It also explains why novice legal writers struggle to understand that which acculturated writers take for granted. A familiar refrain in law school that comes to mind is that professors intentionally "hide the ball," but the reality is that they may not realize they are hiding anything.

Our approach to this project was inspired by and modeled on the work of Linda Adler-Kassner, Elizabeth Wardle, and other scholars nationwide, who successfully participated in a project to identify the threshold concepts of writing studies. In *Naming What We Know: Threshold Concepts of Writing Studies*,[15] they sought to reach consensus on "the content of composition" so as to define their discipline.[16] In so doing, they discovered that theirs was "a philosophical exercise involving exploration as much as consolidation of what [they] know."[17] They also recognized that as a practical matter, the threshold concepts they identified would help them better engage as teacher-scholars, whether in a freshman composition course, supervising doctoral students, or working with faculty in other disciplines.[18]

Just as Adler-Kassner and Wardle sought to articulate the nature of "composed knowledge,"[19] we have sought herein to articulate the nature of composed *legal* knowledge. We too reached out to members of our national community of teacher-scholars to help us identify the content of legal writing. In essence,

---

13. *See* Meyer & Land, *Linkages*, *supra* note 10, at 412; Land et al., *Implications*, *supra* note 10, at 55.

14. Meyer & Land, *Linkages*, *supra* note 10, at 419.

15. *See* NAMING WHAT WE KNOW: THRESHOLD CONCEPTS OF WRITING STUDIES (Linda Adler-Kassner & Elizabeth Wardle eds., 2015) [hereinafter NAMING WHAT WE KNOW]; *see also* (RE)CONSIDERING WHAT WE KNOW: LEARNING THRESHOLDS IN WRITING, COMPOSITION, RHETORIC, AND LITERACY (Linda Adler-Kassner & Elizabeth Wardle eds., 2019) [hereinafter (RE)CONSIDERING WHAT WE KNOW].

16. Kathleen Blake Yancey, *Introduction*, *in* NAMING WHAT WE KNOW, *supra* note 15, at xviii.

17. *Id.* at xix.

18. *Id.*

19. Linda Adler-Kassner & Elizabeth Wardle, *Naming What We Know: The Project of This Book*, *in* NAMING WHAT WE KNOW, *supra* note 15, at 1 (emphasis omitted) [hereinafter Adler-Kassner & Wardle, *The Project of This Book*].

we asked participants, "What is it that legal writers know that is unique to legal writing?" The end result is a combination of concepts that we proposed and those suggested by invited participants, all of whom have long experience in the field. Despite our confidence in the value of these concepts, they represent the work of a relatively small number of legal writing teachers and scholars, and we would have preferred a broader range of contributors. Our hope is that this project marks the beginning of a more robust conversation.

We note here that our vision of legal writing is broad and multiform. It includes varying combinations of writers, clients, exigencies, processes, products, and audiences, encompassing all those operating within the legal writing discourse community. Given the unique mixture of law, legal reasoning, and rhetorical practices in all legal writing,[20] we include here advisory, predictive, persuasive, and transactional legal writing, as well as traditional,[21] clinical,[22] and legal writing scholarship.[23] To be sure, these different genres of legal writing serve different purposes and are aimed at different audiences. Yet we take the position that their expertise derives from the same source: each writer has been trained by and operates within the same legal discourse community.

---

20. *See, e.g.*, James Boyd White, *Law as Rhetoric, Rhetoric as Law: The Arts of Cultural and Communal Life*, 52 UNIV. CHICAGO L. REV. 684 (1985) (describing law as a branch of rhetoric that constitutes a community of shared values) [hereinafter White, *Law as Rhetoric*]; *cf.* Adler-Kassner & Wardle, *The Project of This Book*, *supra* note 19, at 1 (describing the field of writing studies as comprised of composition, rhetoric, and writing studies).

21. By traditional legal scholarship, we mean descriptive, normative and interdisciplinary scholarship that is primarily doctrinal or theoretical. *See, e.g.*, Kristen K. Tiscione & Melissa H. Weresh, *Legal [Writing] Scholarship: Why It Counts*, 6:3 UNENDING CONVERSATIONS 1, 3–9 (2023).

22. By clinical legal scholarship, we mean scholarship derived from teaching students to be lawyers while situated in law practice that describes and assesses clinical pedagogy or develops and critiques practice-based models of the lawyering process. *See* Katherine R. Kruse, *Clinical Scholarship and Scholarship by Clinicians*, 26 CLINICAL L. REV. 307, 307–08 (2019); *see also* Michele Gilman, *The Future of Clinical Legal Scholarship*, 26 CLINICAL L. REV. 189 (2019); Peter A. Joy, *Challenges to Legal Education, Clinical Legal Education, and Clinical Scholarship*, 26 CLINICAL L. REV. 237 (2019).

23. By legal writing scholarship, we mean scholarship that focuses on the creation and interpretation of legal communication and texts. *See* Tiscione & Weresh, *supra* note 21, at 10 (citing Kirsten K. Davis, *A Provisional Definition of "Legal Writing Scholarship*," 2 PROCEEDINGS 6, 11 (2021)).

B. The Positive and Negative Implications of Naming Legal Writing Expertise

To identify the threshold concepts of legal writing is only the beginning of the inquiry. The promise of threshold concepts theory is that once disciplinary expertise is identified, that knowledge empowers us to assess our teaching with a more critical eye and to improve student learning.[24] Somewhat distanced from the law student experience, we too can struggle to articulate the assumptions behind our teaching or the hidden content of the legal writing curriculum. Yet as legal writing teachers, our job is to unpack the complexity of thinking and writing like lawyers, to make conscious that which remains unavailable to practitioners, and to move (back?) from unconscious to conscious competence.[25] By attempting that here, we hope to provide insights for improving curriculum design, teaching methods, and assessment practices in legal writing pedagogy. As discussed in more detail in Chapters Five and Six, these concepts may also serve to promote student well-being and a more sophisticated understanding of the ways in which writing forms our identities as legal professionals.

Although we believe a significant benefit of this project is to help us improve the teaching and learning of legal writing, the project's value is greater than its pedagogical implications. First, to articulate these concepts is to bring them into being for the first time. By the simple act of naming them, we make that which was formerly invisible visible—both to us and potentially to our students. To recast the substance of legal writing as often tacit or implicit knowledge that distinguishes experts from novices casts our discipline in a new light that can be used to improve law student performance overall.[26] It may

---

24. *See* Meyer & Land, *Linkages*, *supra* note 10, at 412 (suggesting the benefits of threshold concept theory in designing effective learning environments); Land et al., *Implications*, *supra* note 10, at 56–57 (explaining that threshold concepts can be used to reevaluate course design and better engage students).

25. *See, e.g.*, Kent D. Beeler, *Graduate Student Adjustment to Academic Life: A Four-Stage Framework*, 28 NASPA J. 163 (1991) describing the progression from unconscious incompetence to conscious incompetence, unconscious competence, and conscious competence in skill mastery).

26. *See* Ray Land, *Preface*, *in* NAMING WHAT WE KNOW, *supra* note 15, at xii (explaining that one benefit of threshold concepts in writing studies is that they are "portable to other knowledge domains") [hereinafter Land, *Preface* to NAMING WHAT WE KNOW].

even encourage law teachers to better appreciate our students' lived experience and focus less on end products and traditional learning outcomes.[27]

Second, to identify the threshold concepts of legal writing is to define the contours or boundaries of our discipline. Like writing studies scholars, we face persistent doubts about "what the field is, whether it is a field, and so on—and on a fairly regular basis."[28] By defining the threshold concepts of legal writing, we stake out for ourselves the nature of our expertise as legal writing teachers as well as the specific skillset we offer students. As Adler-Kassner and Wardle suggest, we know a lot about good legal writing and how to assess it, but we "continue to lose the battle over discussions of writing to stakeholders who have money, power, and influence" but little experience teaching it.[29] To improve the teaching and learning of legal writing, "we must do a better job of clearly stating what our field knows."[30] And to do that, we must develop a shared vocabulary for communicating with each other;[31] perhaps these concepts will help us do just that.

Despite the benefits of this project, we recognize its inherent limitations. First, we recognize that these proposed concepts are highly subjective. Suffice it to say that the end result is a collection of proposed concepts that we claim to know, for now.[32] They are both tentative and subject to debate. Even more important, we recognize that any attempt to concretize a body of knowledge may be experienced as an effort to colonize the curriculum[33] by creating a framework that "include[s] and exclude[s] particular ideas."[34] In so doing we run the risk of imposing "a particular kind of stability and order that privileges

---

27. *See* Yancey, *supra* note 16, at xx.

28. *See* Adler-Kassner & Wardle, *The Project of This Book*, *supra* note 19, at 1.

29. *Id.* at 7.

30. *Id.*

31. *See* Terrill Pollman, *Building a Tower of Babel or Building a Discipline? Talking About Legal Writing*, 85 MARQ. L. REV. 887, 922–25 (2002) (encouraging legal writing faculty to develop a shared vocabulary of legal writing to help develop the substance of the discipline).

32. *See* Land, *Preface* to NAMING WHAT WE KNOW, *supra* note 26, at xiii (acknowledging Adler-Kassner and Wardle's description of their threshold concepts as representing "'final-for-now' definitions of some of what [their] field knows").

33. Meyer & Land, *Linkages*, *supra* note 10, at 422.

34. Linda Adler-Kassner & Elizabeth Wardle, *Editor's Introduction*, *in* (RE)CONSIDERING WHAT WE KNOW, *supra* note 15, at 9; *cf., e.g.*, Teri A. McMurtry-Chubb, *Writing at The Master's Table: Reflections on Theft, Criminality, and Otherness in the Legal Writing Profession*, 2 DREXEL L. REV. 41, 54 (arguing that the absence of teachers of color in the

the past."[35] To balance that risk, we sought consensus on ways of thinking about and practicing legal writing that legal writers share. In particular, we tried to name well-established norms and conventions that novice legal writers should and yet often do not know.[36] That said, we remain open to ways in which we have unintentionally perpetuated dominant norms that marginalize equally valuable but opposing norms and what it means to be an expert legal writer.

C. The Organization of the Book

Both the history and development of threshold concepts theory are more fully explained in Chapter Two, *Introduction to Threshold Concepts Theory*, which draws on Mel Weresh's expertise. In Chapter Three, *The Nature of the Project*, we describe in more detail the inspiration for this project as well as the process we used to develop our proposed concepts.

Chapter Four, *Proposed Threshold Concepts of Legal Writing*, is the heart of the project. It begins with the same overarching assumption as *Naming What We Know*, that legal writing is an interdisciplinary practice and a subject of study.[37] We then divide the field into three categories that serve as organizing principles for the individual threshold concepts. The first category explores concepts relevant to the nature of legal writing as a meaning-making activity. The second category explores concepts that relate to the rhetorical conventions of legal writing, and the third category explains the ways in which legal writing both shapes and constrains the writer's professional identity. Each category is further explained at the outset of Chapter Four, followed by detailed explanations of the related concepts.

Chapter Five, *Implications for Legal Writing Pedagogy*, examines the various ways in which threshold concepts theory and our proposed concepts could be used to improve teaching and learning. Specifically, it explores how

---

legal writing profession disadvantages students by encouraging them to engage in legal reasoning that protects white power and privilege).

35. Linda Adler-Kassner & Elizabeth Wardle, et al., *Recognizing the Limits of Threshold Concept Theory*, *in* (RE)CONSIDERING WHAT WE KNOW, *supra* note 15, at 19.

36. *See* Meyer & Land, *Linkages*, *supra* note 10, at 422 (explaining the value of threshold concepts theory in "evaluating teaching strategies and learning outcomes" despite its limitations).

37. *See Linda Adler-Kassner & Elizabeth Wardle, Metaconcept: Writing Is an Activity and a Subject of Study*, *in* NAMING WHAT WE KNOW, *supra* note 15, at 16.

these concepts might be used to rethink learning outcomes, curricular design, writing assignments and teaching methods, and formative and summative assessments, particularly in a first-year legal writing course.

Chapter Six, *Implications for Professional Identity Formation*, addresses the extent to which the mastery of the threshold concepts of legal writing is at the heart of a student's professional identify formation. In so doing, it furthers the work of American Bar Association Standard 303,[38] helping us think differently about raising students' awareness of their agency and role as legal writers and to encourage them to develop their own authentic voice while balancing creativity with professional norms and ethics.

Finally, Chapter Seven, *Food for Thought: Where Do We Go from Here?* summarizes where we think this work leaves us as writers, scholars, and educators, as well as what is left to be done. It also describes the challenges in defining the legal writing discipline as well and the overall strengths and weaknesses in threshold concepts theory. We close by inviting members of our community to engage in continued conversation on what we got right, what we got wrong, and what we might have missed.

38. 2024–2025 Standards for Approval of Law Schools, Std. 303 (Am. Bar Ass'n 2024) [hereinafter ABA Standards].

TWO

Introduction to Threshold Concepts Theory[1]

Threshold concepts theory is a "theoretical framework"[2] that seeks to identify foundational, transformative ideas or concepts that students must grasp to achieve disciplinary-specific understanding. The term "threshold concept" developed from the *Enhancing Teaching Learning Environments in Undergraduate Courses* project.[3] The project was conducted by teams of academics from universities in the United Kingdom. Its goal was to "develop conceptual frameworks directed at the quality of learning achieved in higher education institutions."[4]

According to Jan Meyer and Ray Land, threshold concepts are disciplinary-specific concepts "akin to a portal, opening up a new and previously inaccessible way of thinking about something."[5] As students pass through that portal, they occupy a liminal space, often moving back and forth between pre- and post-understanding.[6] Once understood, threshold concepts help students construct knowledge that transforms their understanding of the discipline.

---

1. Portions of this chapter are adapted, in part, with express permission from Melissa H. Weresh, *Stargate: Malleability as a Threshold Concept in Legal Education*, 63 J. LEGAL EDUC. 689 (2014) [hereinafter Weresh, *Malleability*].

2. Sarah Barradell, *The Identification of Threshold Concepts: A Review of Theoretical Complexities and Methodological Challenges*, 65 HIGHER EDUC. 265, 266 (2012) [hereinafter Barradell, *Theoretical Complexities*].

3. *See* Land et al., *Implications*, ch. 1, *supra* note 10, at 54.

4. Barradell, *supra* note 2, at 265–66.

5. Meyer & Land, *Linkages*, ch. 1, *supra* note 10, at 412.

6. *See. e.g.*, Land et al., *Implications*, ch. 1, *supra* note 10, at 59–60.

Collectively, threshold concepts "bind a subject together" and are "fundamental to ways of thinking and practising in that discipline."[7]

Threshold concepts differ from core or foundational concepts. Core concepts are conceptual building blocks necessary to understand the subject matter, but they do not lead to a "qualitatively different view of subject matter."[8] For example, understanding the hierarchy of authority is a core concept in legal writing. Legal writers must understand and employ principles of binding and persuasive authority in selecting sources to cite in support of their assertions. Yet this understanding alone does not open up a previously inaccessible way of thinking about legal writing.

In contrast, the malleability of law—the ability to state rules of law more or less broadly to adapt to different situations—is a threshold concept.[9] Novice legal writers often assume that rules of law are found and applied uniformly across situations. Once students come to understand that legal writers construct rules of law tailored to specific circumstances under certain conditions, it fundamentally changes their view of law as a separate body of knowledge and their role—within ethical limits—in framing it.

A. Characteristics of Threshold Concepts

Threshold concepts also differ from core concepts insofar as they possess defining characteristics. Since the introduction of threshold concepts theory, scholars have identified their probable, likely, or essential characteristics as being integrative, irreversible, troublesome, transformative, and bounded.[10]

---

7. Land et al., *Implications*, ch. 1, *supra* note 10 at 54.

8. *See* Meyer & Land, *Linkages*, ch. 1, *supra* note 10, at 415.

9. *See* Weresh, *Malleability, supra* note 1; *see also* ch. 4, Concept 1.4, *infra*, at 42.

10. *See, e.g.*, Land et al., *Linkages*, ch. 1, *supra* note 10, at 415–16. Although additional characteristics such as "discursive" and "reconstitutional" have been proposed, the original five characteristics set forth by Meyer and Land have gained the most traction. *See* Matilda Liljedahl, Per J. Palmgren, & Cormac McGrath, *Threshold Concepts in Health Professions Education Research: A Scoping Review*, 27 Advances in Health Sciences Educ. 1457, 1458 (2022).

1. *Integrative*

Threshold concepts are thought to be integrative, revealing relationships between concepts once perceived as distinct. Meyer and Land explain that threshold concepts "expos[e] the previously hidden interrelatedness of something."[11] Thus, they provide a unifying framework for connecting various aspects and ideas within a discipline, helping students make connections in order to create coherence in their understanding.[12]

This integrative quality helps students begin to process information in a disciplinary-specific manner.[13] For example, understanding the malleability of law is integrative. It requires students to develop a broader understanding of ways in which hierarchies of authority, jurisdictional limits, stare decisis, and precedential value work together in framing rules of law.

2. *Irreversible*

Threshold concepts are "[p]robably irreversible, in that the change of perspective occasioned by [their] acquisition . . . is unlikely to be forgotten, or will be unlearned only by considerable effort."[14] Once learners internalize these concepts, they become integral to the student's cognitive framework, influencing how they approach and think about the discipline. This does not mean that their understanding of the threshold concept cannot be further honed or enhanced. In fact, irreversibility "does not exclude subsequent modification or

---

11. Jan H.F. Meyer & Ray Land, *Threshold Concepts and Troublesome Knowledge (2): Epistemological Considerations and a Conceptual Framework for Teaching and Learning*, 49 Higher Educ. 373 (2005)[hereinafter Meyer & Land, *Epistemological Considerations*].

12. Glynis Cousin, *An Introduction to Threshold Concepts*, 17 Planet 4, 4 (2006) [hereinafter Cousin, *Introduction*].

13. Peter Davies & Jean Mangan, *Recognising Threshold Concepts: An Exploration of Different Approaches* 2, 6, available at https://www.researchgate.net/profile/Jean-Mangan-2/publication/228377119_Recognising_Threshold_Concepts_an_exploration_of_different_approaches/links/02e7e51fb9189eb947000000/Recognising-Threshold-Concepts-an-exploration-of-different-approaches.pdf (unpublished paper) (copy on file with author).

14. Meyer & Land, *Linkages*, ch. 1, *supra* note 10, at 416 (emphasis omitted). Cousin notes that "[f]or teachers this can produce a low ability to empathise with student[s] who have yet to gain mastery. They cannot get back to 'innocence' so to speak." Glynis Cousin, *Threshold Concepts, Troublesome Knowledge, and Emotional Capital: An exploration into learning about others*, *in* Overcoming Barriers to Student Understanding: Threshold Concepts and Troublesome Knowledge, 134, 136 (Jan H.F. Meyer & Ray Land, eds., 2006).

rejection of the concept for a more refined or rival understanding."[15] Yet once learned, threshold concepts are difficult to reject. This too is true of malleability—once a student understands the inherent flexibility of legal rules, they can no longer view the law as fixed or concrete.

3. *Troublesome*

Threshold concepts are often troubling because they "appear counterintuitive, alien (emanating from another culture or discourse), or incoherent (discrete aspects are unproblematic but there is no [obvious] organising principle)."[16] The trouble arises in part because the threshold concept may require students to reject previously held knowledge. This can cause emotional discord as they try to simultaneously accept a new way of thinking while potentially trying to protect established understanding. Students who struggle in this respect have been described as "defended" against crossing the threshold.[17]

Because understanding a threshold concept requires students to integrate new ideas, "[g]etting [them] to reverse their intuitive understandings [may be] troublesome because the reversal can involve an uncomfortable, emotional repositioning."[18] This can be exhilarating for the learner, but might also produce "a sense of disquietude or even loss...as they let go the security of a previously held conceptual stance to enter less certain terrain."[19] As suggested earlier, students may understand certain individual threshold concepts but struggle to integrate them. In those situations, they may fail to appreciate the big picture, what Land et al. refer to as threshold conceptions or the rules of "the underlying game" that explain how the concepts work together.[20]

---

15. Cousin, *Introduction*, *supra* note 12, at 4.

16. Meyer & Land, *Linkages*, ch. 1, *supra* note 10, at 417 (citations omitted); *see also* Caroline Baillie, John A. Bowden & Jan H.F. Meyer, *Threshold Capabilities: Threshold Concepts and Knowledge Capability Linked Through Variation Theory*, 65 Higher Educ. 227, 229 (2012) (describing troublesome knowledge as "challenging, difficult to come to terms with, counter-intuitive or requiring a suspension of disbelief") [hereinafter Baillie, *Threshold Capabilities*].

17. Ray Land, Jan H.F. Meyer & Caroline Baillie, *Editors' Preface*, *in* Threshold Concepts and Transformational Learning x (Ray Land, Jan H.F. Meyer & Caroline Baillie, eds., 2010) [hereinafter Land et al., *Preface*].

18. Cousin, *Introduction*, *supra* note 12, at 4.

19. Land et al., *Implications*, ch. 1, *supra* note 10, at 58.

20. *Id.* at 55–56.

Threshold concepts may also be troublesome because they are conceptually difficult, requiring students to understand, apply, and communicate them at the same time within a new discourse community.[21] As Land et al. explain, "Specific discourses have developed within disciplines to represent (and simultaneously privilege) particular understandings and ways of seeing and thinking. Such discourses distinguish individual communities of practice and are necessarily less familiar to new entrants to such discursive communities or participants who are peripheral to them."[22]

Finally, certain threshold concepts may be troubling because they have become ritualized, tacit, or inert in the discipline.[23] Ritualized knowledge may not carry obvious import; it feels more like "part of a social or an individual ritual: how we answer when asked such-and-such, the routine that we execute to get a particular result."[24] Tacit knowledge is knowledge that is shared within a specific discourse community but rarely made explicit.[25] Inert knowledge "sits in the mind's attic, unpacked only when specifically called for by a quiz or a direct prompt but otherwise gathering dust."[26] As such, it seems to have little connection to the current practice of the discipline or our everyday lives.[27]

Malleability is troublesome for students, in part because it runs counter to the novice legal writer's understanding of the law as concrete or static. It requires students to reject previously held assumptions about the nature of law. It also requires students to understand that as members of the legal writing community, they have both the obligation and the authority to frame rules of law from their perspective or that of their client. The concept of malleability is conceptually difficult because it is hard to learn how lawyers frame rules in different situations and even harder for novices to predict whether their rules fall within acceptable limits. Because expert legal writers make many of these decisions implicitly, often drawing on ritualized, tacit, and inert knowledge, students sense they are failing to grasp the underlying rules of the game.

---

21. *See* Meyer & Land, *Linkages*, ch. 1, *supra* note 10, at 420 (noting that the "discursive practices of a given community may render previously 'familiar' concepts strange and subsequently conceptually difficult").

22. Land et al., *Implications*, ch. 1, *supra* note 10, at 55.

23. *Id.* at 58.

24. Meyer & Land, *Linkages*, ch. 1, *supra* note 10, at 417 (citations omitted).

25. *See id.* at 419 (citations omitted).

26. *Id.* at 418 (describing our understanding of the use of passive voice as inert knowledge in writing) (citations omitted).

27. *See id.*

4. *Transformative*

Threshold concepts are inherently transformative. While not all scholars agree on the essential characteristics of threshold concepts,[28] there is general agreement as to their transformative quality.[29] As one scholar has noted, the "essential property of a threshold concept is its transformative character; one that occasions in varying degrees (attributable to individual differences) epistemic and ontological shifts in the learner."[30] Once students grasp a threshold concept, they experience a resulting shift in perspective or a reorganization of existing knowledge. As such, the transformative quality of threshold concepts has been described as reconstitutive, representing "a shift in learner subjectivity, a transconfiguration of self, of identity; an ontological shift."[31] As novice legal writers come to understand the malleability of law, they are transformed; it affects their understanding of law, legal analysis and advocacy, and their identity as legal writers.

5. *Bounded*

Threshold concepts have been described as likely bounded within a discipline.[32] Meyer and Land explain that they are bounded in such a manner "that any conceptual space will have terminal frontiers, bordering with thresholds into new conceptual areas."[33] Thus, they represent ideas that are foundational to the discipline and essential for meaningful engagement with the subject matter. The bounded nature of threshold concepts has a framing or contextualizing function, helping "to define what the discipline is and what it is not, what is critical and what is peripheral."[34] This characteristic also informs the limit of a concept's applicability to other disciplinary boundaries: "It might be that such boundedness in certain instances serves to constitute the demarcation

---

28. *See* Barradell, *Theoretical Complexities*, *supra* note 2, at 266–67.

29. *See* Sarah Barradell & Tracy Fortune, *Bounded–The Neglected Threshold Concept Characteristic*, 57 Innovations in Educ. and Teaching Int'l 296, 297 (2020) (citations omitted) [hereinafter Barradell & Fortune, *Bounded—The Neglected Threshold Concept*].

30. Baillie, *Threshold Capabilities*, *supra* note 16, at 229.

31. *Id.*

32. Meyer & Land, *Linkages*, ch. 1, *supra* note 10, at 416.

33. *Id.*

34. Barradell & Fortune, *Bounded—The Neglected Threshold Concept*, *supra* note 29, at 297.

between disciplinary areas, to define academic territories."[35] The boundedness of threshold concepts also demarcates a particular threshold of understanding that distinguishes expert practitioners from novices. To the extent that malleability is a concept that informs how law-trained individuals approach the various tasks of legal writing, it is bounded within the discipline.

We note here that "bounded" is the most challenged characteristic in threshold concepts theory, in part because it is considered "the most difficult to interpret" and apply.[36] In contrast, others have argued that "bounded" is the most neglected and yet "non-negotiable" characteristic.[37] Health sciences scholars Sarah Barradell and Tracy Fortune argue that "[e]ach discipline is a type of cultural system shaped by a unique combination of historical narrative, accumulated knowledge and skills, and communities of practice," and students must understand disciplinary boundaries to develop "disciplinary mindsets."[38] Because "[d]isciplines privilege certain knowledge forms that involve an interplay of contextualised knowing, doing and being," the bounded nature of threshold concepts is what enables learners to move toward disciplinary, scholarly ways of thinking.[39] Further, the boundedness of threshold concepts is essential in inter-disciplinary work because it helps us "see the possibilities that can be created when working with people who have different worldviews."[40]

As illustrated in Chapter Four, we adopted the five, generally accepted characteristics of threshold concepts in naming the threshold concepts of legal writing. That said, we elected neither to discard nor prioritize bounded as a limiting characteristic. Thus, several of our concepts may not truly be bounded in the sense that they may also describe concepts relevant to other disciplines. For example, we identify the legal writer's need to develop a level of tolerance for uncertainty as a threshold concept of legal writing,[41] but "uncertainty"

---

35. Meyer & Land, *Linkages*, ch. 1, *supra* note 10, at 416.

36. *See* Anna Wilson et al., *Measurement Uncertainty as a Threshold Concept in Physics* 98, 100 (2010 Paper Presentation at the 16th UniServe Annual Conference) (copy on file with authors) (rejecting "bounded" as an essential characteristic of the threshold concept of "measurement uncertainty" in physics).

37. *See* Barradell & Fortune, *Bounded—The Neglected Threshold Concept*, *supra* note 29, at 297.

38. *Id.* at 298.

39. *Id.*

40. *Id.* (citations omitted).

41. *See* ch. 4, Concept 3.5, *supra*, at 105.

appears as a proposed threshold concept in several disciplines.[42] The fact that legal writing is inherently interdisciplinary encouraged us to take a more flexible view of boundedness as desirable but not to construe it strictly. We return to this potentially controversial decision in Chapter Seven.

B. Liminality as the Stepping Stone to Disciplinary Expertise

The process of mastering a threshold concept has been compared to passing through a portal,[43] but that process is neither simple nor straightforward. As students engage with new conceptual material, they can get "stuck in an 'in-between' state in which they oscillate between earlier, less sophisticated understandings, and the fuller appreciation of the concept" we are trying to teach.[44] Being stuck in the portal is referred to as a liminal state,[45] "a suspended state... in which understanding approximates to a kind of 'mimicry' or lack of authenticity."[46] Moving between pre-liminal, liminal, and post-liminal states of understanding "often involves a degree of recursiveness, and of oscillation."[47] Thus, because "mastery of a threshold concept often involves messy journeys back, forth and across conceptual terrain,"[48] students may "become frustrated, lose confidence and give up...."[49]

Because students in the liminal state may try to hold on to prior understandings when presented with troublesome knowledge, they may resist the

42. *See, e.g.*, Kangmoon Kim & Young-Mee Lee, *Understanding Uncertainty in Medicine: Concepts and Implications in Medical Education*, 30:3 Korean J. Med. Educ. 181 (2018) (emphasizing the need for medical students to develop a tolerance for uncertainty to improve their mental health and patient safety); Wilson et al., *supra* note 36, at 100 (explaining the importance of understanding measurement uncertainty as inherent to the study of physics).

43. *See supra* note 5 and accompanying text.

44. Land, *Implications*, ch. 1, *supra* note 10, at 55.

45. "Liminality" here is derived from Latin, meaning "within the threshold." *Id.*

46. Land et al., *Preface*, *supra* note 17, at x. In attempting to mimic expertise, novice legal writers often focus on the more concrete aspects of a legal problem, explain what experts would view as "self-evident banalities," engage in more summary than analysis, and try to sound lawyerly. *See* Williams, ch. 1, *supra* note 1, at 17–30.

47. Land et al., *Preface*, *supra* note 17, at xi.

48. Cousin, *Introduction*, *supra* note 12, at 5.

49. Land et al., *Implications*, ch. 1, *supra* note 10, at 55.

new understanding in the unstable space, becoming defended learners.[50] As one scholar has noted, the "idea that learners enter into a liminal state in their attempts to grasp certain concepts in their subjects presents a powerful way of remembering that learning is both affective and cognitive and that it involves identity shifts which can entail troublesome, unsafe journeys."[51]

Our students' liminal state can be similarly frustrating for us as we seek to assist them in crossing over the threshold toward mastery. If we think of liminality as signifying our students' attempts to engage with the material, we can begin to see their intellectual struggle as posing unique opportunities for teaching intervention.[52] By identifying those points in the curriculum where students get stuck, we can make adjustments to hasten student learning and "As further explained in Chapter Five, we can rethink the sequencing of curricular material; evaluate "the processes through which learners are made ready for, approach, recognise, and internalise threshold concepts"; and determine "the ways in which learners and teachers recognise when threshold concepts have been internalized."[53]

---

50. Land et al., *Preface*, *supra* note 17, at x.

51. Cousin, *Introduction*, *supra* note 12, at 4–5.

52. *Id.* ("[O]nce a learner enters this liminal space, she is engaged with the project of mastery unlike the learner who remains in a state of pre-liminality in which understandings are at best vague.").

53. Land et al., *Implications*, ch. 1, *supra* note 10, at 56–57.

THREE

The Nature of Our Project

It began with a phone call. Mel Weresh had been studying threshold concepts theory for a few years and had just discovered *Naming What We Know: Threshold Concepts of Writing Studies.*[1] Late in the summer of 2018, she called me, bursting with excitement: "Kris, we need to write a book on the threshold concepts of legal writing." As she explained the theory, we could envision the value in articulating the ways in which legal writers of all kinds understand and practice their discipline. Threshold concepts had the potential not only to help us improve teaching and learning but to define the discipline of legal writing in a completely new way. Mel proceeded to describe her vision of the project, but it did not take long for me to say, "I'm in."

The first thing we did was make a second phone call, to Elizabeth Wardle.[2] She and Linda Adler-Kassner[3] had published *Naming What We Know* in 2015, and we hoped to learn from their experience. We had so many questions, but more important, we wanted to make sure they would be comfortable with our project. To our delight, Elizabeth was incredibly generous in helping us think about threshold concepts in the context of legal writing and how to design and manage the project. "Everyone likes to talk about what they know best," she told us. "The key is to figure out how to get that conversation started." At this point, we had only a vague sense of what our threshold concepts might look

---

1. *See* Naming What We Know, ch. 1, *supra* note 15.

2. Elizabeth Wardle is the Roger and Joyce Howe Distinguished Professor of Written Communication and the Director of the Howe Center for Writing Excellence at Miami University.

3. Linda Adler-Kassner is the Associate Vice Chancellor of Teaching and Learning and a Professor of Writing Studies at the University of California, Santa Barbara.

like but no idea how to tap into the knowledge of experts that so often operates subconsciously.[4]

Elizabeth explained that the best way to tap into expertise was not to ask what legal writers do (or what legal writing teachers teach) but what legal writers *know*. Asking what legal writers do elicits information related to process and products: they investigate facts, conduct legal research, draft contracts, take depositions, write briefs, etc. Asking what legal writing teachers teach elicits information on course content: we teach reading for a specific purpose, the hierarchy of legal authority, analogical reasoning, predictive and persuasive analysis, memos, briefs, etc. While many of these answers relate to threshold concepts, they are not themselves the expression of threshold concepts. As we quickly learned, to ask what legal writers *know* is a completely different question. It prompts ideas on the tacit knowledge that drives expert decision-making, particularly the unique knowledge that legal writers rely on to diagnose and solve legal problems. For us, at least, it began to feel like we had a way to begin.

The next step was to figure out the process we would use to develop our approach and generate individual concepts. We wanted to involve as many members of the legal writing community as possible, but we knew we could not consult *all* legal writing faculty and certainly not all at once. Ultimately, and with permission, we adopted a process that represented a hybrid of the *Naming What We Know* approach and the approach used in the *Feminist Judgments* projects,[5] a series of projects in which legal scholars collaborated to rewrite judicial opinions from a feminist perspective. The feminist judgments projects in the United States were conceived of and launched in part by legal writing colleagues Linda Berger[6] and Kathy Stanchi[7] at the University of Nevada, Las Vegas (UNLV).

---

4. *See* ch. 1, *supra* notes 1–9 and accompanying text.

5. *See, e.g.*, FEMINIST JUDGMENTS: FROM THEORY TO PRACTICE (Rosemary Hunter, Clare McGlynn & Erika Rackley, eds. 2010); FEMINIST JUDGMENTS: REWRITTEN OPINIONS OF THE UNITED STATES SUPREME COURT (Kathryn M. Stanchi, Linda L. Berger, & Bridget J. Crawford, eds. 2016).

6. Linda Berger, Emerita Professor of Law, University of Nevada, Las Vegas, is known for her scholarship on legal writing, law and rhetoric, and the First Amendment.

7. Kathryn M. Stanchi, the E.L. Cord Professor of Law at University of Nevada, Las Vegas, is known for her scholarship on legal writing, law and rhetoric, and feminist legal theory.

To start, in September 2018, we invited a small number of legal writing faculty across the country to act as a core group to conduct initial brainstorming. We hoped their input would help us develop a coherent vision of both process and product. That initial core group consisted of Linda Berger (Emerita Professor of Law, UNLV), Leslie Culver (Clinical Professor, University of Utah S.J. Quinney College of Law), Kirsten Davis (Professor of Law and Provost Faculty Fellow for Generative Artificial Intelligence and Higher Education at Stetson University College of Law), Ann McGinley (Emerita Professor of Law, UNLV), Ruth Anne Robbins (Professor of Law, Rutgers Law School), JoAnne Sweeny (Professor of Law, University of Louisville, Louis D. Brandeis School of Law), David Thomson (Professor of the Practice of Law and John C. Dwan Professor for Online Learning, University of Denver Sturm College of Law), Kristen Tiscione (Professor of Law, Legal Practice, Georgetown University Law Center), and Melissa Weresh (Dwight D. Opperman Distinguished Professor of Law, Drake University Law School).[8] Regrettably, Leslie, Ann, and JoAnne needed to withdraw from the core group based on other commitments, but Leslie and JoAnne returned later to write their own threshold concepts included here.

In March 2019, we held our first core group meetings in conjunction with the Rocky Mountain Legal Writing Conference at UNLV. Our goal was modest—to get our group together for the first time, discuss threshold concepts theory in general, frame the project, and define its scope. From the beginning, our planned agenda fell to the wayside. We found ourselves engaged in a flurry of excited conversations, throwing out ideas and searching for a schema that would help us organize our ideas. Having never conceived of our discipline in this manner, we had trouble collectively passing through the portal that would open up and allow us to access this new way of thinking. At some point late in the afternoon of our first day, the floodgates opened, and concepts started to flow. By the end of the second day, we had compiled nearly a dozen proposed concepts. Over the next several weeks, we reviewed the proposed concepts and each volunteered to draft one or two for our next meeting. For each draft concept, we felt it was important both to explain the concept in our own words and to test it against the five traditional five characteristics: integrative, irreversible, troublesome, transformative, and bounded.[9]

---

8. For more information on the expertise of members of the core group, see participants' biographies, *supra* at xiii.

9. *See* ch. 2, *supra*, at 14.

We met again in August 2019 and were graciously hosted by Kirsten Davis at Stetson Law. We met in sunny Florida for two days, spending the bulk of our time figuring out how to organize our proposed concepts and trying to envision our end product—whether it would be a scholarly work, a textbook, a law review article, or something else. In the afternoon of our first day, something akin to a light bulb switched on, and we tentatively adopted (and further refined) the organizational approach used here.

As you will see in Chapter Four, we ended up with twenty-three individual concepts divided into three main categories. The first category contains concepts that relate to legal writing as a meaning-making activity. At first, we thought of this category as describing the products of legal writing or the substance of what legal writing produces. Ultimately, we revised our view of these concepts as more broadly explaining the function and context of legal writing without regard to specific genres or types. For example, the first concept in this category is that legal writing creates and recreates the law.[10] Expert legal writers know that legal writing is an ongoing conversation among texts and writers across time and distance, in which the meaning of law is negotiated and determined.[11]

The second category contains concepts that relate to the rhetorical conventions of legal writing. From the beginning, we viewed these concepts as describing the process of legal writing, those operating assumptions and rhetorical conventions with which legal writers must conform as members of the legal writing community. The first concept in the second category is that legal writers know that they are engaged in a rhetorical practice even though the law itself denies its rhetorical nature.[12] To be an effective member of the legal writing community, one must balance the operating assumption that law is objective or neutral with the reality that legal writers make myriad rhetorical choices in a messy, creative process that at the end of the day is more art than science.[13]

The third category of concepts relates to the development of individual legal writers, exploring how legal writing both constrains and shapes their professional identities. The first concept in this category is that legal writers understand that to be effective, they must understand the indeterminacy of law

10. *See infra* ch. 4, Concept 1.1, at 36.

11. *See id.*

12. *See infra* ch. 4, Concept 2.1, at 60.

13. *See id.* at 61.

as well as employ the rhetorical skills necessary to communicate its meaning in context.[14]

Throughout the project, we had the sense that these categories came close to but did not hit the nail precisely on the head in terms of what we were trying to express. As a result, we experimented with other organizational structures, but ultimately, we chose this approach as the one that came closest to our vision. We also found that by conceiving of and soliciting concepts as relating roughly to product, process, or writer, we generated some overlap between categories. For example, the notion of legal writing as creative writing appears in Concepts 1.1 (legal writing creates and recreates the law) and 3.5 (legal writers are creative writers). Yet we discovered that by examining the concept of creativity in terms of legal writing as a whole and from the perspective of individual legal writers, we gained new and different insights.

With a good handful of threshold concepts in draft form, we sought input from a larger audience of experts we dubbed our "focus group." In October 2019, we invited roughly fifty legal writing faculty representing expertise from a wide range of law schools to join that group. Their task was to learn a bit about threshold concepts theory, review our draft concepts, and provide feedback. We also asked them to propose additional concepts for consideration. We were thrilled with the enthusiastic response from the focus group, and later that month, we sent out our concepts for review.

With gratitude, we received feedback from Erin Carroll (Professor of Law, Georgetown University Law Center), Chris Coughlin (Professor of Law, Wake Forest University School of Law), Leslie Culver (Utah), Linda Edwards (Emerita Professor of Law, UNLV), Lisa Eichhorn (Director of Legal Writing & Professor of Law, University of South Carolina Joseph F. Rice School of Law), Steve Johansen (Professor of Law & Associate Dean of Admissions, Lewis & Clark Law School), Sherri Keene (Professor of Law, Legal Practice, Georgetown University Law Center), Derek Kiernan-Johnson (Teaching Professor, Colorado Law Boulder), Brian Larson (Emeritus Associate Professor, Texas A&M University School of Law), J.C. Lore III (Distinguished Clinical Professor and Director of Trial Advocacy, Rutgers Law School), Kristen E. Murray (Interim Dean and Professor of Law, Temple University Beasley School of Law), Noah Messing (Lecturer in Legal Practice, Yale Law School), Julie Oseid (Professor and Morrison Family Director of Lawyering Skills, University of St. Thomas School of Law), Terry Pollman (Emerita Professor of Law, UNLV),

14. *See infra* ch. 4, Concept 3.1, at 91.

Anne Ralph (Associate Dean for Academic Affairs and Strategic Initiatives; Morgan E. Shipman Professor in Law, The Ohio State University Moritz College of Law), Sarah E. Ricks (Distinguished Clinical Professor of Law, Rutgers Law School), Nantiya Ruan (Professor of Law, UNLV), and Kathleen E. Vinson (Professor of Legal Writing and Director of Legal Writing, Research, and Written Advocacy at Suffolk University Law School).

Their feedback was both insightful and incredibly helpful. Overall, it fell primarily into two categories: questions or concerns related to the overall scope and structure of the project and reactions to specific or proposed concepts. With regard to the first category, some members of the group questioned our inclusion of all legal writing as opposed to practitioner writing; others questioned what might be construed as undue emphasis on legal writing in the context of litigation as opposed to transactional practice or legal scholarship. Although we struggled with both of these concerns, our goal was to understand the expertise shared not just among practitioners, but also by law-trained judges, legislators, podium law faculty, and legal scholars. Each contribute in unique ways to the functioning of our legal system, and together they comprise the legal writing community.

What we hope to have articulated are the nuggets of expertise that unite all members of the community of legal writers. As for any undue emphasis on litigation, we take the position that understanding the law as a meaning-making activity, in which legal writers conform with disciplinary-specific assumptions and conventions and, at the same time, shape and enact their professional identities is as applicable to transactional lawyers, regulatory lawyers, judges, and legal scholars as to litigators.

With regard to the second category of feedback, our focus group questioned certain assumptions built into the project as well as the accuracy of certain concepts themselves. For example, as a whole, members of the focus group resisted most the notion that legal writers create and recreate the law (Concept 1.1) and that the law denies its rhetorical nature (Concept 2.1). In the first instance, several participants thought we had pushed the envelope too far by including all legal writing genres, such as legal memoranda and briefs. In their view, the idea that all legal writing creates and recreates the law "seems a little misleading, at least as to the writing that lawyers, as opposed to judges, do." In drafting a memorandum of law, can a lawyer truly be said to create law as opposed to report or apply it? From our perspective, all legal writing is creative in that the writer selects and relies on a unique combination of facts, law, conventions, and tradition to accomplish their particular goals. In that sense, all legal writers participate in an ongoing conversation about the contingent nature of law and how it applies to specific situations.

We also stand by the concept that law is a rhetorical practice that tends to deny its rhetorical nature. Experienced legal writers know that although the law does not recognize itself as rhetorical (i.e., constructed by a community of legal writers), to write about and within the law is the "very profession of rhetoric."[15] Despite this tacit knowledge, legal writers tend to state what the law is as if it were definitive or clear.[16]

To involve as many experts in our field as possible, we made a final call for proposals of additional concepts in October 2020. At the same time, we spoke publicly about the nature of our project and invited participation at two conferences: the 2021 Association of Legal Writing Directors biennial conference and the Eighth Applied Legal Storytelling Conference. We received a good handful of proposals but not nearly as many as we had hoped. Due to COVID-19, both conferences were virtual, and we attribute at least some of the low response rate to COVID burnout and to our inability to create excitement about what may have seemed at that time too abstract a project.

Since then, David Thomson, Linda Berger, and Ruth Anne Robbins worked with our focus group authors, providing specific feedback and shepherding their revisions, while we all refined own threshold concepts. Meanwhile, Mel Weresh and Kris Tiscione drafted the remainder of the chapters, and Kirsten Davis provided valuable feedback. Overall, our progress has been frustratingly slow due to professional and family commitments, and we often found ourselves on competing schedules. Now, nearly eight years later, we are proud to share this work and publicly thank all those who participated for their valuable contributions.

---

15. *See infra* ch. 4, Concept 2.1, at 60.

16. *See infra* ch. 4, Concept 3.6, at 111 (noting that legal writers tend to say "the law is X," as opposed to "I have determined the law is X").

FOUR

Proposed Threshold Concepts of Legal Writing

This chapter represents our collective effort to propose some, not all, threshold concepts of legal writing. Our goal has been to identify the tacit expertise that guides experienced legal writers.[1] These concepts represent new knowledge that can help us—as teachers of legal writing—hasten student learning and teach better for transfer. By bringing these concepts into being, we hope to better shape and define the contours and boundaries of the legal writing discipline, inform our own writing practices, and launch new scholarly investigations. As indicated in Chapter One, we do not conceive of these concepts as definitive or static.[2] At the moment, they are best characterized as the concepts we know for now and as best as we understand them.

A. Legal Writing Is a Disciplinary Activity and a Distinct Subject of Study

Similar to Adler-Kassner and Wardle, we begin with the overarching concept that legal writing is an interdisciplinary practice and a distinct subject of study.[3] Each of the individual concepts are derived therefrom. By "interdisciplinary," we mean that legal writing operates in practice, pedagogy, and scholarship at the intersection of law, rhetoric, and composition. This distinct

1. *See* ch. 1, *supra*, at 5–6.

2. *See id.* at 9.

3. In Naming What We Know, the authors adopted a similar overarching concept for writing studies ("Writing is an activity and a subject of study."). *See* ch. 1, *supra* note 15, at 15.

practice—in all its forms—is a subject worthy of study separate from legal doctrine or composition theory, and it involves both the creation and interpretation of legal texts.[4]

By legal writing, we mean to include all law-related texts: the law itself (primary authority ranging from constitutions to administrative regulations), texts about the law (secondary authority ranging from treatises to law review articles), legal analysis and argument (such as opinion letters and briefs), legal instruments (such as letters of intent and other contracts, deeds, wills, etc.), and legal scholarship, including law review articles. In our view, all experienced and effective legal writers acquire and employ some or all of this knowledge, regardless of the nature of their role in the legal writing community.[5] Legal writers thus include legislators, regulators, judges, administrative law judges, practicing attorneys, law professors, and law-trained legal scholars. As one member of our focus group put it, we mean to include all those who engage in legal writing and "wield the power of law."

As explained in Chapter Three, the concepts are divided into three categories: concepts that relate to (1) the nature of legal writing as a rhetorical practice within which the meaning of law and its application to specific facts is negotiated and determined, (2) the process of legal writing in the course of which legal writers must conform with certain rhetorical conventions as acculturated members of the legal writing community, and (3) the nature of legal writers: ways in which legal writing shapes and constrains legal writers and their professional identity.[6] A graphic illustration of our concepts is set forth below in Table 1.

---

4. *See* ch. 1, *supra* note 23 and accompanying text.

5. *See* ch. 1, *supra* notes 20–23 and accompanying text.

6. *See* ch. 3, *supra*, at 26–27.

Table 1 Legal Writing Is a Disciplinary Practice and a Distinct Subject of Study

1. Legal writing is a meaning-making activity.
(the products of legal writing: concerning the nature of legal writing as a rhetorical practice in which meaning is negotiated and determined)

1.1 Legal writing creates and recreates the law.
Melissa H. Weresh and Kirsten K. Davis

1.2 The foundational role of legal writers is to construct arguments about the meaning of language.
Linda L. Berger

1.3 Legal writers understand that the malleability of law gives them latitude in articulating legal principles.
Melissa H. Weresh

1.4 Legal writers understand that "framing" is necessary to open the door to legal remedies and to connect with an audience.
Linda Berger

1.5 Facts in law are not "truth" but are advocated by lawyers and determined by an adjudicator.
Ruth Anne Robbins

1.6 Legal writing involves a blend of rules and storytelling, with stories offering a bridge between the law and facts and giving meaning and context to legal rules.
Sherri L. Keene

1.7 Legal writing is neither right nor wrong.
Melissa H. Weresh

1.8 Legal writing wields and perpetuates dominant power, but it can also be used to disrupt power.
Kristen K. Tiscione

2. Legal writing is a rhetoric with distinctive rhetorical conventions.
(the process of legal writing concerning the rhetorical conventions with which legal writers must conform)

2.1 Legal writers know that they engage in a rhetorical practice even though the law itself tends to deny its rhetorical nature.
Kirsten K. Davis

2.2 Legal writers read actively, efficiently, and effectively, for the purpose of solving specific problems.
Kristen K. Tiscione

2.3 Legal writers must gather and understand both fact and law before they can proceed.
Kristen E. Murray

2.4 Legal writing relies on a flexible understanding of sources of authority.
Kristen K. Tiscione

2.5 Legal writers construct rules of law based on their client's factual circumstances and the arguably relevant sources of law in a given jurisdiction at a specific point in time.
Kristen K. Tiscione

2.6 Legal writers use deductive reasoning, in combination with other forms of reasoning, to reach convincing yet necessarily probable conclusions.
Kristen K. Tiscione

2.7 Precedent is the site for negotiating the validity of competing claims, and analogical reasoning is the primary tool by which legal writers make their case for validity.
Leslie Culver

2.8 Legal citations are concise arguments that serve as proxies for proof and professionalism.
Kristen K. Tiscione

2.9 Legal writers use different genres of writing in response to differences in their goals, stance, and audience.
David I.C. Thomson

2.10 Legal writing requires typographic judgment.
Derek Kiernan-Johnson

continues

continued

3. Legal writers learn their constraints and identities within a professional practice as writers and readers.
(the nature of the expert legal writer: concerning ways in which legal writing shapes and constrains legal writers and their professional identities)

3.1 Legal writing involves ethical and persuasive choices about what constitutes "good" arguments within a specific rhetorical context.
Linda L. Berger

3.2 Legal precedent provides both guidance and boundaries for legal writers.
JoAnne Sweeny

3.3 The expert legal writer knows that time is needed for legal writing because the legal writer is creating something new through a synthetic and recursive process that requires a multi-layered approach, multiple revisions, and an ongoing internal dialogue.
Julie A. Oseid

3.4 Legal writers are creative writers.
Kristen K. Tiscione

3.5 Legal writers internalize conditions of uncertainty.
Melissa H. Weresh

3.6 Legal writing's conventionality makes legal writing identifiable and credible to legal audiences but also potentially exclusionary and confusing for some writers.
Kirsten K. Davis

3.7 Legal writers form and enact their professional identity through legal writing.
Melissa H. Weresh

B. Category One: Legal Writing Is a Meaning-Making Activity

This category contains concepts related to the nature of legal writing as a rhetorical practice in which meaning is negotiated and determined. In short, like all writing, legal writing constitutes a meaning-making activity.[7] As Kirsten Davis and Melissa Weresh explain in Concept 1.1, legal writing creates and recreates the meaning of law through a series of conversations among members of the legal discourse community. The concept of law as continually evolving surprises novice legal writers, who often come to law school assuming that their task as legal writers is "to find and apply the law" as though it exists apart from the language used to express it in a given context. As students begin to understand the nature of law, they begin to understand their role in shaping it.

---

7. *See* Heidi Estrem, *1.1 Writing is a Knowledge-Making Activity*, *in* NAMING WHAT WE KNOW, ch. 1, *supra* note 15, at 19.

In Concept 1.2, Linda Berger explains that as part of that creative process, the fundamental role of legal writers is to make arguments about the meaning of legal language. As novices become familiar with their role in legal writing, they begin to understand the positive and negative constraints associated with meaning-making and how the meaning of laws changes over time and in different contexts.

In 1.3, Melissa Weresh expands on the notion of the evolution of law, explaining the threshold concept of malleability—the degree to which the law and facts in legal writing can be stated with varying degrees of breadth but must fall within a reasonable zone of interpretation. Relatedly, in Concept 1.4, Linda Berger explores how legal writers not only contribute to the meaning of law but do so by framing the rhetorical situation.[8] By emphasizing certain priorities and principles and excluding or downplaying others, the legal writer commits to and creates the lens through which the legal issue at hand may be understood and analyzed.

In Concept 1.5, Ruth Anne Robbins shifts to the role of facts in legal writing. As she observes, legally significant facts are more determined than "found." Ultimately, legal writers view facts as neither true nor false but as relevant or determinative. In Concept 1.6, Sherri Keene explains that stories play a fundamental role in legal writing, bridging the gap between facts and law as they give meaning and context to legal rules. As Keene observes, the law is comprised of stories. For example, opposing parties tell competing stories as part of the decision-making process, and in turn, judges consider those competing stories and choose a story of their own that ultimately becomes law.

In Concept 1.7, Melissa Weresh observes that just as facts are neither true nor false, legal writing cannot be said to be either right or wrong. Instead, it is the product of discretionary choices made in pursuit of specific client goals, and law-trained readers tend to evaluate legal writing as more or less effective as opposed to true or false. Finally, in Concept 1.8, Kristen Tiscione explores the inherent power legal writers yield in the legal discourse community by influencing who is authorized to speak, on what matters, and when. She argues that although legal writing can be said to perpetuate power, it can also be used to disrupt it.

---

8. *See generally* Lloyd Bitzer, *The Rhetorical Situation*, 1 PHIL. & RHETORIC 1 (1968) (explaining that rhetors respond to perceived exigences in an effort to persuade the appropriate audience to effect desired change).

1.1 Legal writing creates and recreates the law.

Kirsten K. Davis and Melissa H. Weresh

Legal writing is an ongoing meaning-making conversation among texts and writers across time and distance. As Learned Hand observed, the law "stands as a monument slowly raised, like a coral reef from the minute accretions of past individuals, of whom each built upon the relics which his predecessors left, and in his turn left a foundation upon which his successors might work."[9]

Thus, legal writing and, in turn, legal writers, create and recreate law.[10] Legal writers who have crossed this threshold know that the law is not static, intractable, or fixed. They understand that legal writers make myriad, creative choices about what the law is, including how to articulate its contours, or what the law should be. As novices engage with this concept, they begin to understand the ways in which legal writing and legal writers shape legal meaning.

Understanding this threshold concept opens conceptual boundaries for legal writers as they begin to understand that cases, statutes, and even scholarly articles are as much raw source material for constructing arguments about what the law can or should be as they are sources of authority for stating what the law is. Their proposed meaning is then subject to the conversation and contributions of other legal writers whose voices may refine, adapt, or reject the proffered, constructed meaning. Put another way, "[w]ritten authorities are not law, but cultural resources for lawyers engaged in the practice of law. Law is the ongoing process of giving written authorities meaning in the context of disputes over what they mean in and for particular situations."[11] Legal writers are thus engaged in the process of creating and recreating legal meaning.

By understanding this concept, legal writers begin to see themselves as sculptors, not scribes, and view law as being in a constant state of change. Entering this threshold often implicates the liminal state where legal writers lean into or shy away from their role in constructing meaning. Even so, as they cross the threshold, legal writers begin to understand their own professional

---

9. Learned Hand, *Book Review*, 35 HARV. L. REV. 479, 479 (1922) (reviewing BENJAMIN N. CARDOZO, THE NATURE OF THE JUDICIAL PROCESS (1921)). While Hand was referring to the process of common law development, legal writers create meaning in the process of using all legal sources to construct texts.

10. *See* White, *Law as Rhetoric*, ch. 1, *supra* note 20, at 691 (asserting that we might consider law "as a community of speakers of a certain kind; as a culture of argument, perpetually remade by its participants").

11. Leigh Hunt Greenhaw, *"To Say What the Law Is": Learning the Practice of Legal Rhetoric*, 29 VAL. U. L. REV. 861, 866 (1995).

identity in the context of legal meaning-making; they envision themselves as "a participant in the perpetual remaking of the language and culture that determines who [the lawyer] is."[12]

The notion that legal writing is a creative and re-creative process rather than a mechanistic one of determining the singular meaning of a set of rules could be characterized as an "episteme" or part of the "underlying game."[13] For the novice, understanding the legal writer's agency in creating the law is thus troublesome and transformative. The idea that everyday legal writers contribute to the development of law challenges long-standing notions that the law is fixed. Nonetheless, once this threshold is crossed, legal writers understand their participation in the ongoing conversation about law in a way that is irreversible.

This threshold concept integrates a number of unrelated core and threshold concepts, such as malleability, rule synthesis, precedential value, *stare decisis*, analogical reasoning, and organizational structures of legal writing—each of these concepts is integrally connected with the creative process.

1.2 The foundational role of legal writers is to construct arguments about the meaning of language.

Linda L. Berger

Expert legal writers understand that the heart of their work is to build arguments about the meaning of language. These arguments center on how the language of the law should be interpreted and acted upon in a particular rhetorical setting. The lawyer constructs arguments designed to persuade an au-

---

12. *See* White, *Law as Rhetoric*, ch. 1, *supra* note 20, at 691; *see also* Concept 3.6, *infra*, at 109.

13. *See* ch. 2, *supra*, at 16; *see also* David Perkins, *Constructivism and Troublesome Knowledge*, *in* OVERCOMING BARRIERS TO STUDENT UNDERSTANDING: THRESHOLD CONCEPTS AND TROUBLESOME KNOWLEDGE 33 (Jan H.F. Meyer & Ray Land, eds., 2006). Perkins explains that "disciplines are more than bundles of concepts. They have their own characteristic epistemes [or] manners of justifying, explaining, solving problems, conducting inquiries, and designing and validating various kinds of products or outcomes." *Id.* at 42. He observes that "[l]earners often encounter difficulties playing the 'epistemic games', as they might be called, that go with the disciplines [and further that] difficulty with particular disciplinary concepts may derive from difficulty with the underlying episteme." *Id.* at 42–43. In this respect, understanding this concept implicates the threshold concept of malleability, or the latitude a legal writer has in expressing legal principles. *See* Concept 1.3, *infra*, at 40.

dience that the language leads (naturally, inevitably) to an outcome that would make things better for the lawyer's client or for society as a whole.

Many students enter law school believing that the language of the law has an established and clear meaning. They are initially troubled when they discover that the primary role of legal writers is not to find and apply the straightforward language of rules to agreed-upon facts, but instead to be engaged in a "conversation by which our words get and change their meaning."[14]

Legal writing focuses specifically on the meaning and import of the language that governs the most significant relationships among individuals, organizations, and governments within our society. This language—mostly found in written texts, but also used orally in promises, oaths, and pledges—spells out a spectrum of obligations and rights, stretching from those associated with intimate relationships (wedding vows and wills) to those growing out of commercial dealings (sales contracts and rental agreements) to those reflecting societal and cultural norms (legislation, judicial opinions, and Constitutions).

Arguments about the meaning of legal language begin with words and phrases and include the many kinds of symbols used to communicate, such as numbers, graphs, images, gestures, and design elements. The legal writer's arguments about meaning extend not only to the language and symbols, but also to whether different constructions of the facts match the language of the law. Think, for example, of the classic hypothetical barring "vehicles in the park": the ensuing arguments address not only the meaning of the term *vehicle*, but also whether increasingly unlikely concrete examples match any of the proposed meanings (automobile, motorcycle, bicycle, child's scooter, tricycle, baby carriage, walker, wheelchair).

The foundational role for legal writers—to construct arguments about the meaning of language—is different from the role of writers in other disciplines. This is primarily because the law exists rhetorically, in the form of language, and its rhetorical existence constitutes its essence.[15] The rhetorical nature of the law remains no matter whether the direction of the legal conversation is progressive, repressive, or static. The law advances, or fails to do so, through the conversations ongoing within the rhetorical community of the law.

---

14. James Boyd White, When Words Lose Their Meaning: Constitutions and Reconstitutions of Language, Character, and Community 266 (1984) [hereinafter White, Words].

15. *See* Marianne Constable, Our Word Is Our Bond: How Legal Speech Acts 2 (2014).

In addition, because lawyers so often write on behalf of clients and within an adversarial legal system, legal writers almost always formulate arguments and anticipate argumentative responses, a rhetorical situation with unique constraints. When legal writers represent a client, the legal writer's voice and beliefs sometimes must yield to what will aid the client and persuade the reader. Because legal writers anticipate being read by other attorneys and judges, expert legal writers know that their arguments about the meaning of language are bounded not only by their own imaginations but also by the requirements that they fit within the context of existing legal doctrine, acknowledge hierarchies of authority, and refer to existing texts.

While arguments about the meaning of legal language construct the law, the law in turn creates the rhetorical community within which legal writers think, speak, write, and act. The law establishes "roles and relations and voices, positions from which and audiences to which one may speak, and [gives] us as speakers the materials and methods of a discourse."[16]

In this way, as they learn to read and discuss cases, novice legal writers are beginning to learn how to think and act in the world they are entering, a rhetorical culture of argument. Their role is to imagine the experience of the legal writer by arguing the current case and anticipating the counterarguments within their own imaginations: "If I were the lawyer in this case, what would I do?"[17] By imagining the arguments they would make on behalf of a client, legal writers not only are preparing to tell a story, they are deciding how to "claim a meaning" for it.

Claiming a meaning is an imaginative interpretive act: the meaning of language changes over time and across cultures and through countless prior interpretive arguments, decisions, and actions. The lawyer's arguments will vary depending on the context in which the language is currently being used as well as on the presence and interpretation of other words and other texts. As one example, some legal writers on the U.S. Supreme Court now argue that the *color-blind* quality of the Constitution supports a position diametrically opposed to the original use of the phrase. Rather than supporting guarantees of equal access to educational opportunities, these attorneys claim that a color-blind Constitution requires courts to reject government programs designed to redress racial inequities.

---

16. White, Words, *supra* note 14, at 8–10.

17. *Id.*

Claiming a meaning also is a social rhetorical activity. Even though the act of writing itself may be solitary, the legal writer is always writing for a client and to various audiences. Each of these audiences understands that language is used for different purposes and in multiple ways. As a result, the expert legal writer must become a more careful reader and user of language.

The concept that their role is to make arguments rather than to find and apply the law is initially troublesome because it introduces uncertainty about whether the novice legal writer is "doing this right." Once the concept becomes part of the writer's deeper understanding, it transforms the way that legal writers value their work. Experienced legal writers value legal arguments not because they provide closure, but because they provide "the open hearing in which one point of view, one construction of language and reality, is tested against another."[18] An open hearing becomes possible because of the capacity of legal language to allow for multiple ways of reading the law and because of the legal writer's responsibility in different rhetorical settings to imagine multiple ways of reading. When legal writers use the language of the law to support different points of view and different constructions of reality, they are opening up and enriching the legal conversation. In the process, they help make room in the law for multiple voices. Recognizing that result makes an irreversible change in the legal writer.

1.3 Legal writers understand that the malleability of law gives them latitude in articulating legal principles.

Melissa H. Weresh

Legal writers understand that the law is not a static set of rules that are applied uniformly across situations. Rather, the disciplinary expert understands that the law is malleable[19] and can be stated and utilized in legal analysis and communication with varying degrees of breadth within a reasonable, ethical zone of interpretation.[20]

---

18. *Id.* at 8.

19. *See generally* Weresh, *Malleability*, ch. 2, *supra* note 1.

20. *See* Jane Kent Gionfriddo, *Thinking Like a Lawyer: The Heuristics of Case Synthesis*, 40 TEX. TECH L. REV. 1, 13–18 (2007). Gionfriddo explains that "lawyers must evaluate the significance of each case in relationship to all other cases in the group and then hypothesize possible explanations of the court's implicit meaning. Depending on the particular group of cases, more than one explanation might reasonably be inferred from the cases." *Id.* at 14. In both an objective analysis and in argumentation, the lawyer's inferences must fall within a "reasonable zone of right explanations." *Id.* at 13–18.

The rule of law from a particular case, or a synthesized rule of law from a number of cases, can be stated broadly so as to apply to a variety of situations, or more narrowly, such that certain situations fall outside of its zone of application. Statutes and constitutional provisions are subject to interpretation as well. This means that legal principles are flexible rather than rigid and adaptable to different interpretations. This flexibility, or malleability, enables the legal writer to contribute to the meaning-making function of legal writing.[21]

Even so, understanding malleability requires the expert to understand the limits of this flexibility, both in terms of the reasonable zone of interpretation of any given legal principle and the ethical limits of the articulation of law and legal reasoning. It also requires the writer to understand and tolerate the degree to which the law is both certain, in terms of cases relying on established precedent, and uncertain, in terms of understanding that judicial opinions select and prioritize certain facts and elevate certain legal principles and policies.[22]

Understanding that the law is malleable (to a degree, given the reasonable parameters of interpretation for a particular legal principle) is a threshold concept. Crossing the threshold to understanding requires a student to integrate several important legal concepts, such as jurisdiction, *stare decisis*, and precedent. It also requires the disciplinary expert to think critically and analytically, considering how the underlying policy implications of legal principles impact the ability of the writer to broaden or constrain those principles.

A thorough understanding of malleability is bounded within the legal discipline because novices tend to believe that the law is certain and static. Understanding malleability represents a paradigm shift, defying the novice's preconceived notions about the certainty of law and changing their understanding of legal analysis and legal writing as meaning-making activities.

Malleability of law is also troublesome and transformative. The idea that the law can be adapted or molded is often objectionable or counter-intuitive to the novice, challenging their assumptions about the stability of law. Accepting that the law is both certain and uncertain may be alien to the novice, who may initially reject or resist such an understanding. Nonetheless, once the novice understands that the law is malleable, she has crossed a threshold of understanding and her legal reasoning is transformed in a way that is irreversible. Understanding that the law is malleable forever changes the disciplinary expert's way of viewing the law, permanently transforming the expert's way of thinking and practicing within the law.

---

21. *See* Concepts 1.1 and 1.2, *supra*, at 36 & 37.

22. *See* Concept 3.5, *infra*, at 105.

1.4 Legal writers understand that "framing" is necessary to open the door to legal remedies and to connect with an audience.

Linda L. Berger

Because no writer can meaningfully convey all the details that make up even a single incident, the writer selects from among the details and presents the chosen ones. When the chosen details are placed within the context of a frame, the description becomes meaningful. Selection of the details and framing of their presentation is common to writing in many fields, but framing in legal writing has a distinctive cast: no insult, injury, or dispute will be heard in a legal forum unless it fits within an appropriate frame.

In this way, the necessity for framing the dispute may exclude people and problems, and it guarantees that any description of the setting will be incomplete. But the process of framing may also be used to bring attention to overlooked details and to expand access to legal remedies. By framing a previously unrecognized problem with a new perspective, legal writers may construct new rhetorical situations and propose fitting resolutions for the people and problems they encompass. When first described, "rhetorical situations" were thought to provide the setting for a rhetorical response when the writer discovered a pre-existing exigence that called out for a solution.[23] Experienced legal writers have learned that they not only respond to naturally created rhetorical situations, they also create new rhetorical situations. New rhetorical situations are created when the legal writer—in conjunction with the client—frames a previously unrecognized failure or lack of solution in a way that the audience accepts.[24]

The purpose and result of framing are to select and foreground some aspects of the situation, making them appear more accessible and more significant, while shifting other aspects to the background. Framing allows the writer to signal the reader about "what is at stake in a rhetorical situation." Through framing, the legal writer not only "promote[s] a particular problem

---

23. *Compare* Bitzer, *supra* note 8, *with* Richard Vatz, *The Myth of the Rhetorical Situation*, 6 PHIL. & RHETORIC 154, 154 (1973).

24. *See* Mark A. Hannah & Michael J. Cedrone, *The Pervasiveness of Rhetoric in Lawyering*, *in* DELIA B. CONTI, LINDA L. BERGER, MICHAEL J. CEDRONE, MARK A. HANNAH, MELISSA E. LOVE KOENIG & JULIE A. OSEID, LAW AND RHETORIC: A PRIMER 264–66 (2023) (describing Richard Vatz's "more open, creative understanding of rhetorical situations" as inviting lawyers to view their work as acts of co-authorship, as co-creating with their client" the rhetorical situation "through which the client's issue will be addressed and resolved").

definition," but also supports a specific "causal interpretation, and approach to resolve an issue."[25]

The exclusionary force of framing becomes apparent to novice legal writers early in their reading and discussion of case law when they are told that some details of a dispute just don't count because they are not relevant to whether the dispute fits within the frame being discussed—a tort, a crime, a contract, or any other category established in the law. The necessity for framing the incident to fit an existing slot is a significant constraint on writers, clients, and the development of the law. Absent a fit within a pre-existing legal category, relief through legal channels may be denied to deserving individuals or groups. Moreover, because framing necessarily leaves the reader with an incomplete picture, it lends itself to the introduction of biases or stereotypes.

The expansive force of framing becomes most apparent when it empowers writers to construct new rhetorical situations or to reconfigure the categories already found in the law. Because legal categories are constructed, rather than existing in nature, the description of a legal category and the selection of one category over another is the author's prerogative. The legal writer begins with the same basic set of information and changes the frame to provide a different way of seeing, and that different way of seeing shifts the meaning of what happened.[26] Just as a new perspective shifts the meaning of the facts, it can affect the characterization of the legal issue.

As essential as it is to open the door to a legal forum, framing is similarly essential to persuasion. For persuasive purposes, framing helps forge identification by helping the writer make connections with an audience. The implicit comparison to a well-known frame (analogy, metaphor, story) helps the reader manage the details and reach a more general understanding of the whole. And when the selected frame resonates favorably with the audience member because it is familiar and comfortable, the implicit comparison helps the writer nurture a shared understanding.

In general, we learn by comparing new information with the embedded knowledge structures[27] we have constructed in our minds through our personal experiences and social and cultural interactions. Effective framing relies

---

25. *Id.* at 271.

26. Linda L. Berger & Kathryn M. Stanchi, Legal Persuasion: A Rhetorical Approach to the Science 128–33 (2018).

27. Linda L. Berger, *How Embedded Knowledge Structures Affect Judicial Decision Making: An Analysis of Metaphor, Narrative, and Imagination in Child Custody Disputes*, 18 S. Cal. Interdisc. L.J. 259 (2009).

on this learning process by encouraging the reader to "connect the pieces of the puzzle in order to see a particular picture."[28] Readers are more likely to make connections when the writer implicitly compares the current incident to the more resonant filters and frames the reader already carries in her mind. That is, connections may more easily be made when the selected frame draws on comfortable or conventional fact examples (analogies), images (metaphors), and plots, settings, or characters (story elements). Once a connection is made, the reader may be persuaded to transfer reasoning and outcomes from the familiar filter or frame to the current incident.

Beyond the "entry frame," legal writers make framing decisions about both the facts and the law. For example, the legal writer may use framing to present the facts in a way that helps her develop an overall theory of the case. Presenting a fact-based storyline in a particular way—using characters, actions, setting, and plot points—allows the writer to frame the situation as calling out for the application of one set of legal rules rather than another.[29] Similarly, crucial framing decisions occur when legal writers are characterizing the law. A broader or more general framing of the rule of law may lead to its application across a wider spectrum of situations, but a narrower framing may result in a surer, but slimmer, slice of application.

Even though they may be deliberate choices by the legal writer, many framing choices are invisible to the reader. But experienced legal writers also use frames more visibly and explicitly. For example, a writer might present current-day exploitation of mineral rights as part of a much larger story-frame of conquering the frontier. Another writer might object to a prosecutor's use of the metaphor-frame of predator in seeking the conviction of a defendant. Such visible and explicit frames seek not only to influence the reader's understanding but also to reorient the reader's perspective. By applying the metaphor of war to drugs or crime, the writer may, for example, subtly incline the reader positively, in favor of arguments to carry out the kinds of policing actions that echo military endeavors, or negatively, against efforts to advance individual healthcare or promote social welfare.

As they gain practice, legal writers recognize additional opportunities for framing: the use of different time frames to shift impressions of causation; the use of an image or analogy to portray an incident as an action or an omission;

---

28. Berger & Stanchi, *supra* note 26, at 3–4.

29. *See generally* Pierre Schlag & Amy J. Griffin, How to Do Things with Legal Doctrine 31–51(2020).

or the use of sophisticated dramatic techniques to shift a story's emphasis from one element to another element of a narrative (for example, from the protagonist to the setting).

Framing is a threshold concept that when understood through experience and practice will reassure the novice legal writer that it is neither unfair nor unethical to leave out some details to present an understandable picture of what happened or what remedies are necessary. At first, encountering the concept of framing is troublesome and will be resisted because it requires novice legal writers to accept that there is no legal remedy for some injuries and wrongs and that it will be necessary to omit details and to recharacterize whole situations in a way that feels slanted.

Over time, the concept of framing is transformative. The experienced writer understands that it is never possible to convey all the facts of a situation in a truly objective or neutral way. Once this reality is grasped, the process of framing becomes an irreversible habit as the writer concentrates on how to connect with the audience most effectively, while realizing that another writer has a similar objective from another point of view.

Framing integrates the writer's understanding of the connection between rhetorical methods (especially the frames provided by implicit comparison with fact analogies, metaphoric images, and stories) and the law. As already mentioned, framing may be viewed as bounded within the discipline of legal rhetoric because of the requirement that an acceptable frame is necessary for a problem to be heard.

1.5 Facts in law are not "truth" but are advocated by lawyers and determined by an adjudicator.

Ruth Anne Robbins

Expert legal writers recognize the contingency of facts and operate to reach what are called fact determinations that are then used to connect the facts to the legal standards. Facts in "the law" do not represent absolute truth; they are determined by a fact-finder. In law, facts are key to any legal determination. Adjudication, legislation, regulation, and private law transactions all derive from the analysis of facts. Facts are at the heart of law; without them, there is no need for legal writing to occur or even for a legal system to exist. But, specialized to law, legal facts are contingent and unsettled until a fact-finder makes a fact-finding determination. Facts are different from "truth," because, in our lived experience—"the facts" as we perceive them—can never be objective. At best, our version of the facts represents only a partial view of "the truth" and reflects our unique perspective. Thus, in law, legal writers must present facts for determination, and fact-finders must create facts through a determination system.

Most easily seen in judicial-based dispute-resolution/public lawmaking, the process of determining facts involves client-centered advocacy by the lawyer and conclusions reached by a fact-finder based on presented evidence and inferences drawn from the presented evidence. A legal dispute in the court system has an assigned, specific "fact-finder," whose role is to make determinations of what constitutes a fact for the purposes of that legal dispute. A fact-finder may be a jury, but may also be a judge (if there is no jury). In other types of legal disputes, the fact-finder may be an arbitrator or mediator. Fact-finding in other types of public lawmaking or private lawmaking is less formal but still exists. Expert legal writers know that even though facts themselves may not represent "truth," they *become* objective truth once the fact-finder makes a fact-finding determination.

Even after a fact-finder adjudicates a fact-finding determination, these determined facts are nevertheless susceptible to challenge in subsequent proceedings. In public lawmaking, those proceedings may involve an appeal from a fact-finder's decision,[30] an amendment to a statute or regulation, or the creation of new legislation or regulation. In private lawmaking, a contract may be modified or ended. Facts, thus, are contingent, dependent on a point of view, perception, and even the passage of time.

Expert legal writers representing clients understand that a critical part of their lawyering obligations must be advocating for client-favorable fact determinations and fact-based inferences. To do that, they must present facts from the client's point of view in an adversarial system. To advocate for fact-finding, legal writers investigate and collect data from a variety of sources that they then assess and select for presentation to the fact-finder. Their process depends on the credibility of the source material and the relevancy of the material to the legal issues. Legal writers understand that the fact-finder will assess the facts for weight of the overall presented facts. Facts are also assessed—though by a lawmaker not a fact-finder—for sufficiency to meet the governing legal standard. Likewise, facts are determined by the fact-finder using the same filtering system. Facts are determined on the basis

30. *See generally* Donald R. Caster & Brian C. Howe, *Taking a Mulligan: The Special Challenge of Narrative Creation in the Post-Conviction Process*, 76 Md. L. Rev. 770 (2017).

of evidence, a lack of evidence, and any appropriate and logical inferences therefrom, particularly those that follow from the way facts are organized in relation to one another.[31] The logical inferences that are drawn are often connected to the narrative line created by the evidence.

Legal writers must understand the legal limitations and legal constructs that govern the determination of facts by fact-finders. These fact-finders have a specific scope of material they may consider when making fact determinations. Facts can be derived from testimony, physical materials (think: weapon, article of clothing, phone messages), or a combination. Fact-finders also make fact determinations based on appropriate inferences gleaned from other facts: this is what we term circumstantial evidence. Evidentiary rules provide the clearest example of legal constructs surrounding fact-finding—those rules refine what types of data may be introduced. In law, both the fact-finder and advocates are constrained by evidentiary rules that limit what can become the basis for fact determinations. In law, every jurisdiction has an established and elaborate set of evidentiary rules that speak to legal relevancy and admissibility, although said evidentiary rules do not always apply (for example, in a motion to suppress hearing).

Legal writers also understand that the facts they present must be constructed from multiple perspectives and potentially conflicting or inconsistent data. To most effectively advocate for the client, expert legal writers understand that they must present selected facts to the fact-finder. The expert legal writer uses a narrative structure as the frame for presentation.[32] As Anthony Amsterdam and Jerome Bruner explain, "facts on the ground" are incognizable until meaning is made through narrative structures.[33] Doing so permits the legal writer to present the facts cohesively and to show plausibility and verisimilitude, even if "truth" remains elusive.[34]

---

31. *See* Ruth Anne Robbins, Steven Johansen & Kenneth Chestek, *Collecting and Assessing the Facts, in* Your Client's Story: Persuasive Legal Writing (3d ed. 2024).

32. Storytelling is further discussed in Concept 1.6, *infra,* at 49.

33. Anthony Amsterdam and Jerome Bruner, Minding the Law 111 (2000).

34. *See* J. Christopher Rideout, *A Twice-Told Tale: Plausibility and Narrative Coherence in Judicial Storytelling,* 10 Legal Comm. & Rhetoric 67 (2013); Cathren Koehlert-Page, *Stranger Than Fiction: How Lawyers Can Accurately and Realistically Tell a True Story by Using Fiction Writers' Techniques that Make Fiction Seem More Realistic than Reality,* 78 La. L. Rev. 907 (2018).

The idea of facts in law is troublesome because novices struggle with the indeterminacy of facts and the idea that facts may be determined even if not fully proven definitively. Novices may be caught up in the idea that legal process is wholly concerned with truth-seeking and may miss the nuance that truth-seeking must always be balanced in law with the guarantees of fairness and due process. Novices will also struggle with the types of facts that may be used, and the relative credibility of fact sources. Novices may under-investigate facts that could prove to be both relevant and persuasive. Circumstantial evidence, in particular, is a troublesome and difficult concept for novices—and sometimes even experienced lawyers—because of the difference between the permissible and impermissible inferences that may be drawn from other presented facts. Moreover, novices may struggle to understand that part of the lawyer's role is in the construction of facts to assist the fact-finder. Legal storytelling plays its own special rule in framing facts,[35] and novices also struggle with the boundaries of ethical storytelling.

Acquiring an expert understanding of fact-finding in the law is also transformative, integrative, and irreversible. Once learned, the concepts associated with fact gathering, fact assessment, fact selection, fact presentation, and fact determination are irreversible. Understanding the interchange between fact selection and legal, logical relevancy makes this an integrative process. For legal purposes, facts must contain legal relevancy; simultaneously, an expert understands that law exists *because* relevant facts drive it. Once the novice legal writer understands the interplay between fact determination and legal reasoning, the learning is irreversible.

Finally, the concept of facts in law is one that is bounded. Legal determination depends not only on truth-seeking but also on the protection of rights through due process and fairness considerations that are embodied in evidentiary rules. Moreover, even when determined, facts may *change* in a subsequent proceeding. For example, in a litigation setting, a different panel of lawmakers may review the determined facts and conclude that the original fact-finding was flawed enough to merit a different outcome. By way of another example, in a regulatory context, fact-finding by an agency is also subject to review and possible reversal. That determined facts may be changed upon review, even if the standards are high to do so, underscores the uniqueness of facts as they exist in law.

35. *See* Concept 1.6, *infra*, at 49.

1.6 Legal writing involves a blend of rules and storytelling, with stories offering a bridge between the law and facts and giving meaning and context to legal rules.

Sherri Lee Keene

"Story" in legal writing refers to a reporting of events offered in furtherance of a legal argument or to support a legal decision. Expert legal writers understand that stories can play a fundamental role in legal analysis as they give meaning to legal rules. Stories offer a cognitive frame for considering the nuances of rule application, accommodating factual similarities and distinctions across cases by placing facts into a familiar context.

Stories are intertwined with rules in legal analysis and play a central role in rule creation and development. Laws are born of stories and also embed stories. Legal process begins with the client's story, and legal argument involves the retelling of this story within factual boundaries established by the law. Opposing legal parties tell competing stories of events relevant to a legal issue as part of the legal decision-making process. Judges consider these competing stories and choose a story of events, and ultimately tell stories in their own legal writing that become law itself.

But storytelling also operates in the law at a more fundamental level as stories explain and offer context for legal rules. "Precisely within the confines of arguably the most logos-dependent sections of a legal document, we see stories being told."[36] Legal writing incorporates story to forge a connection between law and facts and breathe life into legal rules. Each rule explanation tells a story of the law and its application to facts in prior cases. Moreover, rule explanations collectively tell a story of how the law has developed. Understanding these stories of the law allows legal writers to make connections and distinctions between prior cases and determine the boundaries of the law for a legal issue.

Facts are naturally understood in a cognitive story frame and disparate facts are often insufficient alone to convey meaning. While a novice legal writer might assume that the law simply requires an understanding of relevant legal rules and a "matching" of facts to law, legal analysis often requires a deeper and more nuanced understanding of events to resolve legal questions. Legal writers often craft rules from the implied meanings of relevant cases. In this process,

---

36. Christy DeSanctis, *Narrative Reasoning and Analogy: The Untold Story*, 9 Legal Comm. & Rhetoric 149, 151 (2012).

legal writers describe prior cases in story form emphasizing and deemphasizing aspects of these legal stories to highlight common themes or point out differences. Where a prior case offers a similar story, a legal writer may analogize the law to the current facts and frame the story to show why a court should rule consistently with that prior case based on the principle of *stare decisis*. Legal writers can also highlight distinguishable facts of a prior case to illustrate where a court might depart from case precedent.

A legal novice might assume that rule explanations are not detailed enough to be referred to as a story. Yet it is not the length of the reporting that defines what is story and what is not. Indeed, story is defined by its metaphorical nature and ability to tap into one's existing understanding and to bring that meaning into one's assessment of new events. Indeed, stories "are cognitive instruments and also means of argumentation in and of themselves."[37] Like all stories, legal stories can carry meaning that goes beyond what the legal writer describes. In bringing these cognitive frameworks to legal rules, stories enhance our understanding of facts and law and facilitate legal decision-making.

Understanding the fundamental role that stories play in legal analysis is transformative as it changes the way that a student views the law and legal practice. A novice legal writer might expect that stories play a role in law, particularly as a tool for advocacy. However, a novice legal writer would not expect for story to play an integral role in legal analysis. Once transformed, a legal writer learns that law does not involve a simple process of applying law to facts, but rather a complex process of making meaning that is established by exploring law in a contextual frame. Once the legal writer understands the role of story in law, they appreciate the ability of legal writers to explain and shape the meaning of the law through storytelling.

Once a student learns that legal analysis involves not only rules, but storytelling, this understanding is irreversible and cannot be unlearned or disregarded. A legal novice might expect to move from rule to application even if a gap exists between the law and facts. An expert legal writer understands that the space between the legal rule and the events of a case must be bridged by story. Once a legal writer understands the role of story in connecting law to facts they will rely on the story as a cognitive frame to give meaning and make connections. After learning of the connection between rules and story in legal analysis, the legal writer then recognizes the stories in all forms of legal

---

37. *See* Ruth Anne Robbins, *An Introduction to Applied Legal Storytelling and to this Symposium*, 14 Legal Writing: J. Legal Writing Inst. 3, 6 (2008).

writing including legal decisions. Going forward, a legal writer will resort to using story to make meaning and realize there is no other way to effectively make this connection.

The use of story in legal analysis can be troublesome for a novice legal writer and thus difficult to understand. The law is presented as based on logic with law being applied through a simple matching of law to facts that produces consistent and fair results. On the other hand, storytelling is often associated with emotion and persuasion, and thus perceived inappropriate to use in legal analysis. The concept of legal analysis as a process that is deeply intertwined with storytelling is something that a new legal writer would not expect. A novice legal writer might struggle to acknowledge the role of story in law or with their own role of crafting legal stories to engage legal rules and give meaning to law.

Understanding the role of story in legal analysis is integrative as it brings together legal rules and storytelling, as well as logos and pathos in legal analysis. A novice legal writer quickly learns that legal rules and story work hand in hand, and that stories serve a function in the law that goes beyond evoking emotion to help bring meaning to legal rules. Nonetheless, understanding the relationship between law and story also reveals spaces where stories can tap into our existing notions of how the world works and challenge legal writers to make sure that legal storytelling is grounded in evidence and not based on false assumptions.

Stories are bounded as they operate uniquely in the law. All humans process information in cognitive frames and tap into existing stores of knowledge when confronted with a new event. Yet, the process of connecting new events to existing knowledge frames is distinct in the law as this is made explicit in legal analysis. Legal writers explicitly tell the stories of prior cases when assessing a new case. While stories can also play a more hidden role in legal decision-making, offering a familiar cognitive frame, the mechanism for explicitly inviting some stories into the analytical process appears to be specific to the law.

1.7 Legal writing is neither right nor wrong.

Melissa H. Weresh

The products of legal writing are subject to a variety of discretionary choices made by the legal writer. In this way legal writing is not typically evaluated as right or wrong, correct or incorrect, but as more or less effective. While a legal document can certainly be wrong in the sense that it misreads or misunderstands the law or grossly mischaracterizes the facts, most forms of written legal prediction and argument are only more or less probable. This is due in part to the discretion the legal writer has in articulating the facts and legal principles; the ambiguities that arise in the law as it is interpreted, contested, and developed; and the way in which legal writing is subject to persuasive rhetorical techniques.[38] Because legal writing is a meaning-making activity situated in an ongoing conversation, it cannot be evaluated as right or wrong.

Legal writing, like others forms of writing, is capable of being evaluated based on various conventional criteria, such as clarity, coherence, persuasiveness, and adherence to legal principles. Legal writing is also subject to ethical constraints relating to the presentation of facts and law such that those statements can be wrong in the sense that they mischaracterize fact or law. Even so, legal writing relies on the author's articulation of legal principles which themselves may be uncertain or, where settled, subject to interpretation, and the representation of facts which have been curated by the writer.

Moreover, legal writing incorporates inferences and professional judgment calls, and is dependent on context, objective, and intended audience. When taking a position on a legal issue, in either a predictive or persuasive context, legal writers have a degree of latitude when framing the issue and when stating both facts and legal principles. Legal principles are malleable, meaning they can be stated broadly or narrowly. This means that the writer has a degree of discretion in articulating the contours and analysis of a legal issue.

The inability to assess legal writing as right or wrong is based on more than the threshold concepts of framing and malleability. Facts in legal writing do not merely exist; rather, they are selected by the writer. Some may be prioritized; others may be obscured.[39] This is a function of the discretion the legal writer has in her role as an advocate, a person who is meant to persuade an

---

38. *See, e.g.*, White, *Law as Rhetoric* ch. 1, *supra* note 20, at 684. White explains:

> In the law ... [the] means of persuasion can be described with some degree of accuracy and completeness, so that most lawyers would agree that such-and-such a case or statute or principle is relevant, and another is not. But the agreement is always imperfect: one lawyer will see an analogy that another will deny, for example. And when attention shifts to the value or weight that different parts of the material should have, disagreement becomes widespread and deep. Ultimately, then, the identity, the meaning, and the authority of the materials are always arguable, always uncertain. There is a sense in which the materials can be regarded in the first instance as objective, external to the self; but they are always remade in argument. Their discovery is, in a sense, an empirical process, their reformulation and use an inventive or creative one.

Id. at 689–90.

39. *See* Concepts 1.3 & 1.4, *supra*, at 40 & 42.

audience to the writer's view of the matter, whether it be the client's objective in representation or the writer's position in the context of legal scholarship. When these articulations fall within a range of reasonable interpretation and consequent articulation of applicable law and a thorough and accurate statement of key facts (albeit skewed in favor of the writer's position), legal writing may adhere to ethical and conventional constraints while at the same time avoid being right or wrong in the sense of being correct or incorrect.

In addition to relying on the framing of legal issues, the curation of facts, and the articulation of legal principles that may reflect discretionary decisions by the writer, legal writing may also not be viewed as right or wrong due to the ambiguity and evolution of law. The law may include gray areas which fail to provide concrete answers to legal questions. Certain cases or principles may be subject to legal sources that are in conflict, or that fail to align in a uniform legal rule. That the law is constantly evolving may also introduce uncertainty in the sense of "correctness" as precedent is reinterpreted or overruled.[40] Legal writing is also often informed by policies that emerge, change, or are refined, resulting in evolving perspectives through which to consider legal issues. Students engaging in legal writing must grapple with these vagaries, understanding that there is rarely a definitive right or wrong answer.

Legal writing is also influenced by the conventions and persuasive techniques employed within legal discourse. Legal writing is designed to present matters in a light most favorable to the entity or institutional objective on whose behalf the writing has been prepared. This can introduce subjectivity and/or bias in the writing, making it possibly more persuasive but not necessarily right or wrong.

At the same time, the latitude a legal writer has with regard to presenting facts and legal principles is not unfettered but is constrained by ethical rules and conventional standards and expectations applicable to the type of legal document or context in which the writing is produced. While legal principles are able to be stated broadly or narrowly, they must ultimately, and ethically, reflect a reasonable zone of interpretation.

For example, in a case where a landlord is held liable for failing to warn tenants about a known loose guardrail in a common stairwell, an acceptably broad articulation of the ruling might be "a landlord has a duty to warn tenants about known, non-obvious dangers on the premises." An acceptably narrow articulation of the ruling might be "a landlord must warn tenants about a known

40. *See* Concept 3.5, *infra* at 105.

loose guardrail in a common area." It would not be accurate or ethical to state the court's holding as "Landlords are liable for all injuries on their property" or, conversely, "Landlords for condominium complexes will only be liable to tenants for guardrail-related injuries occurring on second floor stairwells in buildings erected before 1982."

Students often enter law school with an understanding that making legal arguments on behalf of a client relies on applying established law to a fixed set of facts, making objective claims and presenting information accurately, and arriving at the justifiable result. Novice legal writers therefore aspire to be right or wrong—to be in a position where the answer to a legal question is either correct or incorrect. Legal writing presents students with a new paradigm in which both interpretation and application of legal principles to curated facts involves choices made within the context of multiple perspectives. In this respect a student's understanding of the "accuracy" of legal writing is a bounded understanding within the legal disciplinary culture.

The ability to understand and perform legal writing in this sense requires students to integrate their prior understanding of judging professional writing from the perspective of right or wrong together with the subjectivity of certain elements of legal writing (e.g., latitude of articulating legal principles and selecting key facts, ambiguity of law, and selection and prioritization of rhetorical choices). It also requires them to integrate understanding of other concepts of legal analysis, including critical analysis of legal texts, the consideration of alternative perspectives, and the anticipation of counterarguments. Understanding that legal writing is neither right nor wrong encourages students to approach legal texts and authorities critically and creatively, assessing the credibility of legal sources and the relative strength of legal arguments. By integrating these concepts students are able to understand the complexity of legal issues and to construct legal writing that evidence nuanced arguments.

The concept that legal writing is neither right nor wrong is likely troublesome for students on various levels. Students may feel uncomfortable with the notion that there is a lack of certainty in legal writing, and that legal writing can be evaluated as more or less persuasive, even in a predictive context where the writer must justify the basis for her prediction. This is because such arguments and predictions rely upon the writer's selective choices in articulating law and facts. This concept can be juxtaposed with the notion that legal writing represents truth-seeking in the absolute sense of right/wrong or correct/incorrect. This concept may challenge students' notions of law and justice, and of writing and knowledge in a disciplinary context that seeks to establish which side of any contested dispute in the law is demonstrably justifiable. The concept requires students to recognize and embrace the inherent ambiguity and complexity of legal reasoning. It may further be intellectually challenging for students to understand and simultaneously perform aspects of legal writing that are more subjective and those that must adhere to relatively objective criteria.

The concept that legal writing is neither right nor wrong, once mastered, is irreversible. Students cannot return to a prior understanding that law is fixed such that its representation in legal writing can be evaluated objectively. By accepting uncertainty in the law and the degree of discretion and range, students begin to appreciate that legal writing is not a straightforward exercise of identifying the correct answer but rather a dynamic process of constructing analysis within the bounds and conventions of the discipline.

Grasping this threshold concept transforms students' understanding of legal writing. When a student understands that legal writing does not communicate a definitive right or wrong answer, she experiences a paradigm shift, altering her focus from finding the "correct" interpretation to exploring competing perspectives. Recognizing this nature of legal writing has ethical implications, encouraging students to consider more deeply the consequences of their choices in crafting legal writing. Understanding that legal writing is neither right nor wrong helps students navigate uncertainty in legal analysis and fosters an understanding of the complexity of the discipline.

1.8 Legal writing wields and perpetuates dominant power, but it can also be used to disrupt power.

Kristen K. Tiscione

Legal writing is an instrument of social power that constructs knowledge by selecting what does and not count as truth.[41] In law, those "in power"—de-

---

41. *See, e.g.*, ANDREW ALTMAN, CRITICAL LEGAL STUDIES: A LIBERAL CRITIQUE 15–16 (1990); Louis B. Schwartz, *With Gun and Camera Through Darkest CLS-Land*, 36 STAN. L. REV. 413, 417 ("Law is an instrument of social, economic and political domination, both in the sense of furthering the concrete interests of the dominators and in that of legitimizing the existing order."); *see also* MICHEL FOUCAULT, POWER/KNOWLEDGE: SELECTED INTERVIEWS AND OTHER WRITINGS 1972–77 131–33 (Colin Gordon, ed., Colin Gordon et al. trans., Pantheon Books 1980) (arguing that knowledge is the result of power yielded within a social order, and this power prescribes particular rules and categories which define the criteria for legitimating knowledge and truth within that order); Kate Veira et al., *Literacy is a Sociohistoric Phenomenon with the Potential to Liberate and Oppress*, *in* (RE)CONSIDERING WHAT WE KNOW, ch. 1, *supra* note 15, at 37 (explaining that

termined largely by socio-economic status and positions of authority within the profession such as lawyers, judges, and law professors—construct our legal reality by controlling the subjects and nature of discourse. In so doing, certain perspectives, realities, and truths are elevated, while others are marginalized or silenced. The power of legal writing lies partially in its ability to prescribe who is authorized to speak, on what matters, and when; in short, to "control the narrative."

First and foremost, legal writers understand that they have an obligation—both moral and ethical—to work within the confines of the law. Put differently, there is an outer limit to a legal writer's creative license, a point at which zealous arguments or positions strain credulity and threaten credibility.[42] For example, *stare decisis* demands that legal writers make claims with adequate foundation in the law, and any argument to extend, modify, or reverse the law must be made in good faith.[43] Under the American Bar Association's Model Rules of Professional Conduct, all practicing lawyers must also avoid making dishonest, deceptive, fraudulent or misleading statements.[44] Judges, too, are required to behave ethically by performing their duties impartially, competently, and diligently.[45] And in the "give and take" of scholarly debate, legal scholars must also be mindful of similar limits on the reach of their normative arguments.

By operating within these constraints, legal writers preserve existing principles of law and, in turn, legitimize the existing social order. In so doing, legal writers directly or indirectly marginalize and silence minority points of view. As participants in this rhetorical process, legal writers may advance legal outcomes that operate as truth even though that truth may, at times, be rooted in outmoded assumptions, bias, or prejudice.

Yet, at the same time, legal writers know that while they participate in perpetuating dominant discourse, they can also employ their power to disrupt it. Within ethical limits—that reasonable zone of interpretation[46]—legal writers

---

reading and writing practices that "resonate[ ] with the power dynamics with which [they] come into contact can never be neutral).

42. *See* Concepts 1.3, *supra*, at 40 & 2.5, *infra*, at 71.

43. Model Rules of Prof. Conduct rr. 3.1, 8.4 (2025) [hereinafter Model Rules]; *see also* Fed. R. Civ. P. 11.

44. Model Rules, *supra* note 43, r. 8.4.

45. *See* Model Code of Jud. Conduct rr. 2.1–2.16 (2025).

46. *See, e.g.*, Concept 1.3, *supra*, at 40.

use their imagination and creativity to frame legal situations and rules of law from their client's perspective, distinguish binding precedent on the basis of differing facts and circumstances, pose novel interpretations of law, argue for a change in existing law, or even challenge the neutrality of the decision-maker. Although the dominant discourse transmits power, it also creates "a hindrance, a stumbling block, a point of resistance and a starting point for an opposing strategy" that leaves open the possibility of change.[47]

In Peter Elbow's terms, legal writers play "the doubting game," seeking to advance outcomes that might be inconsistent with existing precedent by finding error in it.[48] For example, "reasonableness" is a familiar legal standard used to evaluate behavior in a variety of legal contexts, but it is arguably rooted in the white male experience.[49] As such, it may disadvantage different but equally reasonable responses to particular facts and circumstances.[50] By doubting the continued validity of "the reasonable man" standard and its underlying assumptions, legal writers have challenged the dominant male view that this standard connotes."[51]

---

47. Michel Foucault, 1 The History of Sexuality: An Introduction 108 (1978); *see also* Victor Pitsoe & Moeketsi Letseka, *Foucault's Discourse and Power: Implications for Instructionist Classroom Management*, 3 Open J. Phil. 23, 25 (2013) (citing Foucault in arguing that formalist teaching practices constitute a kind of order that privileges particular theories and conceptions of humankind); Chris Weedon, Feminist Practice and Poststructuralist Theory 107 (2d ed. 1996) (citing Foucault in arguing for a form of feminist poststructuralism that can help bring about social change).

48. Peter Elbow, *Appendix Essay, The Doubting Game and the Believing Game—An Analysis of the Intellectual Enterprise, in* Writing Without Teachers 147, 148–51 (1973) (making a case for the believing game in seeking truth by believing each alternative and determining which seems "truest").

49. *See, e.g.*, Lucy Jewel, *Does the Reasonable Man Have Obsessive Compulsive Disorder?* 54 Wake Forest L. Rev. 1049 (2019) (explaining that the standard reinforces inequality by adopting the reasonable man's privileged persona and formalist approach to legal reasoning).

50. *Id.* at 1068 (arguing that the "reasonable man" is dedicated to enlightenment principles of rationality that were often used "to justify racial oppression, inequality, and violence").

51. *Id.; see also, e.g.*, Randy T. Austin, *Better Off with the Reasonable Man Dead or the Reasonable Man Did the Darndest Things*, 1992 B.Y.U. L. Rev. 479; David E. Seidelson, *Reasonable Expectations and Subjective Standards in Negligence Law: The Minor, the Mentally Impaired, and the Mentally Incompetent*, 50 Geo. Wash. L. Rev. 17 (1981); Genevieve Frances Steel, *Constructing the Trident of the Reasonable Person: Enough Is Enough! It's Time for The Reasonable Indian Standard*, 12 Elon L. Rev. 62 (2020).

The legal writer's role in perpetuating and disrupting either the status quo or the majority view is troubling to novice legal writers, who often assume their job is to find, not create answers. Early in their legal careers, they do not expect to be called on to make discretionary choices that carry such significant weight. Once they realize the range and enormity of the legal writer's task, they are understandably daunted by the power they wield as legal writers. This realization is integrative in that it requires them to understand a variety of concepts, such as malleability,[52] the lawyer's creative role in framing legal issues, the relevant facts, and legal rules; [53] the nature of authority;[54] and the uncertainties inherent in the nature and practice of law.[55] Legal writers who view themselves not only as advocates but as active and equal participants in a system resistant to change are irreversibly transformed. Having passed through this portal, they can no longer view their role as a neutral actor in a system that requires them only to apply clear rules to definitive fact. A mature understanding of the relation between power and knowledge in law is likely bounded but only to the extent that it concerns legal knowledge.

C. Category Two: Legal Writing Is a Rhetoric with Distinctive Rhetorical Conventions

The threshold concepts gathered here identify significant rhetorical conventions that distinguish legal writing from other kinds of communication. In our view, the primary rhetorical convention is that legal writers deny that they are being rhetorical when they are writing to a decision-making audience.[56] Legal writing focuses on what the law is, while at the same time downplaying the contingent and fact-specific nature of its assertions. By ignoring that their assertions rely on proposed interpretations of law, legal writers engage in the fiction that their work rests on definitive results. As Kirsten Davis emphasizes in Concept 2.1, the important point for novices to

---

52. *See* Concept 1.3, *supra*, at 40.

53. *See* Concepts 1.4 & 1.5, *supra*, at 42 & 45 and 2.4 & 2.5, *infra*, at 69 & 71.

54. *See* Concept 2.4, *infra*, at 69.

55. *See* Concept 3.5, *infra*, at 105.

56. *See infra* Concept 2.1, at 60; *see generally* Gerald Wetlaufer, *Rhetoric and Its Denial in Legal Discourse*, 76 VA. L. REV. 1545 (1990) (describing this fundamental feature of legal writing ranging from advocacy to scholarship).

grasp is that legal writers deny that they are "engaged in rhetoric," while at the same time participating in an ongoing conversation, subject to change, and heavily influenced by its context.[57]

The rest of the concepts within this category identify smaller-scale yet distinctive conventions associated with the products of legal writing.[58] In Concept 2.2, Kristen Tiscione explores the threshold concept of critical reading in the context of legal writing. Engaged in an "intensely rhetorical practice,"[59] legal writers engage with legal texts actively, efficiently, and effectively, with a specific purpose in mind, such as giving advice or making legal arguments. In Concept 2.3. Kristen Murray explores the threshold concept that legal writers are often surprised to learn: that they must gather both law and fact before they write, processes that are both interdependent and recursive.

In Concept 2.4, Kristen Tiscione explores the concept that legal writers have a unique understanding of legal authority as subjective, fluid, relative, uncertain, and malleable. In Concept 2.5, Tiscione explores the legal writer's understanding of the contingent and contextual nature of rule synthesis, demonstrating once again the dual role of legal writers in stating and creating the rule of law. In Concept 2.6, Tiscione describes how legal writers use deductive reasoning in conjunction with other forms of legal reasoning to reach convincing yet necessarily probable conclusions.

Leslie Culver builds on the probabilistic nature of legal writing in Concept 2.7 by explaining that the primary tool for negotiating validity in law is analogy. As Culver explains, in our common law system, legal writers use analogical reasoning to determine the kind of authority or reasons the court has already determined valid in similar circumstances and then rely on those in justifying their client's position. In Concept 2.8, Tiscione highlights the disci-

---

57. *See infra* Concept 2.1, at 60; *see also* Greenhaw, *supra* note 11, at 866 (describing law as "the ongoing, persuasive use of legal language to resolve problem situations.... Law is the ongoing process of giving written authorities meaning in the context of disputes over what they mean in and for particular situations").

58. *See* Neal Lerner, *2.3 Writing is a Way of Enacting Disciplinarity, in* NAMING WHAT WE KNOW, ch. 1, *supra* note 15, at 41 (explaining that "[m]any specific disciplinary genres—e.g., legal briefs, SOAP notes, mathematical proofs—reflect the values those disciplines assign to particular kinds of evidence, particular forms of argument, and particular expectations for the transaction between readers and writers in particular rhetorical situations").

59. *See* Concept 2.1, *infra*, at 60.

pline-specific nature of legal citation as concise arguments, which serves as a proxy for proof and professionalism.

In Concept 2.9, David Thomson turns to different forms of legal writing, each of which has its own conventions derived from varying rhetorical situations.[60] Legal writers learn not only to identify and intuit the characteristics of particular genres, but also to find opportune moments to adapt and change them. Finally, in Concept 2.10, Derek Kiernan-Johnson explains that persuasion in legal writing relies in part on typographic judgment. Since legal writing eventually appears in some form of text, whether in print or online, expert legal writers understand the importance of design elements in persuading their audience.

2.1 Legal writers know that they engage in a rhetorical practice even though the law itself tends to deny its rhetorical nature.

Kirsten K. Davis

Legal writers participate in a broader discourse community—the law—which has its own disciplinary-specific rhetorical commitments, one of which is, as Gerald Wetlaufer suggests, to deny that the law itself is rhetorical, or, in other words, to deny that the law is constructed by a community of writers that deploys its own disciplinary-specific commitments.[61]

To be a member of the community of legal writers, to cross the threshold from "writer" to "legal writer," novices must understand and embrace this troublesome duality. That is, legal writers become irreversibly transformed when they recognize that although the law does not readily recognize itself as rhetorical, to write about and within the law is the "very profession of rhetoric."[62]

To write within the law requires the writer to hold these conflicting ideas as equally true. This paradox is troublesome for novices. The legal texts that compose what we commonly think of as "the law" represent themselves as

---

60. *See also* Charles Bazerman, *2.1 Writing Speaks to Situations Through Recognizable Forms, in* NAMING WHAT WE KNOW, ch. 1, *supra* note 15, at 35; Bill Hart-Davidson, 2.2 *Genres are Enacted by Writers and Readers, in* NAMING WHAT WE KNOW, ch. 1, *supra* note 15, at 39; *see generally* Katie Rose Guest Pryal, *Genre Discovery 2.0*, 28 BARRY L. REV. 1 (2023) (exploring ways in which legal writers can discover a genre's conventions by studying it) [hereinafter Pryal, *Genre Discovery*].

61. *See* Wetlaufer, *supra* note 56, at 1548.

62. *Id. at* 1555.

anti-rhetorical, as somehow beyond or outside of rhetorical construction. Law, Wetlaufer suggests, is a rhetoric of foundations and deduction and "relies, above all else, upon the denial that [law] is a rhetoric that is being done."[63] This denial results in law's disciplinary-specific rhetorical commitments, which include among others, the appearance of objectivity; a dedication to closure of controversies, clarity, relevance and orderliness; a belief in binary judgment, one right answer; and a reverence for hierarchy and authority.[64] This anti-rhetorical rhetoric "shapes our advocacy, our judicial opinions, our scholarship, and our teaching."[65] What results from these rhetorical commitments is legal writing that appears to express a singular, objective, tidy truth about the human condition and human relationships.

In contrast, experienced legal writers are empowered by the knowledge that writing within the law means engaging in an intensely rhetorical practice. An experienced legal writer makes myriad rhetorical choices in a messy, creative, recursive thinking and writing process, where the texts of the law are viewed as resources for thought and argument, not as inflexible rules, policies, or scientifically certain principles.[66]

To write within the law means understanding that the rhetoric of legal practice—the practice that generates legal texts—is a rhetoric of plural meaning and values, argument and counterargument, malleability, interpretation, subjectivity, and impermanence. Writing within the law means recognizing that the product of the legal writer's work is the result of making countless rhetorical choices within pre-established discursive boundaries.

This duality is a troubling concept for the novice legal writer. To be empowered, a legal writer must be comfortable performing in this liminal space, where what she writes contributes to a larger discourse that treats the law as fixed and universal and resists the notion that it was conceived of and written by anyone in the first place. Legal writers are transformed when they recognize this inherent tension between law's self-identifying anti-rhetorical rhetoric and the deeply rhetorical world of what legal writers actually do: create and recreate the law through a never-ending process of argument and meaning-making.[67]

---

63. *Id.*

64. *Id.* at 1551–52.

65. *Id.* at 1549–50.

66. White, *Law as Rhetoric*, ch. 1, *supra* note 20, at 684.

67. *See* Concepts 1.1 & 1.2, *supra* at 36 & 37.

Standing at this threshold, novice legal writers move from uneasy feeling to conscious recognition of what this duality means to them as individuals and as legal writers. On one side of the threshold, legal writers sense but often cannot explain a feeling of ineffectiveness or illegitimacy as a legal writer. That is, they sense that law's rhetoric devalues their individual voice and suppresses multiple (and marginal) perspectives in its texts. But novices are often without words to explain how this de-voicing works—through a rhetoric of objectivity, closure, certainty, and singularity. If novices never cross this threshold, legal writing for them is less creative, engaging, and self-affirming. Instead, it can be an emotionally draining practice of paraphrase, attempting to find "the one right answer" in legal texts with one singular meaning, and conveying that right answer objectively, correctly, and clearly.[68]

Once across this threshold, the legal writer is irreversibly transformed. The troublesome feeling becomes a conscious recognition of the paradoxical nature of the law: that, even though the law has anti-rhetorical discursive commitments, legal writers construct the law with their own creative rhetorical practices in a culture of argument. They understand that this paradox requires integrating the numerous foundational writing and thinking skills they have learned in law school that will allow them to work effectively at the intersection of rhetorical practice and authoritative discursive conventions. Legal writers who have crossed this threshold learn to value their own voices within the law; they are creative within law's disciplinary boundaries,[69] and they can bring fresh perspectives to the law while at the same time using the law's language to speak within the law.

2.2 Legal writers read actively, efficiently, and effectively, for the purpose of solving specific problems.

Kristen K. Tiscione

Legal writers are expert legal readers.[70] Legal writers understand the differences between reading for pleasure, for learning, and for specific legal ob-

68. See Molly Fajans and Mary Falk, *Against the Tyranny of Paraphrase: Talking Back to Legal Texts*, 78 CORNELL L. REV. 163 (1993).

69. *See* Concepts 3.5 and 3.6, *infra*, at 105 & 109.

70. *See, e.g.*, RUTH ANN MCKINNEY, *Introduction*, in READING LIKE A LAWYER: TIME-SAVING STRATEGIES FOR READING LAW LIKE AN EXPERT, xiii (2014) (describing exceptional lawyers as expert readers) [hereinafter MCKINNEY, READING LIKE A

jectives, such as giving clients advice, making a legal argument on their behalf, or writing a scholarly article on the weaknesses of particular legal doctrine. Unlike novice legal writers, experts approach legal texts with a particular purpose in mind that influences the way they read and interact with them.[71] As members of a community engaged in "an intensely rhetorical practice,"[72] legal writers understand that reading is not simply the transmission of knowledge from writer to reader.[73] Instead, it is a transaction between writer and reader, wherein "meaning exists in the mind of the reader and must be actively constructed from the text."[74]

Legal writers thus engage actively with legal texts, "comprehend[ing, analys[ing], interpret[ing] and evaluat[ing]"—in hopes of using them to advance their specific purposes.[75] As an initial matter, the reader's specific objective informs how she interacts with the text. For example, there is a difference between reading the law for general advice-giving and reading it to file a complaint. If the purpose is to advise a client starting a trash disposal service on how to avoid nuisance claims, the legal writer might read to summarize the general principles of law, the various types of claims, and the facts and circumstances associated with successful claims against disposal-type services. However, if the legal writer needs to draft a nuisance complaint on behalf of a client who lives near a noisy manufacturing plant, they will read the same case law differently, focusing in on the claim best suited to their client's specific facts and circumstances and the most analogous cases (e.g., involving claims of excessive noise).

LAWYER]; *see also* Alex Steel, *Succeed, Question, Repeat: Threshold Concepts and Variation Theory in Understanding How Law Students Build Competency*, 53:3 LAW TCHR. 231, 241 (2019) (arguing that critical reading is a threshold concept to be mastered in legal education) [hereinafter Steel, *Succeed, Question, Repeat*].

71. *See* MCKINNEY, READING LIKE A LAWYER, *supra* note 70, at 97 (noting that expert readers approach the same text from a different perspective and with different questions based on their purpose); *see also* Leah Christensen, *The Paradox of Legal Expertise: A Study of Experts and Novices Reading the Law*, 2008 B.Y.U. Educ. & L.J. 53, 70 (noting that experts keep their purpose in mind "to read more effectively and efficiently").

72. *See* Concept 2.1, *supra*, at 60.

73. Alex Steel et al., *Critical Legal Reading: The Elements, Strategies and Dispositions Needed to Master this Essential Skill*, 26:1 LEGAL EDUC. REVIEW 187, 189 (2017) [hereinafter Steel et al., *Critical Reading*].

74. *Id.; see also* Concept 1.2, *supra*, at 37.

75. Steel et al., *Critical Reading*, *supra* note 73, at 189.

Legal writers also develop rhetorical strategies for reading legal texts efficiently and effectively. They begin by assessing their context: What is the nature of the text (a judicial decision, brief, law review article, etc.)?[76] For example, legal writers understand they cannot make full sense of an appellate decision without first understanding the procedural posture of the decision below and the reason for the appeal. If they recognize the genre of the text, the legal writer will already be familiar with its compositional and stylistic conventions, making it easier to find and assimilate relevant sections of text.[77] Then, legal writers consider who wrote it and for what purpose? Who was the intended audience? What is the main idea (holding, rule of law, major argument, etc.)?[78] And, if relevant, is it binding on my client or does it affect my purpose in any way?

With both purpose and context in mind, the legal writer reads selectively, deciding which parts to read and re-read carefully and which parts can be skimmed or ignored.[79] For example, in reading case law to draft a nuisance complaint, the legal writer may be able to skim parts of judicial decisions that address claims other than nuisance that arose out of the same facts. In contrast, when zeroing in on the pertinent sections, they read carefully, seeking to extract principles that apply to their client's complaint and ultimately create rules of law that are accurate, comprehensive, and favorable to their client.[80] As Ruth Ann McKinney describes it, legal writers are masters at "decoding the words in the texts and reaching behind the words to the many possible meanings that could be attributed to the law they're reading."[81]

---

76. *See* Mary Beth Beazley & Monte Smith, Legal writing for Legal Readers 3 (2014) (explaining that knowing the context "helps readers understand new information") [hereinafter Beazley & Smith, Legal Readers]; Christensen, *supra* note 71, at 76–79 (explaining that lawyers and judges pay more attention than novice legal readers to the context of case decisions, including "both the context within which they [are] reading and the context within which the case was decided"); *see also* McKinney, Reading Like a Lawyer, *supra* note 70, at 105–10 (encouraging students to use internal and external cues to get valuable context for reading cases in casebooks).

77. *See* Concept 2.9, *infra*, at 83.

78. *See, e.g.*, McKinney, Reading Like a Lawyer, *supra* note 70, at ch. 6 (reading for the main idea) & ch. 9 (using who, what, when, where, why, and how to understand context).

79. *See* Beazley & Smith, Legal Readers, *supra* note 76, at 23.

80. *See* Concepts 1.4, *supra*, at 42, and 2.4, *infra*, at 69.

81. McKinney, Reading Like a Lawyer, *supra* note 70, at xiii; *see also* Christensen, *supra*, note 71, at 54–55 (explaining how effective legal writers read).

Finally, legal writers evaluate as they read, seeking to make connections either between new information and existing schemas of knowledge or new information and personal experience.[82] As McKinney explains, they do not assume the text is written by "an authority whose contributions are beyond their reach."[83] Instead, to make meaning out of the text, they "make judgments about the content of what they're reading..., learning from the author but also forming opinions about the content, style, validity, and power of what they're reading."[84] For example, is the text compelling and well-written? Does the reasoning make sense? Am I convinced? They also consider their own thoughts and feelings on the subject matter of the text, the author's writing style, the author's potential biases or assumptions, and the contributive value of the text.[85] For example, do I agree with this outcome? Has the outcome been engineered to achieve the author of the text's goals? What does this case add to my existing knowledge? And what assumptions or worldview did the author bring to this text?

This bundle of critical reading skills does not come easily to novice legal writers. As undergraduate students, novices may have viewed their role as student readers quite differently, willing to receive and to learn new information but not necessarily engage with it critically. Thus, it is troubling for students to realize that reading in law is not a passive activity. They must adjust to the changing purposes for which they read legal texts, recognizing, for example, that reading cases to prepare for doctrinal classes is different from reading cases to resolve a client dispute.[86] Beginning law students must come to appreciate that appellate decisions in casebooks are edited and organized to illustrate legal principles and that their objective is to synthesize those principles, often applying them to different hypothetical scenarios. However, in a legal writing course, students read unedited cases in order to engage in predictive or persuasive legal analysis, culling relevant information to articulate legal principles applicable to the client's claim or charge.

---

82. Beazley & Smith, Legal Readers, *supra* note 76, at 3 (explaining that legal readers understand new information better when they have prior knowledge to "attach it to"); Christensen, *supra*, note 71, at 74 (explaining that expert legal readers use their prior knowledge and experience to construct meaning within the text).

83. McKinney, Reading Like a Lawyer, *supra* note 70, at 153.

84. *Id.*; Christensen, *supra*, note 71, at 79–80 (explaining that expert legal readers are not afraid to question the quality of a judicial decision, including the result and the writing).

85. *See* McKinney, Reading Like a Lawyer, *supra* note 70, at 154.

86. *See, e.g.*, Beazley & Smith, Legal Readers, *supra* note 76, at 24.

It is also troubling to read a host of new genres within a community of discourse with which one is entirely unfamiliar and seek to find one's bearing, let alone have an opinion about a text's validity or value. The novice legal writer often feels like an outsider,[87] keenly aware of the concepts of mandatory and persuasive authority,[88] and ill-equipped to form independent opinions about what they are reading. Students often feel they lack authority and agency to speak in their own voice, questioning their ability to challenge an appellate court decision or state a definitive rule of law.

Yet once students realize that legal reading is "critical 'reading against the grain' activity in which the lawyer interrogates a text and makes independent judgments about its meaning and veracity,"[89] they are irreversibly transformed. At some point during their first year of law school, students begin to understand their role as a critic, and not just as a consumer, of legal texts. For example, they begin to take more confident positions in disagreeing with a court's reasoning and stating rules of law.

Learning to read like an expert is integrative as well, helping students build connections among primary authorities (e.g., how statutes relate to cases), synthesize cases on the same legal issue within the same jurisdiction, and even understand how the legal topics they are studying work together, to name a few examples. And the more students read, the more they build patterns or frameworks for future understanding. In terms of the final threshold characteristic, whether or critical legal reading is bounded, legal reading skills do share some of the same features across disciplines, such as reading for a purpose or as members of a particular discourse community. However, to the extent that critical reading *in law* is equivalent to reading—and usually writing—"like a lawyer," it is likely bounded.

2.3 Legal writers must gather and understand both fact and law before they can proceed.

Kristen E. Murray

Legal writing cannot proceed until both the facts and the law have been gathered. "Gathering" includes the actions of finding and reviewing the facts and the law for relevance and completeness as well as interpreting and present-

87. *See* Concept 3.6, *infra*, at 109.

88. *See* Concept 2.4, *infra*, at 69.

89. Steel et al., *Critical Reading*, *supra* note 73, at 190.

ing both in writing. The task of the legal writer is to gather all the relevant and available facts and all (or nearly all) the relevant law, though the writer ultimately may need not present them all in writing; the legal writer will ultimately be discerning about what should be included in the final written product.

The acts of gathering facts and law need not be done in a particular sequence and cannot be fully separated because the relationship between the two is symbiotic: the facts point to what law governs and the law governs which facts have relevance and legal significance.

The task of fact-gathering can be troubling for new legal writers because legal writing reflects facts that are both constructed and determined.[90] Facts must be gathered from a variety of sources (such as documents and interviews) and, when possible, verified. The legal writer must then assess the facts based on their credibility, relevancy, weight, and sufficiency.

New legal writers may also struggle with two concepts that seem to be at odds with each other: on the one hand, facts are often not objectively true, but are understood subjectively, from the perspective of a particular individual. However, ultimately, the "true" facts may be determined by a key player in the legal hierarchy: the fact-finder. Novices may have a hard time understanding that something may be true but not provable, and thus not something that can be presented as fact.

Gathering the correct set of legal rules requires identification of the issue and of the jurisdiction governing the issue, both of which depend on the underlying facts. Broadly speaking, "the law" is "that set of legal rules that apply within any given jurisdiction."[91] All legal writers must gather the law whether they are writing a multi-issue appellate brief or answering a discrete, legal question. Unlike disciplines where the writer must gather *enough* authority to make their point, legal writing requires that writers gather all, or close to all, the relevant authority for a particular point. Legal research "is an analytical task in which you narrow the field of all legal information available to the subset of information necessary to assess an issue."[92] This process of gathering is unique among disciplines. It also poses a daunting task for new legal writers. What is relevant? What constitutes authority? The task can seem endless, if

90. *See* Concept 1.5, *supra*, at 45.

91. Beazley & Smith, Legal Readers, *supra* note 76, at 15.

92. Amy Sloan, Basic Legal Research: Tools and Strategies 11 (6th ed. 2015).

not impossible: how can the novice legal writer be sure that they have found everything? How could they know what they have not found?

Both gathering tasks must be done within law's hierarchies. New legal writers must first learn what could and should be gathered before they can attempt to gather it. This means first understanding the systems underlying law's hierarchies: the concepts of jurisdiction and hierarchical levels of authority. It also means understanding *stare decisis* (following the most recent decision or precedent) and the related question of relevance.

However, legal writers are also taught how to operate within these systems, how to read the authority they have gathered for relevance and usefulness, and how to be sure (or as close to sure as is possible) that they have gathered all the law there is to gather. Paradigms like information literacy help these concepts take root. (Information literacy allows individuals to "recognize when information is needed and have the ability to locate, evaluate, and use effectively the needed information."[93]) These concepts become integrated and internalized over time. Once internalized, the task of gathering is less daunting.

Only once both the facts and the law are gathered can the lawyer move forward with the legal writing task at hand. Only through the gathering of both facts and law can the legal writer arrive at the set of facts that have legal significance and the authority that is most relevant. Only through the recursive process of determining how the law points to relevant facts and vice versa can the legal writer be sure the project is ready to move forward.

To an outsider, the concepts of "fact" and "law" appear much simpler than they do once inside the discipline. An insider knows that neither fact nor law is objectively determined and inflexible. Once understood, these concepts transform new legal writers—they know that legal analysis is not based on a fixed set of facts or a fixed set of rules, and they understand that gathering facts and law is a necessary prerequisite to building rules and identifying which facts are relevant and useful to the task at hand.

Thus, the process of gathering fact and law is soon internalized and irreversibly affects the way the legal writer perceives the relationship between foundational authority and writing writ large. Much non-legal writing starts with an idea or a thesis. Legal authority tells the writer what she can write but also what she cannot. And yet, at the same time, the gathered authority can

---

93. Am. Library Ass'n, Presidential Comm. on Info. Literacy: Final Report (available at https://www.ala.org/acrl/publications/whitepapers/presidential).

offer opportunities for interpretation and reinterpretation. But it must first be gathered and understood.

As legal writers gather the law, they must also confront law's hierarchies. The information they gather must be primary authority, it must be from the relevant jurisdiction, it must be from an appropriate tier of the hierarchy, it must involve the issue at hand, it must not have been previously overturned or otherwise successfully challenged or modified. Thus, the gathering of facts and law involves many aspects that a new legal writer might not initially perceive to be related, such as jurisdiction and *stare decisis*.

The concept is bounded because the relationship between the gathering of the facts and law for legal writing is unique among disciplines that require the attribution of authority. The legal writer's task is not to gather "sufficient" facts or "enough" law to support a thesis, it is to gather all—or as close to all—of both as is possible. Once gathered, the legal writer can determine whether the conclusions are justifiable under existing law.

At the beginning of the writing process, facts are necessarily tied to the research process because facts are what legal researchers use to generate search terms. Later in the process, taken together, gathering the facts and the law allows the legal writer to determine which facts are legally significant or will determine the outcome. Ultimately, legal writers use these facts to engage in legal reasoning or argument, whether the authority invoked is clearly stated, synthesized, or otherwise constructed.

2.4 Legal writing relies on a flexible understanding of sources of authority.

Kristen K. Tiscione

In law, "authority" refers to primary and secondary sources of law that arguably affect or control the outcome of a given situation (e.g., judicial decisions, administrative regulations, and treatises). When we talk about the "hierarchy of authority," we mean the ranking assigned to different types of authority. In general, we teach law students that constitutional provisions supersede statutes, which supersede judicial decisions. Further, we explain that the weight of authorities differs; they can be binding or persuasive. In theory, binding authority dictates the outcome, whereas persuasive authority provides useful guidance, but what constitutes binding authority depends on the circumstances. For example, federal judicial decisions on either federal or state law bind lower federal courts in their jurisdiction but not their corresponding state courts, and so on.

Despite the seeming rigidity of this hierarchy, experienced legal writers know that the concept of authority is not absolute. In any given situation, what constitutes binding and persuasive authority is open to debate. The answer depends on a number of factors, including the nature of the legal issue, the authority in question, and the timing and location of a given dispute. But it also depends on the creativity of the legal writer, who understands the flexibility they have in characterizing the law. Whether an authority is considered binding or persuasive will be influenced by the ways in which the writer interprets its terms; frames the issue, significant facts or controlling rules of law; and argues that binding case law is either controlling or distinguishable.

The nature and use of legal authorities are troublesome for beginning legal writers, who get stuck when trying to determine whether authority is binding or persuasive as a technical matter and what persuasive really means. They often find it difficult to decide which authorities to rely on, how much authority they need, and whether they have chosen "the right" authority. As they struggle with core concepts relating to the nature of federal and state courts, subject matter jurisdiction, and "who binds whom," they often fail to comprehend this deeper understanding of authority. Once they grasp the core concepts, they quickly realize that the rules are not as easy to apply in practice as they had initially hoped. Their struggle is due in part to the fact that this deeper understanding often functions below the surface, in the form of unspoken rules and shared community norms.

A full understanding of the nature and use of legal authority is integrative in that it combines a number of core and threshold concepts relating to the creativity of the legal writer and the malleability of law.[94] Once a legal writer understands that the weight of authority is subject to debate, they can no longer view legal authority as existing apart from the words used to express it. To understand the role the legal writer plays in selecting, constructing, and applying legal authority is to be irreversibly transformed. The most significant transformation occurs when legal writers begin to trust their own judgment on what authority to select in support of their arguments, how much they need, and how to construct and apply their synthesized rules of law.

The legal writer's understanding of authority is likely bounded. All writers and scholars select and cite evidence to support their arguments or findings in

---

94. *See* Concepts 1.1 & 1.3, *supra*, at 36 and 40.

a manner consistent with their community's expectations. However, the complexity of the legal system is such that the supporting authority changes based on the nature of the legal issue, when and where it arose, the relevant and applicable law, whether that law is binding or persuasive, the client's particular facts and circumstances, and the legal writer's selection and use of authority in such a way as to present the best argument possible on behalf of their client's goals.

2.5 Legal writers construct rules of law based on their client's factual circumstances and the arguably relevant sources of law in a given jurisdiction at a specific point in time.

Kristen K. Tiscione

Legal writers synthesize rules of law from arguably relevant legal sources, including constitutional provisions, statutes, administrative regulations, and judicial decisions.[95] Guided by these sources as well as the hierarchy and weight of authority, legal writers piece together a complete picture of the law in a given jurisdiction at a specific point in time. Often, they are called on to articulate a "synthesized rule" of law that applies to their client's situation. Legal writers know that their synthesized rules must be comprehensive, reasonable, accurate, and tailored to their client's circumstances. At the same time, they know that their rules will be vulnerable to criticism if they omit important information that arguably affects the rule. Moreover, if they misrepresent the law, their lack of candor may constitute an ethical violation.[96] With experience, legal writers become comfortable with the tension between stating rules that benefit their clients and accurately representing the law.

Legal writers know synthesized rules of law are created.[97] Rule synthesis is an inherently subjective process in which legal writers choose the authorities they find useful and largely leave out those they do not. Synthesized rules rarely

---

95. *See, e.g.*, RUGGERO ALDISERT, LOGIC FOR LAWYERS: A GUIDE TO CLEAR LEGAL THINKING 131–34 (3d ed. 2012), https://jm919846758.wordpress.com/wp-content/uploads/2022/04/lflgclt.pdf [hereinafter ALDISERT, LOGIC FOR LAWYERS]; Jennifer M. Cooper, *The Science of Legal Synthesis*, 95 ST. JOHN'S L. REV. 285 (2021); Gionfriddo, *supra* note 20; Dan Hunter, *No Wilderness of Single Instances: Inductive Inference in Law*, 48 J. LEGAL EDUC. 365 (1998); Anita Schnee, *Legal Reasoning "Obviously,"* 3 LEGAL WRITING: J. LEGAL WRITING INST. 105 (1997) [hereinafter Schnee, *Legal Reasoning*].

96. See MODEL RULES, *supra* note 43, at r. 3.3.

97. *See* Concept 1.1, *supra*, at 36; White, ch. 1, *Law as Rhetoric, supra* note 20, at 690.

account for all past outcomes or predict the outcome in all future cases. The primary function of the rule in each case is to state the law for the purpose of resolving the case at hand in the client's favor. The same rule of law in a different jurisdiction with a different set of facts and circumstances would likely be quite different.

Legal writers also know that their synthesized rules cannot be proved with certainty and are at best impermanent.[98] Any number of legal writers could generate any number of rules to explain the outcome in a selected line of cases.[99] Thus, when it comes to the correctness of a synthesized rule, "the only assessment criteria are rhetorical."[100] Moreover, synthesized rules are subject to change as soon as the next legal writers—judges or advocates or both—rely on and characterize them for their own purposes in a future case.

Despite their subjective and impermanent nature, synthesized rules of law play a major role in a legal system that relies on notions of *stare decisis* to ensure predictability and fairness in judicial outcomes. *Stare decisis* requires that like cases be treated alike, that is, the same rules of law should be applied to sufficiently similar cases to reach the same or similar result. Yet the role of legal writers in rule synthesis underscores the extent to which law is not a set of determinate rules but a rhetorical practice.[101]

Beginning law students find it counter-intuitive and troubling to learn that legal writers create rules of law as opposed to find them. Instead of asking, "Is this the *right* rule?" students must learn to ask, "Does this rule fairly characterize the law and frame it in such a way that favors my client? Will it serve to favorably resolve the case at hand?" The subjective, impermanent, and case-specific nature of synthesized rules is transformative and irreversible. The novice

---

98. *See, e.g.*, Cooper, *supra* note 95, at 309:

> Each individual case may be capable of producing *more than one rule*, depending on the lawyer's need, especially where a rule is implied rather than explicitly stated. Lawyers often disagree on the rule extracted from a single case.... Even if relying on the same authorities, synthesized rules may differ. While advantageous for persuasive writing and advocacy, this inherent subjectivity can be confusing for novices learning how to analyze "objective[ly]."

See also Hunter, *supra* note 95, at 390 (a synthesized rule is "at best a contingent, persuasive warrant used to justify a preferred outcome"); White, *Law as Rhetoric*, ch. 1, *supra* note 20, at 689 (explaining that when it comes to "the value and weight that different [legal sources] should have, disagreement becomes widespread and deep. Ultimately, then, the identity, the meaning, and the authority of the [sources] are always arguable, always uncertain").

99. *See, e.g.*, Hunter, *supra* note 95, at 390–91.

100. *Id.* at 390.

101. *See* White, *Law as Rhetoric*, ch. 1, *supra* note 20.

legal writer is transformed when they discover their own agency in framing legal rules. They are further transformed when they realize they have both the authority and the obligation to frame rules based on existing precedent as well as on their client's needs. Once a legal writer understands the conditional nature of legal rules, their understanding of law is irreversibly changed.

The process of synthesizing legal rules is also integrative, calling on legal writers to develop a complex understanding of authority, their role in creating law, and the need to frame rules of law in a way that is both accurate and beneficial to the client. Although the concept of synthesis—the mental process of combining ideas—is not unique to law, its particular application to legal writing makes it worthy of inclusion here.[102]

2.6 Legal writers use deductive reasoning, in combination with other forms of reasoning, to reach convincing yet necessarily probable conclusions.

Kristen K. Tiscione

Legal writers understand that legal analysis often proceeds deductively, applying principles or rules of law to a specific set of facts and circumstances.[103] As participants in a rhetorical process, they also understand that their conclusions are not likely to be certain because their premises are rarely indisputably true.[104] Thus, the legal writer's goal is to make predictions or construct arguments that are both reasonable and convincing.[105] To do so, they combine

---

102. *See* ch. 2 *supra*, at 18–19 (explaining the "bounded" nature of threshold concepts).

103. *See, e.g.*, ALDISERT, LOGIC FOR LAWYERS, *supra* note 95, at 83 (describing deductive legal reasoning as "begin[ning] with the premises and arriv[ing] at a conclusion); Schnee, *Logical Reasoning*, *supra* note 95, at 106–07 (explaining that legal writers use deduction to apply general rules to specific situations).

104. *See* ARISTOTLE, RHETORIC 2.25, 1402a–1403a (c. 333 BCE), *reprinted in* THE RHETORIC OF ARISTOTLE (Lane Cooper, trans., 1932) (explaining that syllogistic arguments in rhetoric are often based on probabilities) [hereinafter ARISTOTLE, RHETORIC]; JAMES A. GARDNER & CHRISTINE P. BARTHOLOMEW, LEGAL ARGUMENT: THE STRUCTURE OF LEGAL ARGUMENT AND ADVOCACY) §7.1, at 74 (3d ed. 2020) (explaining that legal writers can create the impression of certainty by grounding the major premise in authority and the minor premise in evidence) [hereinafter GARDNER & BARTHOLOMEW, LEGAL ARGUMENT].

105. *See, e.g.*, EDWARD P.J. CORBETT & ROBERT J. CONNORS, CLASSICAL RHETORIC FOR THE MODERN STUDENT 43 (4th ed. 1999) (explaining that the reader will accept the conclusion if they accept the premises); GARDNER & BARTHOLOMEW, LEGAL ARGU-

deduction with other forms of reasoning, such as inferential, narrative,[106] and analogical reasoning.[107]

Legal writers know that deductive reasoning in law resembles syllogistic reasoning in that it comprises a major and minor premise.[108] Yet even if the reasoning is valid,[109] the conclusion may still be subject to debate. While legal writers are obliged to represent both law and fact as accurately and comprehensively as possible,[110] their premises are framed from their client's perspective.[111] As opposing parties present the case from their client's point of view, they will exploit potential vulnerabilities in either premise. Thus, legal writers strive to anticipate their opponent's perspective and, to the extent possible, preempt counterarguments that lead to different conclusions that might also be reasonable and convincing.[112]

MENT, *supra* note 104, § 1.1, at 4 (explaining that deduction in legal reasoning "provides the requisite appearance of certainty," making "the outcome seem as certain and as mechanical as the output of a mathematical equation").

106. *See* Concept 1.6, *supra*, at 49.

107. *See* Concept 2.7, *infra*, at 77.

108. *See, e.g.*, GARDNER & BARTHOLOMEW, LEGAL ARGUMENT, *supra* note 104, § 6.2, at 54 and § 7.1, at 74 (explaining the major premise as the writer's characterization of the law and the minor premise as the characterization of fact or law and fact) ; Schnee, *supra* note 95, at 107–09 (describing the major premise in legal deduction as a general rule of law and the minor premise as the process of applying the rule to the facts).

109. In this context, validity refers to the soundness of the inference (i.e., whether the reasoning makes sense), not the truth of the premises. *See, e.g.*, ALDISERT, LOGIC FOR LAWYERS, *supra* note 95, at 103 (explaining that "[l]ogical validity is concerned with the relation between propositions, rather than with the content of the propositions themselves").

110. *See, e.g.*, FED. R. CIV. P. 11 (factual contentions must have evidentiary support, and legal claims must be warranted by existing law or by a nonfrivolous argument for changing or establishing new law); MODEL RULES, *supra* note 43, r. 3.1 (a lawyer shall not make any claim without "a basis in law and fact for doing so that is not frivolous, which includes a good faith argument for an extension, modification or reversal of existing law") & 3.3 (a lawyer shall not knowingly make a false statement of fact or law and must disclose controlling adverse authority).

111. *See, e.g.*, ARISTOTLE, RHETORIC, *supra* note 104, at 1.1, 1355a (explaining that rhetorical premises are comprised of "things contingent and uncertain such as human actions and consequences"); GARDNER & BARTHOLOMEW, LEGAL ARGUMENT, *supra* note 104, § 3.7, at 29 (explaining that "an advocate's view of the law is dictated... by the client's position"); *see also* Concept 1.4, *supra*, at 42.

112. *See* ARISTOTLE, RHETORIC, *supra* note 104, at 2.25, 1402a–1403a (explaining that syllogistic arguments are refuted through counter-syllogisms, which in rhetoric are based on probabilities).

In the legal writing community, the fact that legal writing does not produce scientific or absolute truth does not diminish its value. As Aristotle might say, why would we bother to argue about matters that are certain?[113] Given the inherent uncertainty in legal analysis, legal writers understand that in the process of resolving legal disputes, a decisionmaker's role is to compare competing arguments to find the best truth possible under the circumstances.[114] The goal is to achieve justice, not truth.[115]

Legal writers use deductive reasoning in conjunction with other forms of reasoning, such as inductive, inferential, narrative, and analogical reasoning. For example, legal writers induce rules of law applicable to their client's unique situation, which are then applied deductively to a set of facts (the minor premise).[116] In formulating premises, legal writers may infer certain facts from the existence of other facts (e.g., minor premises based on circumstantial evidence). Legal writers use narrative reasoning both to tell their clients' stories and to explain synthesized rules, explaining the underlying story of the cited cases.[117] And in applying legal rules to facts, legal writers use *stare decisis* and analogical reasoning to persuade the decisionmaker that the cited cases are either controlling or distinguishable.[118]

---

113. *See id.* at 1.2, 1357a (explaining that rhetoric involves "things about which we deliberate—things for which we have no special art or science").

114. *See, e.g.*, ALDISERT, LOGIC FOR LAWYERS, *supra* note 95, at 33 (explaining that judges make value judgments in choosing between competing arguments to resolve disputes); *see also* Concept 1.5, *supra*, at 45.

115. *See* ALDISERT, LOGIC FOR LAWYERS, *supra* note 95, at 8 (explaining that common law rules are "treated not as final truths, 'but as working hypotheses, continually retested in those great laboratories of the law, the courts of justice'"); ARISTOTLE, RHETORIC, *supra* note 104, at 1.1, 1355a (explaining that sound decisionmakers strive to achieve both truth and justice by weighing probabilities [matters of opinion]").

116. *See e.g.*, ALDISERT, LOGIC FOR LAWYERS, *supra* note 95, at 79 (explaining rule synthesis in logic terms as inductive generalization); *see also* Concept 2.5, *supra*, at 71.

117. *See, e.g.*, DeSanctis, *supra* note 36 (explaining the connection between analogy and storytelling); Stephen Paskey, *The Law is Made of Stories: Erasing the False Dichotomy Between Stories and Legal Rules*, 11 LEGAL COMM. & RHETORIC: JAWLD 51, 52 (2014) (arguing that "the analytical moves we think of as rule-based reasoning are often a form of narrative reasoning").

118. *See, e.g.*, ALDISERT, LOGIC FOR LAWYERS, *supra* note 95, at 80 (describing analogical reasoning in law as "identify[ing] the number of respects in which the compared cases, or fact scenarios, resemble one another (let us call these resemblances positive analogies) and the number of respects in which they differ (negative analogies)"); *see also* Concept 2.7, *infra*, at 77.

The complicated use of deductive reasoning, in conjunction with other forms of reasoning, is often troubling for novice legal writers. First, they tend to be unaccustomed to anticipating the legal reader's needs and expectations. Second, confronted with the need to write in a logical and linear manner, some students feel inhibited, constrained, or frustrated, wishing to write more naturally or be more creative.

Some students latch on to heuristics such as IRAC (issue, rule, application, conclusion) or TREAT (thesis, rule, explanation, analysis, re-statement of thesis),[119] mistaking the analytical process they represent with a formula for all legal analysis. Others resist it as too rigid. Both groups fail to appreciate the flexibility these heuristics envision. Despite their common usage, these heuristics and their value have been debated since the beginning of the discipline.[120] Threshold concepts theory suggests that students who rely too heavily on them may be substituting simpler understandings for more sophisticated ones,[121] suggesting that we should make the limitations of these heuristics clearer to students.[122]

Adopting a deductive yet flexible approach to legal writing is transformative and irreversible. With time, novice legal writers begin to understand that deductive reasoning is at the heart of the common law tradition. It paves the way for their creativity, evidenced by their selection of authorities, their framing of rules, how they apply those rules to selected facts, and the conclusions they draw therefrom.[123] And the student who moves past the rigidity of the

---

119. *See* Christy DeSanctis & Michael Murray, Legal Writing and Analysis (3d ed. 2021).

120. *See, e.g.*, Diane Kraft, *CREAC in the Real World*, 63 Clev. St. L. Rev. 567, 570–75 (2015) (describing varying views on the use of IRAC and related heuristics).

121. *See* Steel, *Succeed, Question, Repeat*, *supra* note 70, at 234 (explaining that IRAC is an example of a formula that can make it difficult for students to cross the threshold because it teaches mimicry rather than the underlying concept).

122. Some international scholars have also identified IRAC as the mnemonic for teaching "legal reasoning" or "thinking like a lawyer" more generally. *See, e.g.*, Kenneth Yin & Carmela De Maio, *Transformative, Troublesome and Liminal: Does the Presentation of Legal Reasoning in the Legal Studies Curricula in Higher Education Institutions Satisfy the Characteristics of A Threshold Concept?* 57:1 Law Tchr. 1, 5 (2023). *But see* Weresh, *Malleability*, ch. 2, *supra* note 1, at 707–08 (arguing that concepts such as "legal reasoning" and "thinking like a lawyer" are too broad to reflect threshold concepts).

123. *See, e.g.*, Gardner & Bartholomew, Legal Argument, *supra* note 104, § 3.7, at 29 (explaining that the malleability of law "makes legal advocacy a creative and challenging exercise"); *see also* Concept 3.4, *infra*, at 102.

heuristics used to teach deduction recognizes that for a variety of reasons, not all legal issues fit neatly within the prescribed pattern.

Understanding the role of deduction is integrative in the sense that students begin to see how important it is to read with a view toward framing premises,[124] it enables as opposed to stifles creativity,[125] it satisfies the legal reader's expectations in various legal writing genres,[126] and works with other forms of reasoning to make convincing yet probable arguments based on statutes, common law, policy, and even non-legal sources.[127] Although deductive reasoning is ubiquitous, given its particular application in law, as well as the specific ways with which it interacts with other forms of legal reasoning, it is likely bounded. As Aristotle explained, legal argument (rhetoric) is the counterpart to pure logic (dialectic) in that it too deals with "such things as fall, in a way, within the realm of common knowledge, things that do not belong to any one science."[128] Yet rhetoric is distinguished both by its reliance on probable proof and its appeals to logic, character, and emotion.[129]

2.7 Precedent is the site for negotiating the validity of competing claims, and analogical reasoning is the primary tool by which legal writers make their case for validity.

Leslie P. Culver

Because the law is malleable,[130] **legal writing produces probable results.**[131] **For** each legal assertion, different value claims (or conclusions) compete for validity.[132] Of all the forms of legal reasoning, the primary tool for negotiating

---

124. *See* Concept 2.2, *supra*, at 62.

125. *See* Concept 3.4, *infra*, at 102.

126. *See* Concept 2.9, *infra*, at 83.

127. *See, e.g.*, Concept 2.7, *infra*, at 77.

128. Aristotle, Rhetoric, *supra* note 104, at 1.1, 1354a.

129. *Id.* at 1.1, 1354a–1354b.

130. *See* Concept 1.3, *supra*, at 40.

131. *See, e.g.*, Concept 2.5, *supra*, at 71.

132. *See* Geoffrey D. Klinger, *Law as Communicative Praxis: Toward a Rhetorical Jurisprudence*, 30 Argumentation & Advoc. 236, 238 (1994) (emphasizing that decisions in individual cases "reflect[ ] the mores of a particular culture").

validity in law is analogy.[133] This is because in our common law system, analogical reasoning is the critical space where the legal writer determines the kind of authority or reasons (i.e., the evidence) the audience (i.e., the court) found sufficient to justify the probability that a particular choice was valid. Legal writers then rely on that accepted or sufficient reasoning to justify their client's preferred outcomes.

This concept is troublesome. Casting adequate doubt on the validity of alternative outcomes requires the legal writer to understand the relationship between rhetoric and analogical reasoning in legal analysis. First, rhetoric is argumentation in cases where indisputable, deductive proof is unavailable or impossible, and thus the boundary of rhetoric extends to those things upon which we can deliberate.[134] Second, the law is shaped and developed through the deliberation of legal precedent. And determining which legal precedent is most relevant is the very process of analogical reasoning.

Viewing the role of analogical reasoning in this way is troublesome because it may not be intuitive for novice legal writers to accept that legal decisions are context dependent and rarely provide a clear or correct answer to their client's legal question. Rather, the experienced legal writer's aim is to determine which claim(s) the audience has already accepted as valid.[135] From there, the writer can make conscious choices on how to argue for the desired outcome (i.e., whether the writer should rely on reasoning the audience has already deemed valid or assert another, perhaps less accepted, interpretation as valid).

This concept is transformative. Understanding that legal conclusions are the product of probabilities transforms the writer's perception of the role that precedent plays in legal decision-making, and it shifts how they approach selecting precedent.[136] Thus, the primary driver for evaluating probable choices

---

133. *See id.* (explaining that the primary tool for deciding cases is analogy because "precedents serve as guides rather than timeless answers); STEVEN J. BURTON, INTRODUCTION TO LAW AND LEGAL REASONING 26 (2d ed. 1995) (explaining that "[r]easoning under the doctrine of precedent is mainly by analogy, which basically requires that like cases be treated alike").

134. *See* ARISTOTLE, RHETORIC, *supra* note 104, at 1.2, 1357a.

135. *See, e.g.*, O. V. Tiaglo, *Logic of Legal Reasoning*, 2022(2) ANALYTICAL AND COMPARATIVE JURISPRUDENCE 349, 349 (explaining that "legal validity is determined directly and mainly by the value of the right not by the value of formal or material truth").

136. Cousin, *Introduction*, ch. 2, *supra* note 12, at 4 (discussing a "conceptual shift" as one that is assimilated into a learner's biography, becoming part of who they are, how they see the law and how they feel and experience the law).

rests in studying precedent for premises that the audience already accepts or considers reasonable (or valid).[137]

Conscious case selection is paramount as support for asserting that a particular claim is more probable than another. Yet the higher probability of one claim does not prevent a lawyer from advocating for a different (or less than probable) conclusion. For example, legal writers may agree that a statute or principle is relevant, "[b]ut the agreement is always imperfect: one lawyer will see an analogy that another will deny, for example. And when attention shifts to the value or weight that different parts of the material should have, disagreement becomes widespread and deep. Ultimately, then, the identity, the meaning, and the authority of the materials are always arguable, always uncertain."[138] But by knowing what evidence the audience has previously accepted as valid, the lawyer can better frame the argued-for outcome in their client's case.

This concept is irreversible. When legal writers gain awareness that value claims (or conclusions) of individual cases must compete for validity, they no longer view the law as a monolith but as a function of the rhetorical process where the outcome is chosen from a number of possible outcomes. Both legal assertions and conclusions thus reflect the nature of law as fluid, malleable, and capable of change over time.[139] The dynamic nature of the law triggers in the lawyer an irreversible awareness to be prepared to assert one claim as more valid than another.

This concept is integrative because it connects rhetoric to the malleability of the law.[140] If we conceive of rhetorical argumentation as being concerned with actions and decisions, then rhetoric's primary goal is to invite an audience to identify and interpret the law in a way to make the best case for the client that the law permits.[141] It has a profound impact on a legal writer's selection of authority, the reasoning used to justify their claims, and their mode of argumentation.

Finally, this concept is bounded. Understanding the law as a function of probabilities provides legal writers with insight as to how critical analogical

---

137. *See* Kurt M. Saunders, *Law as Rhetoric, Rhetoric as Argument*, 44 J. LEGAL EDUC. 566, 572 (1994).

138. White, *Law as Rhetoric*, ch. 1, *supra* note 20, at 689.

139. *See* Concept 1.3, *supra*, at 40, and 2.5, at 71.

140. *See* Concept 1.3, *supra*, at 40.

141. CHRISTOPHER W. TINDALE, PRINCIPLES OF THEORY AND PRAC. 23 (2004); James Boyd White, *Legal Knowledge*, 115 HARV. L. REV. 1396, 1400 (2002).

reasoning becomes in the administration of justice. Legal writers understand that the law is not regarded as a set of truths and falsities. Rather, when the legal writer reads controlling law in a judicial opinion, they understand not to equate that law with absolute truth. More appropriately, they understand that "controlling" law represents the claim that the audience determined to be more valid than any other choice set before it.

2.8 Legal citations are concise arguments that serve as proxies for proof and professionalism.

Kristen K. Tiscione

As with all disciplines, legal writing has its own citation practices.[142] Across legal writing genres, citations function as concise arguments in support of legal assertions and uniquely convey through signals the manner in which the writer relies on the cited source.[143] In their construction, citations also reflect the legal writer's understanding of the expectations of the legal discourse community and, as a result, can bolster or threaten the writer's credibility.[144] Unlike novices, expert legal writers understand that citations do more than help readers locate sources; whether in text or footnotes, citations work in concert with the primary text to convey the writer's substantive content.

Because the legal reader is a doubting reader,[145] legal writers must provide adequate citations in support of their assertions. As a substantive matter,

---

142. *See, e.g.*, Lerner, *supra* note 58, at 40–41.

143. Kris Franklin, "*. . . . See Erie.*": *Critical Study of Legal Authority*, 31 U. ARK. LITTLE ROCK L. REV. 109 111 (2008) noting that "understanding citation requires understanding the ways that lawyers and judges characterize and use law").

144. For example, the typeface used depends on the genre; one form is used for law review articles and another for court documents and legal memoranda. *See, e.g.*, THE BLUEBOOK: A UNIFORM SYSTEM OF CITATION, Bluepages B2 & Rule 2 (22d ed. 2025) [hereinafter BLUEBOOK].

145. *See, e.g.*, Bryan A. Garner, *Know Thy Reader: Writing For The Legal Audience*, 98 MICH. BAR J. 46, 46 (Nov. 2019) (describing the legal reader as impatient, easily disappointed, and skeptical by nature); Michael J. Higdon, *The Legal Reader: An Exposé*, 43 N.M. L. REV. 77, 107 (2013) (explaining that a legal reader "reads skeptically, constantly assessing the strength and accuracy of the analysis") (citing Linda H. Edwards, LEGAL WRITING: PROCESS, ANALYSIS, AND ORGANIZATION 162 (3d ed. 2002)); RICHARD K. NEUMANN, LEGAL REASONING AND LEGAL WRITING: STRUCTURE, STRATEGY, AND STYLE 48 (2009) (explaining that legal readers read in "bad faith" "not because lawyers are particularly nasty people, skepticism simply causes better decisions"); *cf.* Elbow, *supra* note

"citations transfer information about the cited authority to the reader at the reader's point of need."[146] A well-constructed citation concisely provides everything the legal reader needs to know about why the authority has been cited, how it supports or detracts from the writer's argument, and where to find the source should the reader wish to do so. Expert legal writers know that citations are integral to legal writing "because they know that their audiences will use the information coded in those citations to assess the merits of their legal analyses."[147]

Signals, a component of citation practice, communicate not only the weight of the cited authority but also the manner and degree to which the authority supports or contradicts the legal writer's assertions. Expert legal writers understand "the centrality of the interpretive work that signals do" [148] in ways that novices do not. Even the absence of a signal sends a message to the reader, indicating that the cited authority directly supports the assertion, with the remainder of the "supporting" signals indicating the degree to which the authority provides inferential support.

Similarly, the "contradictory" signals indicate the degree to which the cited authority calls the assertion into question, a legal writing convention required by the writer's ethical duty to find and report contrary authority.[149] Expert legal writers also use signals and citations, often with explanatory parentheticals, to provide additional support for their arguments without adding additional primary text.

Legal writers know that in addition to their communicative function, signals and citations also serve to avoid plagiarism by requiring proper attribution and reflect on the writers' credibility.[150] Citation rules permit the use of no signal when directly quoting or paraphrasing text and detail the formatting of quotations.[151] Furthermore, inaccurate or sloppy citations can "make[] [the

---

48, at 169 (explaining that the doubting game requires that the reader "doubt particularly those assertions that seem reasonable, and get opposing propositions to fight each other").

146. Alexa Z. Chew, *Citation Literacy*, 70 ARK. L. REV. 869, 872 (2018) [hereinafter Chew, *Citation Literacy*].

147. *Id.* at 876.

148. Franklin, *supra* note 143, at 118.

149. *See* MODEL RULES, *supra* note 43, r.1.1 (duty of competence) & r. 3.3 (duty of candor toward the tribunal).

150. Chew, *Citation Literacy*, *supra* note 146, at 880.

151. *See, e.g.*, BLUEBOOK, *supra* note 144, RULES 1.2 & 5.

reader] wonder if the whole case is weak,"[152] and particularly poor citations can lead to court sanctions.[153]

That citations are "an important feature of legal discourse"[154] can be troubling to novice legal writers, who often view them as largely ministerial. Recognizing that citations are concise arguments takes time. Legal writing pedagogy may reinforce this assumption, emphasizing form over substance in citation practices.[155] Although most novices are familiar with the need to attribute ideas to cited authors to avoid plagiarism, they are not used to citations contributing substantially to the effectiveness of their writing. As they practice incorporating citations into their writing, novices often "rely on citations to communicate information about the cited authority that readers expect to see in the prose."[156] Yet once they begin to harness the power of signals and citations to support novel and nuanced arguments, they are irreversibly transformed.

To internalize this concept, legal writers must understand legal citations as part and parcel of their reasoning. To achieve this understanding requires them to integrate a host of core and threshold concepts, including "a significant knowledge of legal precedent, including common sources of U.S. law, jurisdiction, and court hierarchies across jurisdictions,"[157] the malleability of law,[158]

---

152. Wayne Schiess, *Ethical Legal Writing*, 21 Rev. Litig. 527 (2002); *see also* Chew, *Citation Literacy*, *supra* note 146, at 887–90 (acknowledging that some readers "use citations as a proxy for quality—assessing the writer's credibility on all matters based on how well the citations are formatted").

153. *See, e.g.*, *United States v. Hayes*, No. 2:24-cr-0280-DJC, 2025 WL 235531, at *14 (D.C. Cal. Jan. 17, 2025) (affirming sanctions against defendant's counsel for incorrectly citing and quoting fictitious case); *Puerto Rico Soccer League NFP, Corp. v. Federación Puertorriqueña De Futbol*, No. 23-1203 (RAM), 2025 WL 1080732, at *3 (Apr. 10, 2025) (imposing sanctions on plaintiff's counsel for sloppy and inaccurate citations); *Precision Specialty Metals, Inc. v. United States*, 315 F.3d 1346, 1357 (Fed. Cir. 2003) (affirming reprimand of appellant's counsel under Rule 11 for distorting authority in part by failing to indicate "emphasis added" to quoted material); *see also* Judith D. Fischer, *Bareheaded and Barefaced Counsel: Courts React to Unprofessionalism in Lawyers' Papers*, 31 Suffolk U. L. Rev. 1 (1997).

154. Chew, *Citation Literacy*, *supra* note 146, at 871.

155. *See, e.g.*, *id.* at 874–76 (explaining that current legal citation pedagogy "obscures the more important question of 'what to cite' with the more urgent question of 'how to cite'"); *see also* Franklin, *supra* note 143, at 113 (noting that for novice legal writers "[i]t is as though the citation speaks for itself and no further elaboration is necessary" in the context of exam writing).

156. Alexa Z. Chew, *Stylish Legal Citation*, 71 Ark. L. Rev. 823, 836 (2019).

157. Chew, *Citation Literacy*, *supra* note 146, at 873.

158. *See* Concept 1.3, *supra* at 40.

the necessity of framing,[159] the creativity of legal writing,[160] and the extent to which legal writing manifests the writer's professional identity.[161] All told, expert legal writers understand that "legal citation matters because it provides a window into larger issues of legal reasoning.... On the whole,... the choice of authority invoked and the context for that authority are, to a surprising extent, at the discretion of the writer."[162] Legal citation practices are likely bounded in the sense that no other discipline appears to use words and phrases as signals to indicate the nature of the support the source provides in combination with such highly detailed and stylized formats.

2.9 Legal writers use different genres of writing in response to differences in their goals, stance, and audience.

David I. C. Thomson

Legal writing is instrumental in the sense that its various forms respond to the needs of a particular community of legal readers at a given point in time. Depending on the purpose, audience, and the appropriate means of communication, legal writing tends to fall within recognizable genres that signal the writer's membership in the legal discourse community and adherence to its agreed-upon conventions.[163] Depending on the form of the legal writing—be it an interoffice memorandum, a letter to opposing counsel, a brief filed in court, a judicial opinion, a contract, or a law review article, to name a few, the audience's expectations about the form and substance will differ.

Legal writing genres can be discovered,[164] articulated, learned, modified, and made to evolve by the addition of new genres, such as email. As each is learned, more is discovered and understood about the discourse community in which legal writers participate. Each genre is constructed over time from

159. *See* Concept 1.4, *supra* at 42.

160. *See* Concepts 1.1 & 1.2, *supra*, at 36 & 37 and Concept 2.4–2.7., *supra*, at 69, 71, 73 & 77; Concept 3.4, *infra*, at 102.

161. *See* Concept 3.7, *infra*, at 114 and ch. 6, *infra*, at 145.

162. *See* Franklin, *supra* note 143, at 112.

163. Tzvetan Todorov, Genres in Discourse 18 (Catherine Porter trans., 1990).

164. Katie Rose Guest Pryal, *The Genre Discovery Approach: Preparing Law Students to Write Any Legal Document*, 59 Wayne L. Rev. 351, 355 (2013); *see also* Pryal, *Genre Discovery*, *supra* note 60.

experience, and genres reflect compositional and stylistic conventions that are widely accepted at a given point in time and context (and sometimes required by rules of citation, for example) within the discourse community of law. For example, many state and federal courts have very specific rules about the format, design, and printing of briefs that are filed in their courts.[165]

Because objectives and styles differ among dispute resolution documents, legislative documents, and transactional documents (for example), genre requirements need to be understood and practiced. The process of learning these objectives and styles takes time and benefits from repeated experience.

Legal writing genres tend to be fairly stable until the needs of the particular legal community change. When those needs change, the expert legal writer will adapt the genre to respond to the new need. For example, changes in legal technology and law practice have reduced the need for the formal written memorandum used by one lawyer to provide legal advice to another lawyer in the same office and often been replaced with the email exchange between the same lawyers to communicate back and forth in a more concise way.

Genres of legal writing are not always obvious, intuitive, or explicit. In practice, they can often be unspoken and assumed as part of the legal culture of which the attorney is a member. The novice legal writer struggles not only with the format and rhetorical conventions of a particular genre but also with the unspoken rules within that genre, and the beginning writer can find this learning troublesome.[166] For example, there is a need to explain one's reasoning in detail in predictive memoranda or email, but the writer need not recount the history of the law as it evolved up to that moment. Much writing training before law school favors the historical approach over the former.

Learning to identify and distinguish the various genres of legal writing leads the novice legal writer to integrate all aspects of what they are learning about legal communication—research, legal analysis, citation, and format—into a cohesive and integrated whole, and this is true of whatever genre they are writing in. To understand genre requirements, the novice must also integrate their knowledge of the legal subject matter with their understanding of different legal audiences and situations. The tone, style, and content of writing that serve to inform a client in a letter depend on the writer's understanding of both the

---

165. *See, e.g.*, Colo. R. App. Proc. 32 (specifying the type size, typeface, paper size, line spacing, margins, binding and reproduction, as well as the length of briefs required in the Colorado Court of Appeals).

166. Williams, ch. 1, *supra* note 1, at 19–20.

specific and the general setting of attorney-client relationships, while legislative bodies may prefer more or less content, a more formal tone and style, and an organizational structure keyed to legislative drafting.

The understanding that legal writing is not one type or format of writing, but rather many, and that each genre responds to specific rhetorical needs—of lawyers, clients, judges, and other audiences—is transformative and irreversible. Students are transformed when they realize that "[n]ot only do I have to learn the general skills of legal writing—clarity, word choice, citation, etc.—legal writing is required in multiple genres, such as memos, briefs, mediation statements, and contracts. So, I also have to learn how to adapt to writing different types of legal documents for different audiences!" Once the writer begins to understand not only different genres but also what components of the genre transfer from one genre to another (or do not), they will be reluctant to return to their initial efforts to force all legal writing into one formula. Ultimately, this process of development also helps them to understand better the needs of each audience for their writing.

Legal writing genres are also bounded within the discipline, since some genres emerge in response to the concrete requirements spelled out by statute, local court rules, or common law, and they are governed by the rules of ethics. For example, when preparing a brief to be filed in the United States Supreme Court, the attorney must know the strict format and printing requirements of the Court, up to and including the color of the cover on their bound brief.[167]

2.10 Legal writing requires typographic judgment.

Derek H. Kiernan-Johnson

Every text must be set; the words and symbols that comprise it must be given shape and arranged on the screen or page. How this is done requires judgment, especially in legal writing.

Typographically savvy legal writers know, when sitting down to write, that they can't rely on software defaults for "general correspondence" or "business letters." A default font such as Times New Roman might be fine for some purposes, but, as Judge Frank Easterbrook put it, Times New Roman is "utterly inappropriate" for litigation documents because it was "designed for narrow

167. U.S. SUP. CT. RULE 33.

columns in newspapers, not for briefs."[168] So too with default one-inch page margins, which aren't nearly generous enough for comfortable legal reading.[169]

As legal readers, these experts can't help but notice—and judge—the typography of documents that cross their desk. They might not go so far as Judge Lynn Hughes, who claims that, using just his typographic judgment, he can scan résumés and reject "more than half" the job applications he receives "from across the room."[170] But these experts will notice when a legal document's paragraph alignment is inconsistent or when a font changes mid-sentence. No less than textual errors, such as typos and grammar goofs, lack of typographic polish in a legal document sends signals about an author and the credibility of their claims.[171]

More importantly, they know that legal typography is about more than polish, or even aesthetics. Instead, as Matthew Butterick notes, legal typography is "primarily utilitarian," and aims to "reinforce the goals of the text."[172] A pretty font that works well on a movie poster will, if used in a legal brief, frustrate judges' desire for legal typography that enhances "reading, understanding, and remembering."[173]

Experienced legal writers also tailor their typography to different audiences. For example, in a memorandum to a supervising attorney, a legal writer might use typographic techniques—such as contrast, repetition, alignment, and proximity[174]—to subtly "ensure that certain points are more clearly brought to the readers' attention."[175] Then, when conveying the same analysis to a different audience, such as in a client letter, the writer might increase the frequency and intensity of typographic reader cues. Finally, in an appellate

---

168. Frank H. Easterbrook, Judge of the United States Court of Appeals for the Seventh Circuit, Challenges in Reading Statutes (Sept. 28, 2007).

169. MATTHEW BUTTERICK, TYPOGRAPHY FOR LAWYERS 141–42 (2d ed. 2015).

170. Bryan A. Garner, *The Aesthetics of Your Pages*, *in* GARNER ON LANGUAGE AND WRITING 98 (2009).

171. *See* MICHAEL R. SMITH, ADVANCED LEGAL WRITING: THEORIES AND STRATEGIES IN PERSUASIVE WRITING 29–30 (3d ed. 2013).

172. BUTTERICK, *supra* note 169, at 29.

173. *AsymaDesign, LLC v. CBL & Assocs. Mgt. Inc.*, 103 F.4th 1257, 1261 (7th Cir. 2024) (critiquing appellant's use of Bernhard Modern, a movie-poster font, in its brief).

174. *See* Ruth Anne Robbins, *Painting with Print: Incorporating Concepts of Typographic and Layout Design into the Text of Legal Writing Documents*, 2 LEG. COMM. & RHETORIC: J.ALWD 108, 126 (2004).

175. Ellie Margolis, *Is the Medium the Message?* 12 LEGAL COMM. & RHETORIC 1, 17 (2015).

brief, the lawyer might refrain from using all but the most conservative typographic techniques.

Expert legal writers have also come to learn that not every legal text wants to be understood. Sometimes the text seeks to serve a different, more troubling purpose, which typography could support. Take, for example, contract disclaimers. As Mary Beth Beazley has noted, some "sellers do not write disclaimers because they want buyers to know things. They write them so they can say to the buyer, 'I told you so. I told you that you can't sue me for violating the warranty of merchantability. So even though that paragraph was hard to read . . . it's your fault that you didn't know that you didn't have that warranty.'"[176] Typographic techniques can obscure meaning as easily as they reinforce it, allowing a lawyer and their client to hide in plain sight.

And so legal writing requires typographic judgment: the judgment to recognize that neglecting to consider how one's words appear on the page is itself a choice (and rarely an optimal one). The judgment to know that, just as one need not be a fashion designer or vocal coach to know how to dress for court and talk to a jury, typographic style can be learned. The judgment to think carefully about a text's audience, goals, and genre so as to tailor a document's appearance to the rhetorical occasion. And, finally, the judgment to know that, like other legal-writing techniques, typography is inevitably ethically fraught.

For new legal writers, it can be troubling to learn that, as self-publishers of consequential texts, they will be responsible not only for their words, but also for how those words appear on the page. Already overwhelmed by the architecture of legal analysis or intimidated by the shibboleths of legal language or citation form, they may decide, at first, that developing typographic savvy is too much. They may also find disquieting the reality that other legal writers are not only using typography to make their texts more readable, but also less so.

But those who weather these initial shocks to learn the basics of legal typography (such as by consulting Butterick's *Typography for Lawyers*)[177] find their approach to writing and reading irreversibly transformed. They become sensitive to how, in an engagement letter, typographic choices can reinforce client comprehension while reflecting a lawyer's professional identity. When reading an opposing counsel's demand letter, they cannot help noticing that letter's typography: is it purposefully designed or thoughtlessly cut-and-pasted

176. Mary Beth Beazley, *Hiding in Plain Sight: "Conspicuous Type" Standards in Mandated Communication Statutes*, 40 J. Legis. 1, 2 (2014).

177. *See* Butterick, *supra*, note 169.

together? They can't help but incorporate these visual cues into how they rate their adversaries and the merits of their claims.

This newfound knowledge integrates several communication concepts. The principles that make legal typography good or bad undergird all legal communication. For example, upon realizing that inconsistent paragraph indentation or line spacing may affect a reader as viscerally as a typo or grammar goof, legal writers see how both reactions involve an underlying principle: attention-to-detail as a proxy for professionalism and reliability.[178]

They also realize that textual reader cues—such as roadmaps, thesis statements, and transition words—are just one way to help readers navigate a text, and that they operate alongside typographic cues like clear heading hierarchies, vertical numbered and bulleted lists, or the use of white space to show how ideas relate. They come to realize how a cognitive persuasive technique for emphasis or deemphasis—such as where to place a "bad" fact within a sentence or paragraph—involves not only language processing but also visual perception.

This new way of seeing opens legal writers' eyes to how non-lawyers use typography: they now appreciate how those who design directional signage for subway systems can make those spaces easier to navigate. They see how book-cover designers use typography to communicate genre, mood, character, or setting.

But these discoveries also reveal how bounded, both practically and rhetorically, legal-writing genres are. Contracts, for instance, are often composed jointly between lawyers at different law firms, using different versions of different software. A specialized typeface that's perfect for the occasion might not render correctly on the other person's computer. A provision that fits neatly on one page might, due to variations in the definition of "single" and "double" spacing across software,[179] spill over, causing cascading misalignments (including to any graphics) throughout the document. These practical concerns might cause a contract drafter to prioritize interoperability over readability.

A brief writer, working alone, with Butterick's *Typography for Lawyers* by their side, might not be so constrained.[180] And legal briefs' argumentative rich-

---

178. SMITH, *supra* note 171.

179. BUTTERICK, *supra* note 169, at 138.

180. *See* BUTTERICK, *supra*, note 169.

ness and narrativity make them a perfect site for typographic expression.[181] Yet they might be equally limited by rhetorical constraints. While most court rules today give brief writers "plenty of typographic latitude,"[182] that doesn't mean individual judges don't have strong typographic preferences. Sometimes we learn of these preferences, such as when Judge Frank Easterbrook, after ruling against a lawyer's client, said of that lawyer's favorite font for 25 years, "we hope that Bernhard Modern has made its last appearance in an appellate brief."[183] More often, judges don't publicly express their preferences. They may not even be consciously aware of them, instead finding a brief's typography "distracting" or "hard to read" for reasons they can't articulate. Or, conversely, also for reasons they can't articulate, they may find a typographically sophisticated brief easier to read, remember, and refer back to.

Making these calls requires judgment. But exercising judgment is what lawyers do. And even a basic understanding of legal typography can be transformative.

D. Category Three: Legal Writers Learn Their Constraints and Develop Their Identities Within a Professional Practice as Writers and Readers

The threshold concepts gathered under this heading explore the ways in which legal writing shapes and constrains legal writers and their professional identities. As Lloyd Bitzer explains, the constraints of a rhetorical situation include "beliefs, attitudes, documents, facts, traditions, images, interests, motives and the like,"[184] but they also include the rhetor's creative contributions—those the writer brings to the discourse and those the reader brings to

---

181. Derek Kiernan-Johnson, *Telling Through Type: Typography and Narrative in Legal Briefs*, 7 J. ALWD 87, 114–21 (2010).

182. Butterick, *supra* note 169, at 218.

183. *AsymaDesign, supra* note 173; Mike Scarcella, *Lawyer's 'Twilight Zone' Font Irks US Appeals Court in Typeface Takedown*, Reuters, June 4, 2024, available at https://www.reuters.com/legal/government/lawyers-twilight-zone-font-irks-us-appeals-court-typeface-takedown-2024-06-04/.

184. Bitzer, *supra* note 8, at 8.

its interpretation. Thus, the constraints of legal writing can be both positive and negative.[185]

Experienced legal writers understand both the freedoms and limitations of the legal discourse community, learning to navigate its constraints in order to create new meaning on behalf of their clients. In so doing, these constraints contribute directly to the writer's development and identity as a legal professional. As Linda Berger explains in Concept 3.1, expert legal writers understand that a "good" argument is one that is judged as "good" by the legal community. Inherent in this process is the need to make ethical and persuasive choices at the same time, which creates ambiguity and discomfort for the novice legal writer.

In Concept 3.2, JoAnne Sweeny explores the legal writer's understanding of authority as part and parcel of their identity formation. Although novice legal writers instinctively form opinions about what the law should or does mean, experts understand that they must leverage the malleability of existing law and their own creativity to fit their arguments within existing precedent.

Experienced legal writers also come to understand the generative, recursive, and time-consuming nature of the writing process. As Julie Oseid explains in Concept 3.3, expert legal writers know that legal writing takes time—time to understand the legal issues, time to find the facts, research the law, frame the law, shape the story, bring that story into being, develop "good" arguments or effective language, and then refine their writing and refine it again. In Concept 3.4, Kristen Tiscione explores the extent to which legal writers come to understand and embrace the creativity they enjoy as legal writers. Novice legal writers prefer to stand behind clear, authoritative statements and accepted legal conventions, whereas expert legal writers know when those statements can be re-framed and those conventions defied. In Concept 3.5, Melissa Weresh acknowledges the extent to which the legal writer's creative license demands that they become comfortable with and even embrace a certain level of uncertainty in their decision-making. In so doing, they maximize their role as advisor and advocate.

In Concept 3.6, Kirsten Davis summarizes the conventional nature of legal writing and its impact on the writer's professional development. As Davis also notes, legal writing conventions serve to make legal writing recognizable, understandable, and credible as legal writing, but at the same time, adhering to these conventions can also depersonalize and alienate novice legal writers.

185. *See, e.g.*, Concept 3.2, *infra*, at 94.

While the law reinforces certain ways of knowing and being, it discounts or silences others. As novices work through what might feel like a process of alienation, they come to learn how and when to challenge dominant narratives and create opportunities for change. Finally, Weresh concludes this category with Concept 3.7, exploring the ways in which legal writing, perhaps more than any other mode of legal communication, both shapes and manifests a legal writer's professional identity.

3.1 Legal writing involves ethical and persuasive choices about what constitutes "good" arguments within a specific rhetorical context.

Linda L. Berger

Expert legal writers understand that their arguments must fall within the bounds of "good arguments" as judged by the practices of their profession. Judgments about whether an argument is "good" in this sense encompass the writers' construction of both facts and law. Because they work in a culture of argument, legal writers are constantly engaged in thinking and talking about how to write, speak, and construct arguments. This conversation generates the written and unwritten (and always subject to change) rules and practices for evaluating arguments.

Novice legal writers typically go through several stages of thinking about the evaluation of legal arguments. At first, they judge every argument as "right" or "wrong." Many beginning writers move on to a position of believing that every argument is fair game because it's "all relative." But the experienced legal writer understands that there are constraints on their creation of arguments and that these emerge from the practices of the profession.

Judgments about what constitutes a good argument will vary by rhetorical situation. Arguments must be tailored to the individual rhetorical situation in which they are constructed: they must be fitting, appropriate, and timely considering the situation's specific audience, purpose, and conventions.[186] The arguments made in negotiations will differ from those filed in court. For example, constitutional arguments, but not those made in a parole hearing, will ordinarily rely on the constitutional text, the history of its adoption, case prece-

186. Jennifer Fletcher, Teaching Arguments: Rhetorical Comprehension, Critique, and Response 52–72 (2015).

dent, policy concerns, and ethical values, while arguments made in negotiations, but not those made in a motion to dismiss for failure to state a claim, may be drawn from knowledge of the personalities and history of the parties involved.

More universally, the expert legal writer understands that the evaluation of good arguments will depend on judgments growing out of the relationships among writer and client, writer and language, writer and readers, and writer and prior texts. Some guidelines for judging arguments are more certain. The ethical rules established by the professional community govern outright misstatements or omissions of law or fact; rhetorical principles provide guidance on how writers can maintain their credibility and the credibility of their claims, while presenting a favorable view of their client's claims and appealing to the decision-maker's values.

Exercising judgment is otherwise more fluid and requires the expert legal writer to learn to manage conflicts in order to maintain each of these relationships over time. For the legal writer, the first significant relationship is with the client. The expert legal writer understands that their first responsibility is to represent the client and that the legal writers with whom they come into contact are similarly representing other parties. Whether an argument is good is judged within the context of this background setting.

Second, as legal writers, we initiate, continue, or rupture our relationship with language whenever we write. When we argue for the preservation or alteration of the meaning of words or symbols, we are making ethical and persuasive choices, and the results may be fleeting or permanent, destructive or beneficial. For every claim that a legal argument twisted the words of a prior precedent beyond the breaking point, there is a claim that the arguments made in a legal text such as the Declaration of Independence created "a new world" and so the language requires broader interpretations. Understanding the extent and limits of their relationship with language makes experienced legal writers more deliberate and careful writers.

Ethical and persuasive choices similarly pervade the relationship between writer and reader. Whenever we write for an audience, we are suggesting identities for ourselves and our readers as well as imagining our effects on others. While testing the limits of language, the writer operates within the constraints of his audience's time and attention. He is required to choose among the arguments he might make, and he is expected to offer "the best performance of the state of his art, as does the lawyer who opposes him."[187]

187. White, Words, *supra* note 14, at 267–78.

Finally, legal writers are required to make ethical and persuasive judgments with respect to the law's shared cultural inheritance. To be understandable and credible, a good argument will make use of the existing body of cases, statutes, understandings, and rules in such a way that the reader recognizes an "allegiance to their common language."[188] The legal writer understands that their work inevitably will be evaluated within the context of these relationships, which together constitute the legal rhetorical community.

The suggestion that whether an argument is good or bad is neither a yes-or-no nor a relative judgment is troublesome for the novice legal writer who does not yet understand the standards and practices of the legal community and so is uncertain about whether their argument meets expectations. Knowing that the writer must situate their legal writing within a particular rhetorical community makes the concept even more difficult to grasp, yet all the more transformative to the writer's thinking. Rather than thinking that constructing a good argument is merely a legal hypothetical, the experienced legal writer knows that they must thoroughly explore the setting so that they can fashion an appropriate and persuasive response.

Once grasped, this concept is irreversible: the maturing writer not only recognizes, but begins to welcome the need to immerse themselves within the setting and the surrounding rhetorical community. Because the writer is required to integrate ideas from rhetoric with ethical rules and community practices as well as the lived experiences of the individuals involved in the situation, the expert legal writer is able to see previously unrecognized connections: how does the ethical rule encouraging zealous advocacy interact with rhetorical thought about maintaining credibility and the client's desires?

Finally, whether this threshold concept is bounded—that is, unique to the discipline of legal rhetoric—is arguable. Many professions impose practice-generated standards. The standards for judging good arguments in legal rhetoric may, however, emerge from a more open and wider range of conversations. For example, judgments about the arguments made by lawyers in political-legal controversies (such as regulating elections) likely emerge from commentary not only by lawyers and judges, but also by citizen-constituents, politicians, news and opinion leaders, scholars, religious leaders, and eventually voters.

---

188. *Id.* at 268.

3.2 Legal precedent provides both guidance and boundaries for legal writers.

JoAnne Sweeny

A unique feature of legal writing is the large role existing law has in shaping the way legal documents are written and even the way lawyers think about legal problems, which can be both helpful and a creative hindrance to legal practitioners. Prior case law can provide guidance in how to shape legal arguments but, in so doing, can limit the arguments a lawyer can make. Judges and lawyers are constrained by the notion of *stare decisis,* and that corresponding adherence to precedent infiltrates every aspect of legal documents. Lawyers who want to advance their client's case must show the judge how prior cases and other primary authority apply favorably to their client's facts. As a result, even though there is room for interpretation, policy considerations and even creativity, all legal writing is ultimately limited by existing law.[189]

Legal precedent sets the terms for every aspect of legal writing. For example, when beginning to work on a legal problem, a legal writer will start by considering the facts provided by the client and "issue spotting" the relevant legal issues within those facts. Which facts are "legally relevant" and, therefore, worth considering is determined solely by comparing those facts to existing law.[190]

Similarly, when a potential claim or defense is identified, lawyers conduct research to discover what the law already says on the subject to determine how their client's facts match with prior law. Ultimately, this prior law, whether in the form of statutes, cases, regulations, etc., dictates the organization and the content of every legal argument. Without some legal authority to support an argument, that argument is not likely to be taken seriously by a judge and, at worst, can be seen as frivolous and, unless the lawyer makes a good faith argument to change the law, potentially worthy of sanctions.

Accordingly, when writing about the law, a lawyer's opinion on how a case should be decided will not be accepted by the court unless it is supported by, essentially, what a judge has previously said about the applicable law. Moreover, it is not enough to simply cite authority; the legal writer's use of precedent must convince a judge that their description of the prior holding (or statute,

---

189. *See* Concepts 1.3, *supra* at 40, 3.4, *infra* at 102; Concept 2.4, *supra* at 69.

190. Of course, later legal research and fact investigation may alter the lawyer's initial assessment of what is "legally relevant" in the case.

etc.) is both accurate and can be reasonably interpreted to support the lawyer's arguments.[191]

This reliance on existing authority can be troublesome for novice legal writers. Law students often struggle with it, particularly when coming from social science or humanities backgrounds where their interpretation of a concept or piece of literature was adequate support for their assertions as long as that interpretation was supported by the text itself. In addition, in the social sciences and humanities, novel interpretations of existing texts are favored in contrast to students simply regurgitating what they have already read. Legal writing, in contrast, is much more tied to what was written (be it judicial opinions, statutes, administrative regulations, etc.) in the past.

Lawyers, therefore, are always governed by prior precedents, and when writing, they make explicit reference to those precedents because it is fundamentally understood that judges follow the law and will not consider an argument that is not grounded in precedent. For that reason, using precedent is how lawyers demonstrate their credibility to the court and attempt to persuade the judge to rule in their client's favor.

Part of what law students learn in their first year is not only how to read different legal authorities but also how to organize them, combine them, and, ultimately, frame them to be used on behalf of their client.

This concept integrates a wide variety of skills and a deep understanding of the law such as issue spotting, rule synthesis and the hierarchy of authorities. The organization of legal authorities requires knowledge of jurisdictional restraints and the hierarchy of authorities (e.g., knowing which sources of law can be used for a certain legal problem—state law or federal law, for example—and which should be discussed first). [192] For example, if there is a constitutional provision or statute that applies, students learn not to start with a case; the provision or statute dictates what is relevant and provides something of a blueprint for the rest of the legal analysis.

Knowing that a statute takes precedence over a court case harkens back to the United States' Constitution's separation of powers principles; legislatures make the laws and courts merely interpret them.[193] This is a simple enough proposition for a student to learn, but common law, which is effectively created

---

191. *See* Concept 2.5, *supra* at 71.

192. For a thorough analysis of the traditional and more modern interpretations of hierarchy of authority, *see* SCHLAG & GRIFFIN, *supra* note 29.

193. *See* U.S. CONST., art. I, § 8 & art. 3, § 2.

by judges, not the legislature, muddies the waters. When there are no statutes that govern a legal issue, students must determine what the law is based solely on court cases, which brings in issues of federalism, court hierarchies, and binding versus persuasive authority.

Consequently, an experienced legal writer knows to consult multiple potential sources of legal precedent including cases, statutes, regulations, and even constitutions. Similarly, legal writing experts know that the law does not fit into neat categories the same way law school classes are organized. A client's case may implicate multiple areas of law, such as a contractual dispute that involves intellectual property claims.

Once legal writers have accepted that they must properly use existing legal authority, this new worldview transforms the way they view their clients' facts—what is legally relevant and what is not legally relevant—and what claims they can credibly make on behalf of their client. Accordingly, this way of precedent-bound reasoning also permanently changes the way lawyers think. Early in their law school careers, students often uncritically follow judicial opinions, and mistake them as infallible interpretations of the law, partially because of how professors train them to read cases[194] and partially because that is how judicial opinions are written.[195]

Over time, students learn to be more critical and even creative as they read cases and use them in their writing assignments, beginning to use techniques like distinguishing or combining cases in novel ways to suit their needs. However, one thing never changes, even for the most activist lawyer: existing law is where all legal writing starts, and this existing law dictates what arguments a lawyer can make. No matter which area of law is implicated or genre of writing is attempted, existing legal authority is an ever-present guide for all lawyers, and it must be properly cited to create effective legal arguments.[196] Indeed, it can be comforting for law students to know that they must start their writing by interpreting someone else's words instead of creating legal arguments out of nothing.

Yet, staying within the law's existing boundaries can be harmful as well, particularly to underrepresented groups whose stories have not yet made it

---

194. *See* Susan McMahon, *What We Teach When We Teach Legal Analysis*, 107 MINN. L. REV. 2511, 2513 (2023).

195. *See* Concept 2.1, *supra* at 60.

196. *See* Concept 2.8, *supra* at 80.

into the law's understanding of the world.[197] Similarly, an over-reliance on rule-based reasoning can preclude arguments based on narrative and storytelling, which are also important for writing persuasively.[198] Substantial literature has been devoted to legal storytelling[199] and its importance to effective advocacy.

Despite these potential harms and limitations, it is only by understanding the law's boundaries, and forcing oneself to work within them, that a legal writer can successfully argue a client's case. Even a lawyer who seeks to change the law must start within its borders before they can hope to force open a new door. Therefore, to become an expert legal writer, one must allow oneself to be constrained by existing authority if only to ultimately tear down that constraint.

3.3 The expert legal writer knows that time is needed for legal writing because the legal writer is creating something new through a synthetic and recursive process that requires a multi-layered approach, multiple revisions, and an ongoing internal dialogue.

Julie A. Oseid

Perhaps the biggest surprise about legal writing is how much time it takes. Knowing that time is required but also limited, the expert legal writer appreciates how much time is needed and also knows how best to use the time available. The expert legal writer knows that every legal writing project forces the legal writer to create something new. Legal writing is synthetic because a legal writer must combine ideas; it is recursive because a legal writer must revisit and revise the writing. The legal writer also knows that legal writing gets slightly easier, but it will always be difficult because legal writing is an act of creation. And it will always take a copious amount of time.[200]

---

197. *See* Marc A. Fajer, *Authority, Credibility, and Pre-Understanding: A Defense of Outsider Narratives in Legal Scholarship*, 82 Geo. L.J. 1845 (1994); *see* Concept 1.8, *supra* at 55; Concept 3.6, *infra* at 109.

198. *See* Kenneth D. Chestek, *The Plot Thickens: The Appellate Brief as Story*, 14 J. Legal Writing Inst. 127 (2007); *see also* Concept 1.6, *supra* at 49.

199. *See, e.g.*, J. Christopher Rideout, *Applied Legal Storytelling: An Updated Bibliography*, 18 Legal Comm. & Rhetoric 221 (2020).

200. The use of technology, including Generative Artificial Intelligence ("GAI"), will likely increase a lawyer's efficiency in all aspects of legal writing. *See* S. Sean Tu, Amy Cyphert & Samuel J. Perl, *Artificial Intelligence: Legal Reasoning, Legal Research and Legal Writ-*

Novice legal writers come with expectations about time because they are experienced writers, but they wildly underestimate the time needed for legal writing. They find this troubling because they have been told they are "good writers," leading them to believe the amount of time they have spent on past writing projects, and the way they have spent that time, will lead to success in legal writing. When moving from novice to expert, the legal writer begins to appreciate that time underpins all aspects of being a legal writer.[201]

In one sense, "time" has the same meaning in legal writing that it does in all situations—it is the part of our life that is measured in minutes, hours, days, weeks, and years. But in another sense, "time" means something different to expert legal writers. First, lawyers often bill time by the minute, so "as a lawyer, time [is] your most valuable commodity."[202] Second, lawyers represent clients, and those clients often control a lawyer's time. Third, court rules dictate strict time deadlines. Finally, legal writers are always conscious of an adversary, so time must be spent not only on generating text, but also on anticipating opposing positions.

Legal writing takes so much time because at its core, writing is thinking and creating.[203] Legal writing is more than simply transcribing a fully formed legal analysis. Instead, a legal writer needs time to integrate a host

---

ing, 25 MINN. J. L. SCI & TECH 106, 122 (2024). Lawyers have relied on electronic legal research for decades, and "using A.I. in legal research cuts the time spent sifting through case law... to a fraction of what it once was, all while being more efficient and relevant." John Campbell, *Ex Machina: Technological Disruption and the Future of Artificial Intelligence in Persuasive Legal Writing*, 5 UNIV. BOLOGNA L. REV. 294, 300 (2020). Many predict that law practice is "on the cusp of a legal technology revolution" because "GAI is particularly powerful for legal writers." Joe Regalia, *From Briefs to Bytes: How Generative AI is Transforming Legal Writing and Practice*, 59 TULSA L. REV. 193, 193 (2024) [hereinafter Regalia, *From Briefs to Bytes*]; *see also* Teresa Phelps & Kevin Ashley, *"Alexa, Write a Memo": The Promises and Challenges of AI and Legal Writing*, 26 LEGAL WRITING: J. LEGAL WRITING INST. 329, 331 (2022) (stating that a document produced with A.I. assistance "can be more thorough, accurate, and certainly more quickly produced than those written solely by a human attorney"). For more on the impact of technology on legal writing, see *infra* Ch. 7.

201. Writing and Rhetoric Professor Doug Downs explains that "time [is] an aspect of virtually everything students need to learn" about contributive inquiry, which he defines as making intellectual contributions to a field. Doug Downs, "*Time Is a Threshold Concept in Writing*": *Expanding Access to Undergraduate Research by Mentoring for Threshold Concepts and Self-Concept*, 84:6 COLLEGE ENGLISH, 613, 623 (2022). Downs points out, "[C]ontributive inquiry [is] an activity that hangs on time, extraordinarily time-intensive and -extensive—*time saturated* –rather than short-term or quickly completable. *Id.* at 619.

202. CHRISTINE COUGHLIN, JOAN MALMUD ROCKLIN & SANDY PATRICK, A LAWYER WRITES: A PRACTICAL GUIDE TO LEGAL ANALYSIS 80 (4th ed. 2024).

203. *See* Concepts 1.1, *supra* at 36; Concept 3.4, *infra* at 102.

of core and threshold concepts, including researching and critically engaging with the law,[204] grappling with legal standards, thinking about potential legal arguments, deciding which legal arguments are most persuasive,[205] creating a persuasive theory,[206] gathering and organizing the facts and law,[207] choosing how to address counterarguments, selecting what should be kept and what should be cut, inserting citations,[208] revising, editing, and proofreading. The legal writer is thinking and writing—again and again—in a synthetic and recursive creation.

A legal writer will have starts, stops, obstacles, and breakthroughs as the writer is writing and creating—all requiring time.[209] This realization is transformative because it is the act of writing itself that leads to the legal writer's best understanding of the legal issues presented in each unique situation. For example, legal writers often see a new argument or approach only while writing. Only the act of writing itself can reveal the holes and weaknesses in the legal analysis.[210] Time is needed to allow the legal writer to return and fix those holes and weaknesses.[211]

Legal writing presents three unique challenges that a novice legal writer must understand to grasp this concept: the adversarial nature of law, the constant distraction in legal practice, and the danger of procrastination.

Due to the adversarial nature of law, the legal writer is in the unique situation of having another legal writer, currently representing an opponent or hired in the future to represent an opponent, suggesting a different resolution to the legal issue. The adversarial nature of law is most obvious in litigation, but there is a potential future opponent even during transactional legal work. For example, a legal writer drafting a contract presents the terms most favor-

---

204. *See* Concept 2.2, *supra*, at 62.

205. *See* Concepts 2.4–2.7 & 3.1, *supra* at 69, 71, 73, 77 and 91, respectively.

206. *See* Concept 1.4, *supra* at 42.

207. *See* Concept 2.3, *supra* at 66.

208. *See* Concept 2.8, *supra* at 80.

209. Legal writers create meaning about the law, and making meaning is "messy, slow, tentative, full of starts and stops." Linda L. Berger, *Applying New Rhetoric to Legal Discourse: The Ebb and Flow of Reader and Writer, Text and Context*, 49 J. LEGAL EDUC. 155, 155 (1999) [hereinafter Berger, *Applying New Rhetoric*].

210. Linda Berger points out that "writing is a process for constructing thought, not just the 'skin' that covers thought." *Id.*

211. COUGHLIN et al., *supra* note 202, at 13 ("Expert legal writers allow themselves the time to re-think and revise so that the readers see—not the thinking process—but a complex analysis, clearly explained.").

able to the legal writer's client, knowing that the other party will advocate for other terms. A legal writer drafting a will knows that a future party may argue for an opposing interpretation of the will or contest the will. When drafting legislation, a legal writer must be prepared for suggested changes from other legislators. A legal scholar anticipates opposition to new ideas. Even judges drafting opinions write knowing that other judges might oppose either the result or the reasoning of the opinion.

Legal writers face numerous and constant distractions—legal writers have many projects and many clients vying for their attention and action. Unlike many other professional writers, legal writers need to build in extra time because they are often called away from their writing, which can interrupt the flow of creating a legal document.

Procrastination is a concern for all writers, but it is particularly dangerous for legal writers. Legal writing must be started early. It takes time for a legal writer to fully understand all the nuances of a legal issue. It takes time to structure a legal argument. It takes time to check for accuracy at every level. Legal writers often face firm deadlines, so there is little room for perfection. Lorne Michaels's advice about a deadline can be instructive for legal writers, "The show [*Saturday Night Live*] doesn't go on because it's ready, it goes on because it's 11:30."[212] Of course, the consequences when a lawyer misses time deadlines can be catastrophic. For example, a lawyer failing to file a habeas corpus petition on time can forfeit powerful claims, including a challenge to the death penalty.[213] Missed deadlines are also the leading complaint in legal malpractice claims.[214] A lawyer's professional duty of diligence also requires avoiding procrastination and meeting deadlines.[215]

---

212. TINA FEY, BOSSYPANTS 123 (2011).

213. *See* Ken Armstrong, *Death by Deadline*, THE MARSHALL PROJECT, PART ONE, (Nov. 15, 2014, 4:30 PM EST), https://www.themarshallproject.org/2014/11/15/death-by-deadline-part-one.

214. Jay Reeves, *Missed Deadlines: Top 2021 Malpractice Claims*, BYTE OF PREVENTION (May 23, 2022), https://www.lawyersmutualnc.com/blog/missed-deadlines-top-2021-malpractice-claims (based on statistics from Lawyers Mutual).

215. The American Bar Association Model Rules of Professional Conduct include comments. The following comment applies to Rule 1.3 Diligence:

> Perhaps no professional shortcoming is more widely resented than procrastination. A client's interests often can be adversely affected by the passage of time or the change of conditions; in extreme instances, as when a lawyer overlooks a statute of limitations, the client's legal position may be destroyed. Even when the client's

Legal writing cannot be separated from the author. The legal writer internalizes and grapples with every decision made while writing. Perhaps a legal writer researches a legal issue and begins writing, only to discover that additional research is needed to respond to a counterargument or to overcome a logical fallacy. Or a legal writer may recognize that a legal argument is difficult to understand because the legal writer did not provide enough context. Or maybe the legal writer identifies something that should be cut. Or the legal writer may question whether the drafted legal writing will persuade a skeptical reader. Even when revising, a legal writer might see that the organization could confuse a reader. In all these scenarios, the legal writer will have an internal dialogue both about the severity of the issue and how to correct it.

Many have noted that there are no great writers, only great rewriters.[216] Rewriting turns adequate legal writing into excellent legal writing.[217] Legal writers cannot skimp on rewriting and should take a multi-layered approach, reviewing the document on a broad and narrow scale. When reviewing the whole document, a legal writer can improve the structure, arguments, persuasion, responses to counterarguments, cohesiveness, and completeness. When reviewing sentences and words, the legal writer can improve grammar, transitions, and word choice. When correcting errors, the legal writer pays attention to details which helps build credibility with the legal reader who is more likely to trust a legal writer who produces polished writing. Each level of rewriting takes time.

The legal writer also must learn how to approach rewriting with humility and resilience. For instance, rewriting at the broadest scale forces the legal writer to recognize that the legal writer may not have adequately explained everything in the first draft. The legal writer must approach the writing with new eyes to consider if anything else should be included or omitted and to

---

> interests are not affected in substance, however, unreasonable delay can cause a client needless anxiety and undermine confidence in the lawyer's trustworthiness.

Model Rules, *supra* note 43, r. 1.3 cmt. 3.

216. Justice Louis Brandeis said, "There is no such thing as good writing. There is only good rewriting." BRYAN A. GARNER, THE ELEMENTS OF LEGAL STYLE 218 (2d ed. 2002) (citing George W. Pierce, *The Legal Profession*, 30 TORCH 5, 8 (1957) (quoting an oral remark by Justice Brandeis)).

217. Revision in legal writing is "constant, recursive, reflective, and responsive." Berger, *Applying New Rhetoric*, *supra* note 209, at 162. Revision is not reserved for the end of a writing project, but it instead "recurs throughout the writing project." *Id.*

check for cohesiveness, completeness, and readability. With humility, the legal writer can see those issues and then redraft to clarify.

Legal writers, often initially resist the concept that legal writing requires more time than they expect. But legal writers are irreversibly transformed once they understand that legal writing is intertwined with thinking about and solving legal issues and that legal writing, rewriting, thinking, and creating require sufficient time. Legal writers are also transformed when they internalize the idea that a legal argument is best explained in a written document that has been imagined, drafted, revised, and polished, perhaps several times.

3.4 Legal writers are creative writers.

Kristen K. Tiscione

Legal writing is, at its core, a creative act, "something akin to painting or literary creation."[218] Although legal writers must operate within legal and ethical constraints,[219] both the malleability of law[220] and the flexible nature of authority[221] empower them to construct, emphasize, and deflect reality through language.[222] They also understand that the flexibility associated with framing facts and legal issues allows for a range of creative options. While novice legal writers tend to rely on authority to find inspiration for their arguments, expert legal writers may craft their arguments first and then look for authority to support them.

The concept of legal argument as the result of a creative process dates back to ancient Greece. The first of the classical canons is referred to as invention or discovery, where the rhetor works with the existing evidence (inartistic appeals) to create arguments grounded in reason, emotion, and credibility (artistic appeals).[223] At least one contemporary legal scholar has suggested that

---

218. Douglas Litowitz, *Legal Writing: Its Nature, Limits, And Dangers*, 49 MERCER L. REV. 709, 722 (1998); *see also* Teresa Godwin Phelps, *The New Legal Rhetoric*, 40 Sw. L.J. 1089, 1094 (1986) (describing legal writing as "disciplined creative activity"); Concepts 1.1–.2, *supra* at 36 & 37.

219. *See, e.g.*, Concepts 1.3, 1.7, 2.5, and 3.1, *supra* at 40, 51, 71 & 91.

220. *See* Concept 1.3, *supra* at 40.

221. *See* Concept 2.4, *supra* at 69.

222. *See* Concept 1.4, *supra* at 42.

223. *See* ARISTOTLE, RHETORIC, *supra* note 104, at I.2, 1355b–1356a.

legal writing requires "even more creativity than works of fiction or poetry."[224] As Nancy Wanderer has noted, legal writers use their imagination to convert existing facts and law into compelling stories, to frame potential legal theories, and to select cases to analogize or to distinguish.[225]

Barbara Blumenfeld describes the creative process of legal writing in terms of four stages: preparation, incubation, illumination, and verification, which lead to "novel and adaptive product[s]."[226] According to Blumenfeld, between preparation (gathering facts and law) and the final end-product, the legal writer engages in the less definable stages of incubation and illumination.[227] Incubation is a period "during which the mind is left to begin solving a problem, connecting the acquired information, without conscious direction, to a precise course or solution."[228] Thereafter, illumination occurs "when the incubated material percolates to the surface: ideas coalesce and the writer may again consciously and with direction choose arguments and approaches or, with document in hand, begin choosing words, phrasing, etc."[229] During incubation and illumination, the writer combines her understanding of the legal audience's expectations with her own judgment.[230]

The concept that legal writing is creative can be troubling for novice legal writers for several reasons. First, students often come to law school expecting their writing experience to transfer directly to legal writing. For example, they may be used to relying on their own observations and opinions as opposed to needing to cite external, supporting authority.[231] They may also be disappointed

---

224. Nancy A. Wanderer, *Legal Writing and Creativity: Polar Opposites or Perfect Partners?* 35 ME. BAR J. 80, 81 (2020).

225. *Id.* (stating that "[d]eciding how to use analogous cases to support arguments in a client's favor probably requires the most creativity of all"); *see also* Daniel E Cummins, *A Portrait of the Lawyer as an Artist*, 30 PA. LAW. 26, 28 (2008) (acknowledging that legal writing is creative despite having to "honor[ ] the requirements of plain language and concise writing").

226. Barbara Blumenfeld, *Rhetoric, Referential Communication, and the Novice Writer,* 9 LEGAL COMM. & RHETORIC 207, 216 (2012).

227. *Id.*

228. *Id.*

229. *Id.* at 216–17.

230. *Id.* at 217.

231. Marie A. Monahan, *Towards a Theory of Assimilating Law Students into the Culture of the Legal Profession*, 51 CATH. U. L. REV. 215, 231 (2001) (noting that many law "students' previous writing allowed for creativity through broad statements often supported only by personal opinion").

to learn that in legal writing, readers prefer clarity and readability over elegant variation and complex sentences.[232] Second, beginning legal writers are often frustrated with formulaic structures and stylistic constraints they perceive as stifling their creativity.[233] Typically, teachers wait until students are more comfortable with the basics of legal analysis and legal writing genres before encouraging them to "be creative."[234] Accordingly, students become frustrated because they feel there is no place for their own voice in legal writing.[235]

Once students integrate the concepts of law as a meaning-making activity, as malleable, as situated in particular facts and circumstances, and yet as conforming with conventions relating to substance and style, they are able to use their imagination to frame rules and arguments. This transformation is irreversible. When students begin to understand the value of their own observations and opinions as long as they are "founded in an accurate assessment of the law, ... their process of becoming a creative legal writer begins."[236] They no longer see themselves as merely scribes or reporters. Moreover, the structures of legal reasoning once experienced as confining become familiar and recognizable paths to achieve client-based goals, "freeing them" from the need to reinvent new organizational structures.[237] The creativity inherent in legal writing is not bounded, nor need it be, to qualify as integral to legal writing expertise.

---

232. Miriam E. Felsenburg & Laura P. Graham, *Beginning Legal Writers in Their Own Words: Why the First Weeks of Legal Writing Are So Tough and What We Can Do About It*, 16 LEGAL WRITING: J. LEGAL WRITING INST. 223, 276 (2010); *see also* Cummins, *supra* note 225, at 28 (acknowledging his realization as a law student that legal writing is creative despite having to "honor [ ] the requirements of plain language and concise writing").

233. Wanderer, *supra* note 224, at 80; *see also* Olivia Ruschill, *Creative, Vulnerable and Bold: Learning the Art of Good Legal Writing*, 91 J. KAN. BAR ASS'N. 14 (2022) (describing her experience as a law student in legal writing).

234. Felsenburg & Graham, *supra* note 232, at 259.

235. *See, e.g.*, *id.* at 298; J. Christopher Rideout & Jill J. Ramsfield, *Legal Writing: A Revised View*, 69 WASH. L. REV. 35, 59–60 (noting that "the seeming loss of the ability to 'be original' is something every law student encounters.... [L]aw students are frustrated by what they see as the lack of 'creativity' in legal writing and analysis.") [hereinafter Rideout & Ramsfield, *A Revised View*].

236. Monahan, *supra* note 231, at 231.

237. *See* Felsenburg & Graham, *supra* note 232, at 298.

3.5 Legal writers internalize conditions of uncertainty.

Melissa H. Weresh

Uncertainty permeates many aspects of legal analysis, including interpreting ambiguous laws, balancing conflicting legal authorities, assessing an ever-evolving legal landscape, evaluating the application of laws to novel facts, determining relevant facts, and predicting outcomes. Legal writers understand that laws and legal precedents are often subject to interpretation and can be vague or ambiguous in certain situations. In some instances, legal writers may encounter conflicting legal authorities that complicate their analysis. Moreover, the law itself is not static and evolves over time through legislative changes, judicial decisions, and societal developments. Facts are not "truth," but are gathered and curated by the legal writer. Despite thorough research and analysis, legal writers acknowledge and accept that there can be uncertainties regarding the outcome of a case or the interpretation of the law by a judge or jury. Tolerating uncertainty involves assessing these conflicts, weighing competing arguments, and making informed judgments based on the available legal reasoning.

One example of uncertainty faced by legal writers is the juxtaposition of the concept of *stare decisis*, grounded in the implicit assumption that cases have been decided "correctly" and therefore merit replication in their application to subsequent cases, and the uncertainty inherent in legal texts. As one author explains, texts are "ill-structured problems," those that are "more complex, conditional, and contingent" and that "do not have easy, final, or agreed-upon solutions" such that they require reflection and "engagement with often conflicting and competing claims."[238] Judicial decisions, like all texts, may represent ill-structured problems "because they are rhetorical artifacts and because they are always the product of a particular historical moment and a unique conjunction of ideologies, power relationships, material conditions, and political, economic, psychological, personal, and social variables."[239] To require the legal writer to simultaneously make sense of, respect the authority of, and apply the principles discerned from these cases to circumstances which, while similar, almost inevitably differ in meaningful ways and predict how the application of these principles will resolve subsequent disputes is an intellectu-

---

238. Patrick Sullivan, *The World Confronts Us With Uncertainty: Deep Reading as a Threshold Concept*, *in* (RE)CONSIDERING WHAT WE KNOW, ch. 1, *supra* note 15, at 117.

239. *Id.* at 117–18.

ally, cognitively and, at times, affectively uncertain undertaking. And yet, that is what is routinely required of the legal writer.

In this respect, uncertainty about the law, the facts, the accuracy about predictions, and the efficacy of certain legal arguments can undermine the sense of authority and credibility that legal writers seek to convey in their writing. This tension between the need to project confidence and the reality of legal uncertainty can create a profound sense of insecurity and instability in the developing identity of the legal writer, requiring them to continuously navigate and negotiate their role as advisor and advocate.

Nonetheless, understanding and tolerating uncertainty is essential for legal writers as it allows them to navigate the role of a lawyer as advisor and advocate. Embracing uncertainty fosters intellectual curiosity, encouraging legal writers to approach cases with creativity and to consider competing perspectives. Moreover, tolerating uncertainty promotes critical thinking skills, prompting legal writers to analyze issues comprehensively and weigh the possibilities and merits of different arguments. It also encourages flexibility in legal reasoning, enabling writers to adapt their strategies in response to changing circumstances. Ultimately, by acknowledging uncertainty, legal writers can embrace and maximize their creative role as advisor and advocate in their professional writing.

Many disciplines have recognized uncertainty as a professional identity threshold concept. For example, in a study of design students, researchers asserted that "a student's acceptance of uncertainty as both an essential and routine part of the practice of designing would (1) permit deeper explorations of design than would have been previously possible and (2) would facilitate movement toward greater understanding of the self as a designer."[240] Similarly, in a study of medical students, researchers concluded that "[m]anaging or embracing uncertainty has been identified as a possible, or even overarching [threshold concept] in multiple medical disciplines."[241] Likewise, tolerating uncertainty is a threshold concept for legal writers, and one that is likely bounded within the constructs of legal analysis and communication.

Legal writers understand that they must tolerate and may, in fact, invite, conditions of uncertainty—this understanding is a part of their professional identity. Mastering legal writing in conditions of uncertainty requires legal

---

240. Monica W. Tracey and Alisa Hutchinson, *Uncertainty, Reflection, and Designer Identity Development*, 42 Design Studies 86, 107 (2016).

241. Sarah E.M. Meek, Hilary Neve & Andy Wearn, *Threshold Concepts and Troublesome Knowledge, in* Clinical Educ. for the Health Pros. 361, 370 (D. Nestel et al. eds., 2020) (citations omitted).

writers to integrate other concepts and threshold concepts. Legal writers must not only understand the malleability of legal principles[242] and the contextualization of facts,[243] but also that these aspects of legal writing make the process less than certain. Beyond the relationship of uncertainty to these other threshold concepts, the understanding and acquiescence that legal writers tolerate uncertainty is part of their identity as professionals, and the recognition of and adaptation to practicing in conditions of uncertainty is thus a professional identity threshold concept.

Confronting uncertainty and adapting to it is troublesome for the legal writer. Navigating uncertainty initially poses significant challenges to the development and maintenance of a cohesive professional identity. Uncertainty challenges the notion of expertise, as legal writers must constantly confront the limitations of their knowledge and expertise in the face of ambiguous legal principles and evolving case law.[244] This can lead to feelings of inadequacy and imposter syndrome, particularly for novice legal writers as they develop their skills and understanding of the law.[245]

Even so, tolerating uncertainty is transformative for legal writers, impacting their understanding of their own expertise, authority, responsibility, and accountability, all aspects of the professional identity of a legal writer.[246] Legal

---

242. See Concept 1.3, *supra* at 40.

243. *See* Concept 1.4, *supra* at 42.

244. *See, e.g.*, Georgina C. Stephens, Mahbub Sarkar, & Michelle D. Lazarus, *'I Was Uncertain, but I Was Acting on It': A Longitudinal Qualitative Study of Medical Students' Responses to Uncertainty*, 58 MED. EDUC. 869, 872 (2024). In this study, though not focused on threshold concepts, researchers describe negative cognitive responses to uncertainty, including descriptors such as "'threat', 'vulnerability', 'doubt', a 'lack of confidence' and even thoughts of 'helplessness'. *Id.* at 872. Related to these cognitive descriptors, participants typically described uncertainty as a threat to one's expertise and credibility." *Id.*

245. David A. Rasch & Meehan Rasch, *Overcoming Writer's Block and Procrastination for Attorneys, Law Students, and Law Professors*, 43 N.M. L. REV. 193, 199 (2013). The authors observe that legal "[w]riting is often a solitary undertaking, and lawyers need to be able to tolerate loneliness, self-doubt, fatigue, dread, delayed gratification, uncertainty, criticism, and overwhelm — yet still continue to write."

246. *See, e.g.*, Stephens et al., *supra* note 244, at 876. In terms of behavioral responses to uncertainty, the researchers found maladaptive responses such as avoidance and inaction, but also adaptive, transformative responses, such as identifying ways to manage uncertainty, including "collecting information where available to better understand a scenario they were uncertain about, advocating for their learning to supervising clinicians, self-regulation of learning and even putting on an act of confidence to help persevere with learning despite enduring uncertainty." *Id.* at 874.

writers are expected to possess expertise and authority in their field. Embracing uncertainty as a threshold concept challenges legal writers to move beyond simplistic views of the law as a set of fixed rules and instead engage with its inherent complexities and ambiguities. Legal writers must similarly move beyond the notion that, as an expert, the legal writer can make guaranteed predictions or unassailable arguments. Accepting uncertainty in legal writing transforms the writer's understanding of expertise and prompts the legal writer to continuously adapt to new situations, necessitating an attitude of life-long learning. By accepting the uncertainty inherent in legal analysis and writing, this threshold concept fosters professional development and intellectual growth regarding how to advise clients and advocate for them despite inherent uncertainty.

Moreover, navigating uncertainty cultivates resilience and adaptability in the professional identity of the legal writer. By learning to tolerate ambiguity and embrace the fluidity of legal reasoning, writers develop the confidence to confront challenges and uncertainties. Recognition of uncertainty indeed serves to normalize it, thereby allowing the legal writer to embrace rather than be stymied by it. This not only enhances their ability to address complex legal issues but also strengthens their sense of professionalism and self-assurance in their role as legal advocates.

Embracing the uncertainty inherent in legal writing is also transformative in initiating the legal writer into the professional community. Legal writing often serves as a means of communication and collaboration within the legal community, establishing the role of the legal writer. Recognizing uncertainty fosters open dialogue and collaboration among legal professionals, as individuals share perspectives, insights, and strategies for addressing uncertainties. Because "the process of law is at once creative and educative," legal writers "are perpetually learning what can and cannot be done with [the language of law] as they try—and fail or succeed—to reach new formulations of their positions [which] also means that both the identity of the speakers and their wants are in perpetual transformation."[247]

Finally, a legal writer who crosses the threshold and thus understands uncertainty as an aspect of professional identity experiences an irreversible transformation. In fact, the legal writer not only accepts the uncertainty characteristic of legal analysis and communication, she may also welcome uncertainty as the "play in the joints" facilitating legal argument. Whereas navigating uncertainty may initially pose challenges for the legal writer, it ultimately serves as a catalyst for growth, transformation, and skills development.

---

247. White, *Law As Rhetoric*, ch. 1, *supra* note 20, at 691.

3.6 Legal writing's conventionality makes legal writing identifiable and credible to legal audiences but also potentially exclusionary and confusing for some writers.

Kirsten K. Davis

Because the law and legal institutions are "conservative" in that they tend to be slow to change and value stability and tradition, professional legal writing is highly conventional. That is, legal writing has a well-worn and familiar way of "doing things"; it adheres to rules and customs that both originate from and are generally honored by those who read and write the law. These conventions make legal writing recognizable, understandable, and credible *as* legal writing to reading audiences.[248] In legal writing, *writing* conventions are not just the conventions of composition (including organization); instead, the conventions for effective legal writing necessarily include *legal* conventions and require the novice writer to integrate both composition and legal concepts. When this integration is accomplished, novices better understand how legal writing is a conventional practice.

Legal writing conventions are institutionalized through rules and are also passed to new legal writers by custom and practice. For example, a convention in litigation-centered legal writing is that representing a legal rule in a document like a brief or motion typically requires the author to include a citation to the legal authority supporting the existence of that rule.[249] When legal writers use authority to establish a legal proposition in litigation documents, they include in their writing a reference to that proposition's authoritative source to show their audience that the legal rule is legitimate.[250] Legal writers know

---

248. *See* Concept 2.9, *supra*, at 83.

249. *See* Concept 2.8, *supra*, at 80; *see also* CAROLYN V. WILLIAMS, THE ALWD GUIDE TO LEGAL CITATION R. 34.1 (2021) ("Legal citations are used in many written situations, including practice based documents...."); JOAN M. ROCKLIN ET AL, AN ADVOCATE PERSUADES 153 (2022)("In addition to conveying your credibility, citations can provide more substantive support for your arguments....“); MODEL RULES, *supra* note 43, r. 1.1 ("Competent representation requires the legal knowledge, skill, thoroughness and preparation reasonably necessary for the representation.") and r. 3.3(a)(2) (describing duty in litigation to reveal directly adverse authority when opponent fails to disclose); FLA. R. OF APP. PROC. r. 9.210(3)(b)(5) (2024) (requiring that the brief include "citations to appropriate authorities" in the arguments on the issues).

250. *See* ROCKLIN ET AL, *supra* note 249, at 153 (noting the purpose of citation).

that authoritative sources have a hierarchy from most to least authoritative.[251] Accordingly, legal writers know the convention of citation in litigation documents expects not only a cite to *an* authority that supports a legal proposition but to *the* highest available authority in the hierarchy of sources, in other words, the authority most likely to persuade the reader of the validity and strength of the legal rule the writer states. In this example of a legal writing convention, a student must integrate their understanding of audience,[252] precedent, hierarchy of legal authority, citation format, citation placement, the power of court rules, and rule synthesis to effectively satisfy the convention of "citing authority" in their legal writing.

Legal writers recognize that conventions are constraints on how writers can address legal exigencies in documents. In other words, conventions of legal writing mark the boundaries for what can and cannot be written in the law and what can and cannot be understood as part of the category of "legal writing." Arguably, the boundedness created by legal writing's conventions is particularly strong as conventions exist not just in the customary practices of writers but in legally enforceable rules and ethics codes.[253] Following these conventions is, in part, what makes a legal writer's communications credible and comprehensible to the writer's audience even when the writer is engaged in an otherwise creative rhetorical practice.[254]

When a novice begins to understand the dominant conventions of legal writing, like the litigation-centered convention of needing to cite to the best legal authority for a proposition, the novice is reoriented to what it means *be* a legal professional. A legal reader, who is likely, in the first instance, to be the

---

251. *See* Concept 2.4, *supra*, at 69; *see* also WILLIAMS, *supra* note 249, at Appx. 1 (listing primary sources by jurisdiction in hierarchical order).

252. Audience is a significant factor in the conventionality of legal writing. Novices must learn that legal writing audiences are not monolithic and that the conventions for the documents legal writers prepare change based upon the audience to whom the document is addressed. In the context of conventionality, this means that different legal documents have different conventions. Transactional documents, like contracts, have their own conventions, which differ from those related to litigation documents. For example, a convention of contract drafting would be to place definitions at the beginning of the contract and in alphabetical order. Another convention is to [mostly] avoid including citations to legal authorities upon which the validity of contracts is based.

253. *See, e.g.*, FLA. R. OF APP. PROC. r. 9.210(3)(b)(5), *supra* note 249 (requiring that briefs include "citations to appropriate authorities" in the arguments on the issues).

254. *See* Concept 2.1, *supra*, at 60.

student's writing professor, will notice unconventional legal writing and will guide a student to avoid violating those conventions. Once a student understands what is important to the readers in their audience for their document, the student cannot "unsee" those conventions. Instead, students undergo internal writing *process* transformations that result in improved conventionality in the written product; students integrate legal writing's conventions as part of their writing style and come to understand the conventions as something necessary to satisfy their reading audience. That is, when a writing professor gives feedback to a student to "cite here," the student begins to internalize legal writing's citation conventions as part of their professional identity,[255] not just as a technique of attribution.

If this integration does not happen, then the novice does not cross the threshold to become a legal writer. But if the threshold is crossed, not only do students make a *conceptual* shift as legal writers when they learn the conventions of legal writing, they make an *ontological* one, to recognize themselves as legal writers, speak in the vocabulary of legal writers, and better imagine and satisfy the needs of their reading audiences.

As a threshold concept, legal writing's conventionality can have some troublesome features that are often the result of contradictions embedded within the conventions themselves. For example, one convention where this troublesomeness arises is the convention that directs a legal writer to avoid writing in the first-person singular when making a legal argument in a court document. In other words, in most instances, a legal writer does not say, "I have determined the law is X." Rather, the writer says, "the law *is* X." This convention of legal writing perpetuates the notion that legal writers "transmit" rather than "invent" the law. Expert legal writers know, however, that the absence of the agent—the "I"—in the writing itself is a fiction. The legal writer is always there, in the document, inventing, creating, organizing, revising, and writing the document into being.[256] Expert legal writers who are writing to a judicial audience learn to live with the tension and paradox caused by a convention that demands a lawyer act with agency but write as if that agency does not exist.[257]

---

255. *See* Concept 3.7, *supra*, at 114.

256. *See* White, *Law as Rhetoric*, ch. 1, *supra* note 20, at 684 (describing law as a constitutive, creative rhetorical act); *see also* Concepts 1.1 & 1.2, *supra*, at 36 & 37; 2.1, *supra*, at 60; 2.3–2.5, *supra*, at 66, 69 & 71; and 3.3, *supra*, at 97.

257. See Concept 2.1, *supra*, at 60.

Another way of thinking about this litigation writing convention is to imagine that legal writers write "as if' the document speaks for the law itself when in reality the document does not. Speaking "as if" results in the legal writer not expressly claiming or taking credit for their own creativity or inventiveness within a legal document. Experienced legal writers know that the conventions of litigation documents make it seem as if the document presents the reader with conclusions that are obvious, predictable, and even predetermined, when they are not necessarily so. In reality, the legal writer has researched the law, read the applicable sources, and is expressing his or her synthesis of what the texts of the law and the facts mean in the context of the particular legal concern the writer is writing about. Experienced legal writers know that one does not find *the* "truth" of the law; instead, one builds an argument that invents a version of what the law *can be* in a particular context. In other words, expert legal writers know the fiction of the "missing I": legal writers are speaking as themselves and on behalf of others, but instead of saying so, legal writers purport not to speak for themselves at all. The writer as agent disappears from the argument.

Novices struggle with the idea that, in many legal writing situations, legal writers do not claim or take credit for their own creativeness or ability to invent something new in legal argument. The "missing I" causes some novices trouble. Some are bothered by the realization that their writing is not merely a "conduit" of the law as it exists somewhere outside themselves, but instead represents their own creativity, analytical skill, and critical thinking applied within the constraints of existing texts. Others are comfortable with the idea that they are creators of legal argument but are troubled by not expressing ownership of those ideas in the way the document is written. Even others are troubled by both ideas.

This is not the only type of trouble that can come from legal writing's conventionality. Conventionality is an expression of power that includes the life experiences of some legal writers and not others.[258] The standards of "good" legal writing are the products of the systems, institutions, and people who have had the power to establish these standards. Some legal writers begin their legal writing journey as members of this powerful group, while others have never been a part of it. This latter group intuits, but, in my experience, often does not always consciously recognize, that legal writing's conventions can have

258. *See* Concept 1.8, *supra*, at 55.

an exclusionary character. Critical scholars, however, have consciously called attention to the nature of this exclusion.[259]

For example, one critique is that legal writing's conventions, at least in Western common law countries, are based on Western ways of knowing, and therefore act to exclude non-Western ways of writing about and within the law.[260] Not all novice legal writers identify strongly with these Western norms. The feeling of "otherness" that can come from writing with conventions that one feels are not one's own (or are at least in conflict with one's own) can be a troublesome feeling. Some legal writers might find themselves adopting conventions that make for a successful legal writer that at the same time seem confusing, inconsistent, or out-of-sync with some aspects of their personal ways of knowing. Yet, integrating the conventions of legal writing into one's notions of a competent professional performance is necessary for crossing the threshold to disciplinary expertise. This internalizing, however, can be emotionally and intellectually costly for some writers and for the legal profession as a whole.

Experienced legal writers who have crossed the threshold recognize the way the conventions of legal writing operate to highlight some ways of knowing and being while discounting or silencing others is only part of the story. They recognize that while legal writing conventions are a kind of entrenchment of a dominant narrative about what can be written about the law, this entrenchment can be resisted, and openings exist for transforming the way legal writing is usually done.[261]

---

259. *See* Leslie P. Culver, *(Un)wicked Analytical Frameworks and the Cry for Identity*, 21 Nev. L.J. 555 (2021) (challenging IRAC as a conventional analytical structure and arguing that privileges some ways of knowing and some voices over others).

260. See the arguments on this point raised in Elizabeth Berenguer et al, Critical and Comparative Rhetoric: Unmaking Privilege and Power in Law and Legal advocacy to Achieve, Truth, Justice, and Equity (2023).

261. One example of this kind of transformative resistance is the scholarly literature of the critical race theory movement which privileges personal narrative in and as legal scholarship. *See, e.g.*, Patricia J. Williams, The Alchemy of Race and Rights: Diary of a Law Professor (1991); *see also* Culver, *supra* note 259; Berenguer et al., *supra* note 260.

3.7 Legal writers form and enact their professional identity through legal writing.

Melissa H. Weresh

It is primarily through writing that lawyers both shape their own professional identities and communicate those identities to the legal community.[262] As expert lawyers come to understand, it is primarily through writing that "writers come to develop and perform identities in relation to the interests, beliefs, and values of the communities they engage with, understanding the possibilities of selfhood available in those communities."[263] Indeed, "[l]earning to write like a lawyer means acquiring a new discoursal identity—one positioned within legal contexts and, in many ways, shaped by those contexts."[264]

Through legal writing, legal writers demonstrate not only their expertise, but also their credibility, commitment to professional norms, and their own personal and professional values and ideology. It is also through legal writing that law students and emerging professionals begin to understand and adapt their role as a professional member of the discipline.[265] They view themselves,

---

262. While scholars have debated the definition of "professional identity" in the context of professional identity formation in legal education, the articulation of this threshold concept views the term broadly, as "more than simply ethics or professionalism." Martin J. Katz, *Teaching Professional Identity in Law School*, 42 COLO. LAW. 45, 45 (2013). Rather, professional identity in this context encompasses "the way a lawyer understands [their] role relative to all of the stakeholders in the legal system, including clients, courts, opposing parties and counsel, the firm, and even the legal system itself (or society as a whole)." *Id.* This conceptualization therefore includes an ethical grounding and deep commitment to professional norms, as well as a sense of the lawyer's role within the profession.

263. Kevin Roozen, *3.1 Writing Is Linked to Identity, in* Adler-Kassner & Wardle, NAMING WHAT WE KNOW, ch. 1, *supra* note 15, at 50–51 (explaining that writing "functions as a key form of socialization as we learn to become members of academic disciplines").

264. J. Christopher Rideout & Jill J. Ramsfield, *Legal Writing: The View from Within*, 60 MERCER L. REV. 705, 744 (2010) (asserting that "to the extent that learning to write like a lawyer means mastering the conventions of legal discourse, we argue that those conventions become not only part of the text, but also part of the writer.") [hereinafter Rideout & Ramsfield, *View From Within*]; *see also* Shelley Kierstead & Erika Abner, *Text Work As Identity Work for Legal Writers: How Writing Texts Contribute to the Construction of A Professional Identity*, 9 LEGAL COMM. & RHETORIC 327, 329 (2012) (emphasizing that, in a study of senior lawyers, research participants acknowledged that "acquiring strong writing skills was very much a part of legal identity").

265. *See, e.g.*, Barbara Kamler & Pat Thomson, *The Failure of Dissertation Advice Books: Toward Alternative Pedagogies for Doctoral Writing*, 37 EDUC. RESEARCHER 507,

and are viewed by other members of the community, through their writing.[266] As novice legal writers become expert legal writers, "the embedded values and beliefs of a discourse shape the[ir] identity [as a] writer."[267]

Novice legal writers often assume that writing is a neutral, ministerial act of recording legal knowledge of substantive law using predetermined formats and conventions[268]—performing a kind of general, conventional literacy within the discipline. This perspective treats legal writing as a mere conduit for information rather than recognizing it as a rhetorical and constitutive practice.

In contrast, expert legal writers understand that writing is not simply a tool for communicating expertise; it actively shapes the legal writer's identity by enacting professional norms, demonstrating credibility, engaging with the ideological dimensions of legal discourse, and becoming a member of the discourse community. Expert legal writers understand that, within any discipline

> [t]here is no general literacy: literacy is always in some way involved in the negotiation of identities and ideologies in specific social situations. Vocabularies, genres, and language conventions are a part of what creates and distinguishes social groups, and thus learning to write is always ongoing, situational, and involving cultural and ideological immersion.[269]

---

508 (2008) (asserting that, in the context of dissertation writing, "texts and identities are formed together, in, and through writing").

266. Kierstead & Abner, *supra* note 264, at 330 (noting that a "lawyer's writing, whether public or private, becomes a representation of the lawyer in the world").

267. Rideout & Ramsfield, *The View From Within*, *supra* note 264, at 724. Reminiscent of the affective journey of traversing a threshold concept, the authors explain that "[t]his can happen when writers incorporate some of the values and epistemologies of a new discourse into their own literacy practices, or it can even happen when writers resist or struggle with some of the values and epistemologies of a new discourse."

268. *See* J. Christopher Rideout, *Knowing What We Already Know: On the Doctrine of Legal Writing*, 1 Savannah L. Rev. 103, 115 (2014) [hereinafter Rideout & Ramsfield, *On the Doctrine of Legal Writing*]. Rideout explains an objective, "common-sense view of what writing is," "a matter of recording what is already known, what already lies outside the writer." In contrast, he notes that "the essence of much legal writing is legal analysis and legal argumentation—acts of thinking that require interaction between writer and audience, writer and subject matter, and writer and language." *Id.*

269. Tony Scott, *3.0 Writing Enacts and Creates Identities and Ideologies*, *in* Adler-Kassner & Wardle, Naming What We Know, ch. 1, *supra* note 15, at 48.

Legal writing is essential for establishing the credibility inherent in professional identity within the legal profession.[270] Effective legal writing requires clarity, precision, and persuasiveness—not just as a technical skill but as a means of enacting professional credibility and competence. Briefs, memos, and contracts do more than convey information; they establish the writer's role as a legal professional. Moreover, the legal writer understands that credibility is reinforced through the strategic use of legal authority, and also in the choices made regarding structure, tone,[271] and rhetorical approach. As such, "[l]earning to write like a lawyer is much more than simply taking on a role. It is taking on a different identity, one inscribed with ways of understanding the world that are constrained by the positions and possibilities available within the discourse of the law."[272]

Further, legal writing is the primary way in which legal professionals internalize and perform professional norms. Writing is not just a reflection of these norms but a site where they are practiced and negotiated. By adhering to specific conventions, styles, and ethical standards, law students and novice legal writers begin to align themselves with the expectations of the profession, demonstrating their integration into the legal community.

At the same time, professional norms are not static. They evolve, in part, through writing. As legal writers gain expertise, they may challenge and refine these standards, contributing to the discipline's ongoing discourse.[273] The ability to navigate these norms—both conforming to and, when necessary, testing their boundaries—is a crucial aspect of professional identity formation. Through writing, legal professionals both adopt and shape the conventions that define the field.

Legal writing is inherently a practice of identity construction, as it reflects and enacts personal values and ideological commitments. The framing of legal issues involves deliberate rhetorical choices that signal a writer's priorities and

---

270. *See e.g.*, SMITH, *supra* note 171 (explaining the importance of, and ways in which to evince, credibility, or ethos, in legal writing).

271. Kierstead & Abner, *supra* note 264, at 329 ("the representation of the lawyer in the world may be reflected in the tone of the document.").

272. Rideout & Ramsfield, *View from Within*, *supra* note 264, at 737.

273. *Id.* at 742 ("learning to write like a lawyer involves construction of a discoursal identity. The discoursal identity is constructed from among the positions and possibilities available within the discourse of the law, and the construction entails accommodation and, to greater or lesser extents, negotiation and perhaps resistance on the part of the writer.").

perspectives.[274] For example, the rhetorical import of framing an issue as one impacting "gun control" versus "gun rights" carries ideological weight, shaping not only legal arguments but also the writer's identity within the profession. In the context of advocacy, legal writers come to understand the ways in which framing and contextualizing legal issues communicates values, and they must navigate how that framing comports with their own ethical and professional values, as well as those of the profession.

While legal writing adheres to formal conventions, legal writers come to recognize that it also allows for creativity and individual expression. The choices a legal writer makes in tone, structure, and argumentation strategies contribute to their professional persona. Through writing, legal professionals negotiate these tensions, continuously shaping their professional identities in relation to the broader legal and ethical landscape.

The concept that professional identity is both formed and enacted through writing integrates understanding of both writing as a process involving an understanding of doctrine and genre as well as the context within which professional identity is formed and communicated. The recognition that

> writing is not merely a matter of recording one's research or thoughts, but it is in fact a process linked to the development of new, professional identities... illuminates how writing in new contexts is not only about learning abstract conventions but also about learning how to *be* within a group with social conventions, norms, and expectations."[275]

The realization of the relationship between writing and professional identity is also troublesome. Novice legal writers view legal writing as a skill, the manner in which they communicate the professional analysis they view as central to their role as lawyers. That those communications go beyond the transfer of information, representing the creation of knowledge and comprising a critical component of professional identity, is a weighty and intimidating prospect.

Indeed, mastering legal writing is troublesome, in part, because of its relationship to identity. As J. Christopher Rideout and Jill J. Ramsfield explain, "questions of the self are one of the reasons why legal writing is such a challenging type of discourse to write and to write well. And we further believe that

---

274. *See* Concept 1.4, *infra*, at 42.

275. Estrem, *supra* note 7, at 56 (emphasis in original).

for beginning legal writers, questions of the self are primary and are one of the central challenges."[276]

The realization that writing enacts identity may also be troublesome as legal writers come to understand the way in which legal writing itself may perpetuate inequities that are steeped but also tacit in law. It is disquieting for the novice legal writer to learn that legal writing "can marginalize conventional moral or social moorings and bury or render invisible ideological considerations."[277] This underscores the way in which legal writing is an ideological activity:

> As we are immersed in discourses through reading, and dialogue with others, we begin to name and understand, *through* those discourses, internalizing the ideologies they carry. Indeed, language learning, and use is a primary means through which ideologies are conveyed, acquired, and made to seem "natural," without obvious alternatives or need of explanation.[278]

For example, once legal writers recognize the way in which unchallenged inequities are instantiated through legal writing conventions such as *stare decisis*,[279] the writer understands her own role in perpetuating the status quo and her agency[280] in challenging the structures the law supports and protects.

Legal writers may also experience the troublesome nature of this threshold concept when they become aware of how their framing of an issue may be at once guided by their objective but also influenced by their own values. By way of example, the environmental lawyer who represents industrial interests but who is also concerned about environmental impacts must struggle with the use of "climate change" to frame an issue that could alternatively be characterized as "global warming." In this sort of troublesome space, the writer understands how ideologies are formed and communicated in legal writing, and how her own professional identity is influenced by, and manifested through, her writing.

Finally, the realization that writing enacts identity may be troublesome because of a shift in self occasioned by becoming an expert legal writer. As Elizabeth Mertz explains, in order to "successfully master [legal] discourse,

276. Rideout & Ramsfield, *View from Within*, supra note 264, at 706.

277. *Id.* at 737.

278. Scott, *supra* note 269 at 49 (noting that "[a]s ideological activity, writing is deeply involved in struggles over power, the formation of identities, and the negotiation, perpetuation, and contestation of belief systems") (emphasis in original).

279. *See* Concept 1.8, *supra*, at 55.

280. *See id.; see also* Concept 3.6, *supra*, at 109.

students must be able to speak in an 'I' that is not their own self, to adapt their position to the exigencies of legal language"[281] and such a transition can constitute an "unmooring of the self from its usual coordinates."[282]

Understanding the relationship between writing and identity is irreversible, representing a permanent shift in perception. When the legal writer acknowledges that writing is not just about technical skill but also about embodying their professional identity, this reshapes their understanding of the purpose and importance of legal writing in their careers. This also transforms the writer's analytical and critical thinking skills as they learn to see beyond surface-level tasks and engage with writing as a means of expressing complex legal arguments and professional judgments. This depth of engagement is a permanent change in their cognitive processes. Recognizing legal writing as an enactment of professional identity means that legal writers integrate ethical standards, professional responsibilities, and personal values of integrity and fealty to the law into their writing. This integration becomes a core part of their professional identity, influencing future writing tasks and professional activities.

Recognition that writing is a manifestation of identity is also transformative. It redefines the role of writing as writers begin to view legal writing as a means for demonstrating their competence, values, and commitment to the legal community. This transformation affects how they approach every legal document, from memos to briefs to scholarly articles. As students internalize the idea that their writing reflects their professional identity, they gain confidence in their ability to contribute meaningfully to the legal field. This confidence extends beyond writing, influencing their overall professional demeanor and interactions.

Finally, understanding the importance of legal writing in enacting professional identity encourages a commitment to continuous improvement and lifelong learning.[283] Students recognize that mastering legal writing is an ongoing process that requires dedication, reflection, and adaptation to new challenges and contexts.[284]

---

281. ELIZABETH MERTZ, THE LANGUAGE OF LAW SCHOOL: LEARNING TO "THINK LIKE A LAWYER" 99, 135 (2007).

282. *Id.* at 137.

283. *See* ch. 6, *infra,* at 153 (explaining that lifelong learning has emerged as a professional identity threshold concept across a variety of disciplines).

284. *Cf.* Concept 3.3, *supra* at 97.

FIVE

Implications for Legal Writing Pedagogy

Many first-year legal writing students expect the only new content to be learned is the law itself. If they have been successful writers in the past, they may assume that "writing is writing" and that legal writing will pose no new challenges. Students unfamiliar with law practice or without much writing experience may not know what to expect. Within a few weeks, almost all students realize that legal writing is far more complicated than they anticipated.

What students do not anticipate is the extent to which "the law" is a rhetorical construct within a community of practice that has its own conventions and expectations. The first-year legal writing course comprises a daunting list of challenges that include learning how to find, read, understand, and translate legal concepts from multiple legal sources; constructing the law in writing, often from a particular point of view; communicating with an audience with whom they are largely unfamiliar in a variety of new writing genres; developing their own voice, agency, and identity as legal writers; and revising their "misconceptions of the nature of the [course] and misguided expectations as to how writing ought to work and go."[1]

When students struggle to assimilate this new knowledge—often all at the same time—they may occupy a liminal space between old and new understandings and capabilities. In that space, they can easily become frustrated, discouraged, and disengaged. In short, they get stuck.[2] As Joseph Williams observed, students taking introductory courses in complex fields often expe-

---

1. Doug Downs & Liane Robertson, *Threshold Concepts in First-Year Composition*, *in* Naming What We Know, ch. 1, *supra* note 15, at 105.

2. Meyer & Land, *Epistemological Considerations*, ch. 2, *supra* note 11, at 375–77.

rience "cognitive overload," which temporarily "degrades [their] powers of written expression."[3]

This chapter explores how threshold concepts can improve and hasten learning in legal writing courses. Section A explains how to identify the sources of cognitive overload—the threshold concepts being taught and when—to determine whether the design of the curriculum needs improvement. Section B offers suggestions for improved teaching methods to provide for deeper learning,[4] and Section C discusses how threshold concepts can be used to improve formative and summative assessment methods. Section D concludes by briefly explaining how threshold concepts theory can help reduce students' frustration and promote well-being.[5]

A. Using Threshold Concepts to Improve Curriculum Design

Threshold concepts give us "a different way of conceptualizing [course] content" and how we teach it.[6] As the scope of legal writing continues to expand in volume and complexity (including new research methodologies, technological innovations such as generative artificial intelligence, and new

---

3. Williams, ch. 1, *supra* note 1, at 20–22 (explaining, for example, that novice legal writers tend to explain basic concepts that acculturated members of the legal discourse community take for granted); *see also* Land et al., *Implications*, *supra* ch. 1, note 10, at 60–61.

4. *See* Jan H.F. Meyer, *Threshold Concepts and Pedagogic Representation*, 58 EDUC. + TRAINING, 463, 469 (2016) (emphasizing that identifying threshold concepts is in itself "unproductive, unless the process provides new insights" into teaching methods) [hereinafter Meyer, *Pedagogic Representation*]; *see also* ch. 1, *supra* note 10 and accompanying text.

5. Rachael Field & Jan H.F. Meyer, *Threshold Concepts in Law: Intentional Curriculum Reform to Support Law Student Learning Success and Well-Being*, *in* KEY DIRECTIONS IN LEGAL EDUC.: NAT'L AND INT'L PERSPECTIVES 143 (2020) (concluding that "the effective teaching of threshold concepts can positively impact on law students' well-being and learning outcomes, and that this process should therefore be integral to, and explicitly prioritized, in curriculum reform in law schools").

6. Donna Cullen, *Threshold Concepts & Troublesome Knowledge in Curriculum Design*, PRINCIPLES IN PATTERNS PROJECT REPORT 2 (2010) (expressing the view that "the overarching theme of curriculum design is indeed surrounded by 'troublesome knowledge' and perhaps even threshold concepts"), https://www.principlesinpatterns.ac.uk/Portals/70/pip%20document%20library/Publications/TacitKnowledge.pdf); Mary Hedges, *Embedding Threshold Concepts: The Use of a Practice –Theory—Practice Cycle*, 19 WAIKATO J. EDUC. 83, 84 (2014).

modes of law practice), it is a struggle to keep pace with these changes. One response is to "stuff" the curriculum with more and more content, "burdening [our]selves with the task of transmitting vast amounts of knowledge."[7] Threshold concepts theory can help us focus on what is fundamental to the course. As Glynis Cousin explains, threshold concepts theory offers "a 'less is more' approach to curriculum design."[8]

As used here, curriculum design refers to course descriptions, stated goals or learning objectives, substantive course content, and the structure and scaffolding of the course. The first step is to map out the content and structure of the semester, including writing assignments. The second step is to identify places where students get stuck and the corresponding core[9] and/or threshold concepts[10] being taught at those junctures.[11] The third step is to make appropriate course adjustments to help students more easily traverse identified thresholds. Each of these steps is illustrated below using the fall semester of a first-year legal writing course as an example.

---

7. Cousin, *Introduction*, ch. 2, *supra* note 12, at 4.

8. *Id.*

9. Core concepts are "important building blocks to learning a discipline that involve students adapting previous knowledge to a discipline context." Steel, *Succeed, Question, Repeat*, ch. 4, *supra* note 70, at 232. giving the concept of a "judgment" or an Act of Parliament as examples of core legal concepts in Australia); *see also* ch. 2, *supra*, at 14. They do not rise to the level of threshold concepts because they do not present troublesome knowledge that irreversibly transforms student understanding. *See* Meyer & Land, *Linkages*, ch. 1, *supra* note 10.

10. Threshold concepts comprise troublesome knowledge, be it "alien, inert, tacit, conceptually difficult, counter-intuitive, characterized by inaccessibility of the 'underlying game', or equally inaccessible super-complexity." Ray Land & Jan H.F. Meyer, *Threshold Concepts and Troublesome Knowledge (5): Dynamics of Assessment*, *in* THRESHOLD CONCEPTS AND TRANSFORMATIONAL LEARNING 61 (Jan H.F. Meyer, Ray Land, & Caroline Baillie, eds., 2010) [hereinafter Land & Meyer, *Dynamics of Assessment*]; *see also* ch. 2, *supra*, at 13–20.

11. *See* Meyer & Land, *Epistemological Considerations*, ch. 2, *supra* note 11, at 377; *see also* Meyer, *Pedagogic Representation*, *supra* note 4, at 469 (urging teachers to routinely review their courses to adopt approaches that prepare students to internalize threshold concepts through active engagement).

1. *Mapping the Fall Semester and Identifying Places Where Students Struggle*

Table 2 below lays out some of the major writing skills taught in the fall. The first column identifies the skill being taught, the second column identifies writing assignment(s) that might be given, and the third and fourth columns represent the core concepts and the threshold concepts being taught, often at the same time. The table will look different based on different syllabi, and this example is intended largely as a springboard for faculty to evaluate their own course design. The ultimate goal is to determine whether the content needs to be rearranged, provide opportunities for deeper, recursive learning, or be more explicit in terms of the threshold concepts being taught. For a similar table on the major skills taught in the spring semester and the accompanying threshold concepts, see Appendix 1.[12]

---

12. *See infra* at 193.

Table 2 Skills Typically Taught in the Fall Semester of a First-Year Legal Writing Course

Skill	Writing Assignment	Core Concepts	Threshold Concepts
Reading case law from the perspective of a practitioner	Case briefs, charts, or summaries of research results	The nature and type of judicial decisions, the difference between edited cases in casebooks and unedited cases that practitioners read	**Threshold Concept 2.2** (legal writers always read with a purpose in mind and develop strategies for reading cases actively, efficiently, and effectively **Threshold Concept 2.9** (legal writers recognize and employ different genres of writing based on the writers' goals)
Engaging in predictive analysis	Some form of legal memorandum or informal communication	"Objectivity" in legal writing; the purpose, audience, scope and stance of memos; the elements of a typical memo	**Threshold Concept 1.2** (the foundational role of legal writers is to construct arguments about the meaning of language) **Threshold Concept 2.1** (legal writers know they engage in a rhetorical practice even though the law tends to deny its rhetorical nature) **Threshold Concept 2.3** (legal writers must gather both fact and law) **Threshold Concept 2.9** (legal writers recognize and employ different genres of writing based on the writers' goals)
Rule synthesis	Separate exercises or as part of a larger writing assignment	Primary versus secondary sources of authority, mandatory and binding authorities, the structure of federal and state courts, the hierarchy of authority, stare decisis, and common law analysis	**Threshold Concept 1.3** (Legal writers understand the malleability of law) **Threshold Concept 2.4** (legal writers have a flexible understanding of sources of authority) **Threshold Concept 2.5** (legal writers construct rules of law for specific contexts) **Threshold Concept 3.2** (precedent both guides and restrains legal writers) **Threshold Concept 3.5** (legal writers must become comfortable with uncertainty) **Threshold Concept 3.6** (legal writing is potentially exclusionary and confusing for some writers) **Threshold Concept 3.7** (legal writers form their professional identity through writing)
Rule application		Applying a synthesized rule to client facts to predict outcome on a given legal issue in a logical and convincing manner	**Threshold Concept 2.6** (legal writers use deductive reasoning to reach convincing yet probable conclusions) **Threshold Concept 2.7** (legal writers use analogy to make their case for validity)
Citing rules of law in support of assertions		When to cite, the duty of candor, the difference between practitioner and scholarly citations, citation formats, signals	**Threshold Concept 2.8** (legal citations are concise arguments that serve as proxies for proof and professionalism)
Rewriting, revising, and polishing		The various stages of the writing process, the difference between first and final drafts, strategies for all phases of the post-writing process	**Threshold Concept 2.10** (legal writing requires typographic judgment) **Threshold Concept 3.3** (legal writers understand that legal writing takes time and is a recursive and reflective process)

a. Reading Case Law from the Perspective of a Practitioner

Early in the fall, students are introduced to strategies for "reading the law." Among other things, students need to become familiar with the nature of primary and secondary authorities; the difference between cases in casebooks and the unedited, unofficial versions they read in the course of conducting legal research; and how to read differently for different purposes.

Students get stuck here for a number of reasons. First, they are unfamiliar with the legal writing genre in general, such as statutes and judicial decisions.[13] Second, students are troubled to discover that in legal writing, they must read the law not only for understanding but also with their client's goals in mind.[14] When confronted with unedited versions of cases online, students often do not know where to focus, what to focus on, and what to do with what they have found. Given the volume to be read, they must develop strategies for reading actively, efficiently, and effectively.[15]

b. Engaging in Predictive Analysis

The first major writing assignment in the fall semester—usually some form of memorandum or email—introduces students to another genre of legal writing: predictive legal analysis.[16] To complete their initial research tasks, students might be given the client's facts and circumstances. As a result, they might not yet fully appreciate the role that gathering and selecting facts plays in law practice.[17] Often, they also assume that the law is relatively easy to find, a bit like taking a book off the shelf. When students realize they are responsible for gathering and selecting the legally significant facts as well as finding and constructing the applicable law, they can get overwhelmed by the number of choices they need to make with little experience in making them.

At the same time, students must become familiar with the tension that exists between accurately reporting rules of law and predicting as favorable an outcome as possible for their client. As novice legal writers, students are not

---

13. *See* Concept 2.9, ch. 4, *supra*, at 83 (legal writers are familiar with legal writing genres).

14. *See* Concept 2.2, ch. 4, *supra*, at 62 (legal writers read actively, efficiently, and effectively).

15. *See id.* at 64.

16. *See* Concept 2.9, ch. 4, *supra*, at 83 (legal writers are familiar with legal writing genres).

17. *See* Concept 2.3, ch. 4, *supra*, at 66 (legal writers gather fact and law).

yet comfortable with the malleability of law. They seek to find definitive rules of law as well as "the right answer," sometimes without appreciating the impact of that answer on their client. Early on, students are confronted with the reality that legal writing is a rhetorical practice even though it operates largely as though it is not.[18] They must also accept that their primary task as legal writers is to construct arguments about the meaning of language.[19]

c. Synthesizing Rules of Law

As part of predictive legal analysis, students are called on to engage in rule synthesis (i.e., framing rule statements or rule formation). Synthesizing legal rules from statutory and/or common law and then applying them to a set of facts represent the jewels of the fall curriculum. Because of the complexity and compression of this conceptual material, individual students understandably struggle, traversing these thresholds at widely varying points throughout the year. In some cases, students may not achieve understanding until the end of the course or even afterwards "because of the time required to build critical mass against any effectual prior knowledge."[20]

To synthesize rules using case law, students must first become familiar with federal and state court structures and hierarchies of authority.[21] Although they may understand the theoretical difference between binding and persuasive authority, novice legal writers find it difficult to apply it to their first writing assignments. With insufficient experience choosing among competing options, students struggle to decide which authorities are more binding or persuasive than others and which to select to support and explain their rules.

Students must learn to piece together relevant primary authority, including binding case law, to induce a rule of law that accounts for the outcomes in all potentially relevant cases.[22] Their rule must state the law accurately and, if

---

18. *See* Concept 2.1, ch. 4, *supra*, at 60 (legal writers know they engage in a rhetorical practice even though the law tends to deny its rhetorical nature).

19. *See* Concept 1.2, ch. 4, *supra*, at 37 (legal writers construct meaning about language).

20. *See, e.g.*, Downs & Robertson, *supra* note 1, at 116.

21. *See* Concept 2.4, ch. 4, *supra*, at 69 (legal writers have a flexible understanding of authority).

22. *See* Concept 2.5, ch. 4, *supra*, at 71 (legal writers synthesize rules for a particular context).

possible, provide for a potentially favorable outcome for their client.[23] In so doing, students must reconcile the malleability of law[24] with the need to state their rules in concrete and definitive terms.[25] Not only are students uncertain about the accuracy of their own rules,[26] they question their authority to create them in the first place.[27] No wonder students prefer to rely on quoted language rather than their own words.[28]

d. Applying Rules of Law

When applying synthesized rules to facts, students must learn to use deductive reasoning to reach logical and convincing conclusions.[29] In so doing, they learn to proceed from the general to the specific, beginning with the rule of law (the major premise) and demonstrating how that rule applies to a set of specific facts (the minor premise). At the same time, they must learn to incorporate other forms of reasoning, such as analogical reasoning to predict or argue for a specific outcome required under *stare decisis*.[30]

Students struggle here as well for several reasons. First, students must learn to write to a new audience without fully understanding its needs and expectations. Second, they may not fully appreciate the instrumental nature of legal writing, which functions here as proof of their assertions.[31] Moreover, they may not understand that in law, deductive reasoning is quasi-syllogistic.

---

23. *See id.*; *see also* Concept 1.4, ch. 4, *supra*, at 42 (legal writers understand the importance of framing) & 3.2, ch. 4, *supra*, at 94 (precedent both guides and constrains legal writers).

24. *See* Concept 1.3, ch. 4, *supra*, at 40 (legal writers understand the malleability of law).

25. *See* Concept 2.1, ch. 4, *supra*, at 60 (legal writers know they engage in a rhetorical practice even though the law tends to deny its rhetorical nature).

26. *See* Concept 3.5, ch. 4, *supra*, at 105 (legal writers must become comfortable with uncertainty).

27. *See* Concept 3.7, ch. 4, *supra*, at 114 (legal writers form and enact their identity through writing).

28. *See* Williams, ch. 1, *supra* note 1, at 18–24 (explaining that novice legal writers tend to focus on concrete language as opposed to abstract concepts and repeat the language of the law in summary form without much analysis).

29. *See* Concept 2.6, ch. 4, *supra*, at 73 (legal writers use deductive reasoning to reach probable yet convincing solutions).

30. *See id.*; *see also* Concept 2.7, ch. 4, *supra*, at 77 (legal writers use analogy to make their case for validity).

31. *See* Concept 2.9, ch. 4, *supra*, at 83 (legal writers are familiar with legal writing genres).

Although the reasoning must be valid, the major and minor premises need only be reasonable, not irrefutable.[32]

To the extent students interpret heuristics like IRAC to represent a formula for writing that is easily replicated or a rigid structure that inhibits creativity, they can quickly become frustrated.[33] On the one hand, students may intuitively understand that these heuristics do not account for the complexity of all legal issues yet feel constrained to follow them. On the other hand, they may feel these heuristics rob them of their voice and creativity.

e. Citing Rules of Law in Support of Assertions

To support their rule statements and case analogies, students learn to use signals and citations in a format both new to them and unique to legal writing.[34] Although students are generally familiar with the use of citations, legal citation is highly stylized and analytically precise. Students must learn to cite authority not only as support for their assertions but also to indicate the nuanced ways in which they rely on it. Given the complexity of legal citation rules, students understandably focus on form over substance. Naturally inclined to seize on concrete concepts,[35] students are more comfortable using citation manuals to construct correct citation format than struggling to understand how signals and explanatory parentheticals function as concise arguments that provide further support and credibility for their analysis.

f. Rewriting, Revising, and Polishing

A well-designed course should help students develop an appreciation for the generative nature of writing and the evolution of drafts through revision. The goal is for students to understand that initial drafts are often teaching drafts written for themselves as opposed to their audience. Students may struggle to accept that writing involves an infinite number of choices and that the quality of their writing improves upon reflection and over time.[36] At the same

32. *See* Concepts 2.6 & 2.7, ch. 4, *supra*, at 73 & 77.

33. *See* Concept 2.6, ch. 4, *supra*, at 73 (legal writers use deductive reasoning to reach probable yet convincing solutions).

34. *See* Concept 2.8, ch. 4, *supra*, at 80 (legal writers use citations as concise arguments).

35. *See* Williams, ch. 1, *supra* note 1, at 18–24.

36. *See* Concept 3.3, ch. 4, *supra*, at 97 (legal writers understand that writing is a recursive process that takes time).

time, they must come to appreciate that their credibility rests in part on producing error-free final drafts that also reflect well on their professional and typographic judgment.[37]

2. *Making Potential Course Adjustments to the Design of the Fall Semester*

Once the operative threshold concepts are identified, the goal is to

> think about constructing a *framework of engagement* within the course that might enable students to experience and gain understanding of the ways of thinking and practicing... that are expected of practitioners within a given community of practice.[38]

In essence, we want students to understand not only how lawyers think, but also to begin thinking like lawyers. The ability to achieve this goal will depend, among other things, not only on the quality of instruction but also on differences in each student's depth and rate of understanding, both before and after they are exposed to conceptual material.[39] For some, the internalization of concepts will be experienced as a "light bulb moment," while for others it will feel more like a "hard slog."[40]

In making design changes, faculty should consider the following questions: Should current course descriptions and learning objectives be modified in light of the threshold concepts actually being taught? Are each of the concepts being taught necessary or appropriate to this particular course? If so, does the current sequencing of concepts make sense, or does it need to be modified, rearranged, or expanded to avoid cognitive overload? Is adequate time devoted to teaching complicated clusters of core and threshold concepts? Are concepts reinforced throughout the semester? And, finally, are any relevant concepts missing?

Appropriate course adjustments include reframing course descriptions and learning objectives to ensure that they reflect what is actually being taught or intended to be taught; refining the focus or adjusting the volume of course content; rearranging the sequence of course content to better scaffold under-

---

37. *See* Concept 2.10, ch. 4, *supra*, at 85 (legal writers use typographic judgment) & Concept 3.7, ch. 4, *supra*, at 114 (legal writers form and enact their identity through writing)

38. Land et al., *Implications*, ch. 1, *supra* note 10, at 57.

39. *See, e.g.*, Meyer, *Pedagogic Representation*, *supra* note 4, at 467.

40. Rebecca Huxley-Binns, *Tripping over Thresholds: A Reflection on Legal Andragogy*, 50:1 LAW TCHR. 1, 12 (2016).

standing; and recognizing that "there [will] need[ ] to be a number of 'takes' and looping back on the conceptual material to be grasped" because learning is rarely a linear process.[41] Once this review is accomplished, revisions can be made to teaching[42] and assessment[43] methods.

Set forth below are typical course descriptions and learning objectives for the fall semester, along with suggested revisions to incorporate essential threshold concepts:

FALL COURSE DESCRIPTION	REVISED DESCRIPTION
Legal Research and Writing I is a foundational course designed to equip first-year law students with the essential skills to effectively analyze legal problems and communicate their findings in writing. Through a combination of lectures, hands-on exercises, and mock client problems, students will learn to draft objective legal documents, such as traditional memoranda, email, and client letters, while developing a precise and professional writing style.	Legal Research and Writing I is a foundational course designed to equip first-year law students with the essential skills to effectively analyze legal problems, and communicate their findings in writing. Through a combination of lectures, hands-on exercises, and mock client problems, students will develop an understanding of "the law" and its communication in legal analysis and writing as both malleable, situational, and contingent. Throughout the semester, students will practice drafting several different genres of predictive legal documents, such as traditional memoranda, email, and client letters while developing a precise and professional writing style, an appreciation for the function and format of legal citation, and an understanding of the role legal writing plays in forming their professional identity.

continues

41. *See, e.g.*, Cousin, *Introduction*, ch. 2, *supra* note 12, at 5; Meyer & Land, *Epistemological Considerations*, ch. 2, *supra* note 11, at 377.

42. *See infra* at 133.

43. *See infra* at 137.

continued

FALL LEARNING OBJECTIVES	REVISED OBJECTIVES
Students will gain proficiency in the following areas: • Identifying and assessing the legally relevant facts in a given client situation • Conducting efficient legal research using traditional and digital resources • Applying to client facts relevant legal principles in case law and statutes • Structuring and organizing clear, concise, and effective legal analysis • Using appropriate legal citation and formatting conventions for a variety of legal documents.	Students will work toward proficiency in the following areas: • Identifying and assessing the legally relevant facts in a given client situation • Conducting efficient legal research using traditional and digital resources • Framing legal rules based on the given facts, the binding jurisdiction, and existing sources of law, with an understanding of the contingent nature of legal rules • Structuring and organizing clear, concise, and effective legal analysis • Citing legal and non-legal sources in support of their analysis, as well as an appreciation for the substantive function of citation in legal writing • Drafting a variety of predictive legal documents, with an appreciation for the purpose and audience of each, the complexity of the legal writing process, and their own professional identity formation as legal writers

The revised versions explicitly add the creative and contingent aspects of rule formation, the role of genre and audience, the substantive use of legal citation, and the writer's role and development in the legal writing process. In so doing, they may better capture the complexity of the course and the discipline-specific expertise students will be expected to acquire.

Changes to the volume and sequencing of content could include modifying the number or breadth of assignments to focus longer or more deeply on the concepts students find most troubling, building in opportunities for students to reengage with the same conceptual material throughout the semester, and saving some of the most difficult concepts for later in the semester. For example, "reading the law" could be taught at the beginning of the semester to teach case briefing for doctrinal courses and again, when students engage in their first legal research assignment. Another example would be to reduce the cognitive overload often experienced when learning rule synthesis and application by having students complete short exercises that break these skills down into their component parts and build toward a longer, more complicated writing assignment.

B. Using Threshold Concepts to Improve Teaching Methods

Teaching methods should be maximized to provide opportunities for deep learning. Improved methods can include designing assignments and class exercises with particular core and threshold concepts in mind, exposing students to the same concepts in familiar but different situations to isolate the nature of the concept, and creating opportunities for reflective and recursive learning.[44]

1. *Designing Assignments and Exercises with Threshold Concepts in Mind*

As suggested above, the typical fall memorandum represents a likely sticking place for beginning law students because it calls on students to juggle a heavy cognitive load.[45] Assignment prompts could articulate not only the objectives of the assignment in terms of core concepts, such as the difference between mandatory and persuasive authority, but also the associated threshold concepts. For example, students could be told explicitly that the assignment is designed to teach them that legal analysis involves understanding the malleability of law and the extent to which legal writers create the applicable rules.[46]

---

44. *See* Land et al., *Implications*, ch. 1, *supra* note 10, at 56–57.

45. *See supra* at 126.

46. *See* Concepts 1.1, ch. 4, *supra*, at 36 (legal writers create and recreate the law); 1.3, ch. 4, *supra*, at 40 (legal writers understand the malleability of law); 2.5, ch. 4, *supra*, at 71 (legal writers create synthesized rules for a particular context); 3.4, ch. 4, *supra*, at 102 (legal writers are creative); and 3.5, ch. 4, *supra*, at 105 (legal writers must become comfortable with uncertainty).

They can also be told that their goal is to reach probable as opposed to certain conclusions.[47]

Class exercises that break the threshold concepts down into manageable parts can reduce overload and frustration. For example, students could be asked to work alone or in groups to discuss the results of their research and then rank them from most to least binding in the context of their assignment. They could also be asked to use their research to outline the general legal rules (e.g., the elements of the relevant cause of action) and select which highly ranked authorities could be cited in support of those rules and why.[48] Finally, students could work alone or together to synthesize legal rules relevant to the assignment.[49] Sharing their different rules can help students develop a deeper understanding of the inherent malleability, creativity, and uncertainty in legal writing, particularly if that goal is made expressly clear.

2. *Exposing Students to the Same Concepts in Familiar but Different Situations to Isolate the Nature of the Concept*

Threshold concepts theory suggests that students should be exposed to the same threshold concept in multiple contexts. As Ray Land et al. explain, "[g]iven the often troublesome nature of threshold concepts, it is likely that many learners will need to... attempt[ ] different 'takes' on the conceptual material until the necessary integration and connection... take[s] place."[50] Mary Hedges explains that students who struggle with specific concepts may "find it difficult to separate the concept from the specific examples used in class or a text."[51] The more practice students have in working with the same concept in different applications, the "easier [it is] for them to clearly identify the concept as distinct from the applications."[52]

---

47. *See* Concepts 2.6 and 2.7, ch. 4, *supra*, at 73 & 77 (legal writers use deductive and analogical reasoning to reach probable yet convincing conclusions); *see also* Concept 3.5, ch. 4, *supra*, at 105 (legal writers must become comfortable with uncertainty).

48. *See* Concept 2.4, ch. 4, *supra*, at 69 (legal writers have a flexible understanding of authority).

49. *See* Concept 2.5, ch. 4, *supra*, at 71 (legal writers synthesize rules for a particular context).

50. *See, e.g.*, Land et al., *Implications*, ch. 1, *supra* note 10, at 59.

51. Hedges, *supra* note 6, at 88.

52. *Id.*

Thus, to highlight the critical features of the threshold concept, future assignments should build on but vary the nature of its application. By controlling some variables and changing others, students can better appreciate how the concept operates under different circumstances.[53] For example, assignments that require students to synthesize rules should vary either in terms of the nature of the rules (e.g., elements versus factors), the context in which rules are applied (e.g., tort versus criminal law), or the writing genre (legal memorandum versus client letter versus memorandum in support of summary judgment). Or, to simplify the transition from predictive writing in the fall to persuasive writing in the spring, the first assignment of the spring could begin with a writing assignment that involves a legal issue with which students are already familiar. Keeping the same legal issue may help students better understand the differences in audience, stance, and tone between predictive analysis and argument.[54]

3. *Creating Opportunities for Reflective and Recursive Learning*

Threshold concepts scholars emphasize the importance of critical reflection to transformative learning.[55] In a 2009 study, for example, computer science students were able to identify the threshold concepts that transformed their understanding and, in some cases, what caused those transformations.[56] Based on student input, the researchers concluded, "Transformation frequently happened when a student faced problems that pointed out the inadequacies of his or her approach. It is at this point... that critical reflection can drive transfor-

53. Gerlese Akerlind, Jo McKenzie & Mandy Lupton, *A Threshold Concepts Focus To Curriculum Design: Supporting Student Learning Through Application of Variation Theory*, (Australian Teaching And Learning Council, 2011), https://opus.lib.uts.edu.au/bitstream/10453/19462/1/2011003880OK.pdf.

54. *See, e.g.*, Steel, *Succeed, Question, Repeat*, ch. 4, *supra* note 70, at 240 (variation theory suggests that students learn concepts more effectively if they encounter them more than once in order to understand "how the concept changes when critical features are changed [*e.g.*, the writing genre]) but non-critical ones remain the same [*e.g.*, the law of the problem]").

55. *See, e.g.*, Meyer, *Pedagogic Representation*, *supra* note 4, at 465 (citing Jan Erik Moström et al., *Computer Science Student Transformations: Changes and Causes*, 41:3 ACM SIGCSE Bull. 181, 184 (2009); *see also* J. Mezirow, Learning as Transformation: Critical Perspectives on a Theory in Progress (2000).

56. *See* Moström et al., *supra* note 55, at 184.

mation."[57] Those transformations manifested in a variety of ways, including "changes in their thinking, identity, behavior, and confidence."[58]

Thus, legal writing students may benefit from reflecting on their own learning and connecting threshold concepts to their own experience.[59] These reflections can take a variety of forms, such as posting reflections to a discussion board, making journal entries, or engaging in small-group discussions. For example, at the beginning of the year, students could be asked to describe what they expect or hope to learn in their legal writing course or what they think it means to write like a lawyer.[60]

As the semester unfolds, students might be asked to explain their current understanding of a particular concept (e.g., reading law from the client's perspective or how legal writing is creative). At the end of the semester, they might explain how their understanding of these concepts has changed over time. They could also be asked to explain how a particular concept applies to events in their own lives (e.g., consider the context-dependent nature of rules as it applies to one dealing with one parent versus the other).[61] Comparing concepts to their own experience helps students make connections between new information and existing schemas of knowledge.[62]

---

57. *Id.* at 184.

58. *Id.* at 185.

59. *See* Matthew Christopher Atherton & Yvonne Nalani Meulemans, *Threshold Concepts Theory as a Pedagogical Tool for Articulating Transformational Learning: An Initial Exploration*, J. TRANSFORMATIVE EDUC. 1 (2020) (explaining that self-reflective writing helps students "think[ ] about their experiences with the 'content' of their education as opposed to the 'content' itself").

60. *See* Anthony Niedwiecki, *Teaching for Lifelong Learning: Improving the Metacognitive Skills of Law Students Through More Effective Formative Assessment Techniques*, 40 CAP. L. REV. 149, 185–91 (2012).

61. *See* Hedges, *supra* note 6, at 86–87 (explaining the benefits to MBA students in posting to an online discussion forum that required them to apply threshold concepts to different situations, including their own life experiences).

62. *See* Concept 2.2, ch. 4, *supra*, at 62 (legal writers read actively, efficiently, and effectively).

C. Using Threshold Concepts Theory in Formative and Summative Assessment

The American Bar Association requires law schools to "utilize both formative and summative assessment methods... to measure and improve student learning and provide meaningful feedback to students."[63] Formative assessment generally provides feedback throughout the course to improve student learning, whereas summative (or evaluative) assessment measures the degree of student learning at various intervals or the end of the course.[64] Best practices include "using evidence from multiple methods and sources of information" to yield "an accurate portrayal of student learning."[65]

Assessment methods should take students' understanding of threshold concepts into account. To ensure "deep learning," course objectives, teaching and learning activities, and assessment tasks should all work together.[66] Because the acquisition of troublesome and transformative knowledge opens up new and previously inaccessible ways of thinking and being, "it follows that such transformations [ ] require a more nuanced and appropriate form of assessment."[67] Assessments can help identify where students are in their journey from pre-liminal, liminal, and post-liminal understanding of troublesome concepts.[68] The goal is to identify and "render visible [the various] sources of conceptual difficulty, at the point in time in which they are experienced" and provide contemporaneous and appropriate feedback.[69]

---

63. ABA STANDARDS, ch. 1, *supra* note 38, STD. 314.

64. *See id.* at Interpretation 314-1.

65. Ruth Jones, *Assessment and Legal Education: What Is Assessment, and What the *# Does It Have to Do with the Challenges Facing Legal Education?*, 45 MCGEORGE L. REV. 86, 101 (2014).

66. Noel Pearse, *An Illustration of Teaching and Assessment Practices of the "Conceptual Framework" as a Threshold Concept*, 20 ELEC. J. BUS. RSCH. METHODS 122, 128 (2022), https://academic-publishing.org/index.php/ejbrm/issue/view/254/33.

67. Land & Meyer, *Dynamics of Assessment*, *supra* note 10, at 63.

68. *Id.*

69. *Id.*

1. *Using Formative Assessments to Teach Threshold Concepts*

Legal writing pedagogy incorporates a variety of formative assessment methods, including:

- rubrics or checklists to guide students in completing assignments or explain their graded performance;[70]
- questions specific to the assignment posed by students when drafts are first submitted to prompt relevant feedback;[71]
- individualized written feedback (margin comments and holistic comments) on writing assignments;[72]
- generalized written feedback about class performance as a whole on writing assignments;
- sample answers written by faculty or students, with or without class discussion;[73]
- live critiquing;[74]

---

70. *See, e.g.*, Jessica Clark & Christy DeSanctis, *Toward A Unified Grading Vocabulary: Using Rubrics in Legal Writing Courses* 63 J. Leg. Educ. 3 (2013); Julie Ross & Diana Donahoe, *Lighting the Fires of Learning in Law School: Implementing ABA Standard 314 by Incorporating Effective Formative Assessment Techniques Across the Curriculum*, 81 U. Pitt. L. Rev. 657, 680–81 (2020); Sophie M. Sparrow, *Describing the Ball: Improve Teaching by Using Rubrics-Explicit Grading Criteria*, 2004 Mich. St. L. Rev. 1 (explaining in detail how rubrics can be used to notify students how they will be or have been evaluated and to provide feedback for the next assignment).

71. *See, e.g.*, Niedwiecki, *supra* note 60, at 188–90 (explaining that questions posed at the time assignments are submitted "begin[ ] a dialogue between the professor and the students regarding the skills in the class, one of the key principles to effective formative assessment.").

72. *See, e.g.*, Daniel L. Barnett, *Triage in the Trenches of the Legal Writing Course: The Theory and Methodology of Analytical Critique*, 38 Univ. Toledo L. Rev. 651 (2007); Kirsten K. Davis, *Building Credibility in the Margins: An Ethos-Based Perspective for Commenting on Student Papers*, 12 J. Legal Writing 73 (2006) Anne Enquist, *Critiquing and Evaluating Law Students' Writing: Advice from Thirty-Five Experts*, 22 Seattle Univ. L. Rev. 1119 (1999); Jane Kent Gionfriddo, *The "Reasonable Zone of Right Answers": Analytical Feedback on Student Writing*, 40:3 Gonzaga L. Rev. 427 (2004/5).

73. *See, e.g.*, Terrill Pollman, *The Sincerest Form of Flattery: Examples and Model-Based Learning in the Classroom* 64 J. Leg. Educ. 298 (2014); Ross & Donahoe, *supra* note 70, at 682.

74. *See, e.g.*, Patricia Grande Montana, *Live and Learn: Live Critiquing and Student Learning*, 27:1 Persp: Teaching Legal Res. & Writing 22 (2019); Amanda L. Sholtis,

- paper conferences to discuss written feedback;[75]
- quizzes;
- peer-review;[76] and
- self-evaluation.[77]

Regardless of the method used, formative assessments should aim to go beyond the content of the assigned problem and teach directly to the relevant threshold concepts. Formative feedback thus reflects not only the student's understanding of "the law of the problem" but also of the underlying knowledge that should transfer to the next assignment. In the absence of both types of feedback, students may move forward unaware of the underlying concepts with which they are still struggling.[78]

Assume that students in the fall semester of a first-year legal writing course have been asked to draft a legal memorandum. The legal issue for purposes of the memorandum is whether the defendant was "driving" while intoxicated under state law once he pulled over to the shoulder of a two-lane road with the engine running. Students must synthesize a rule on what it means to drive, and the binding courts have defined "driving" to mean "operating or in control of" a motor vehicle.

In the discussion section of their memorandum, a student's synthesized rule directly quotes a relevant, ten-year-old case, accurately explaining that "driving is not intended to include parked cars." In the cited case, the defendant, who was intoxicated, was charged while parked in a public parking space with the engine off. As a result, the student's rule is accurate but incomplete for the defendant's problem.

In response to the student's rule on "driving," comments in individualized written feedback or student conferences might include "try to paraphrase rules in your own words," "is this one case most representative of the rule?"

Say What? A How-To Guide On Providing Formative Assessment To Law Students Through Live Critique, 49 STETSON L. REV. 1 (2019).

75. *See, e.g.*, Niedwiecki, *supra* note 60, at 173; Robin S. Wellford-Slocum, *The Law School Student-Faculty Conference: Towards a Transformative Learning Experience*, 45 SOUTH TEX. L. REV, 255 (2004).

76. Ross & Donahoe, *supra* note 70, at 672–80.

77. *Id.*; Niedwiecki, *supra* note 60, at 184–193.

78. *See* Land & Meyer, *Dynamics of Assessment*, *supra* note 10, at 62 (explaining that using traditional modes of assessment, students "can produce the 'right answer' while retaining fundamental misconceptions"); *cf.* Niedwiecki, *supra* note 60, at 177.

or "why did you choose this case when there are more recent cases available?" These comments could be improved by also teaching directly to the underlying threshold concept, such as

- "remember, your goal is to read the cases as a whole and write a rule in your own words that you think accounts for the outcomes in all relevant cases,"
- "synthesized rules should represent the rule of the jurisdiction at the time they are written, but this rule leaves out any case law since the cited case was decided,"
- "this case may be useful as part of your rule, but it is so old that the reader may question your credibility,"
- "since this case is easily distinguishable on its facts, consider whether this case alone accurately conveys the law relevant to the defendant's case,"
- "it can be intimidating to state rules in your own words when you are unsure about their accuracy, but as a legal writer, part of your job is to become comfortable with uncertainty and take a certain amount of risk. My job is let you know if those rules are effective."

Assume also that the student was invited to submit questions specific to their memorandum when the assignment was due. In this case, the student expressed feeling uncertain about their synthesized rules and asked if their rules were correct and they had cited the right cases. In our experience, students know precisely where they are struggling, even if they do not yet have the words to explain their misunderstanding. In this case, the feedback proposed above would also serve to validate the student's concerns and reassure the student that their experience with uncertainty was normal.

Class exercises should provide further formative feedback and improve students' understanding of the various facets of relevant concepts such as rule synthesis. One exercise might consist of students working together to review sample discussion sections (either models of varying strength written by faculty or student samples with varying strengths and weaknesses). The goal would be for students to analyze the differences among the rules on "driving," rank them, and then explain their rankings to the class.[79]

---

79. *See* Moström et al., *supra* note 55, at 185 (explaining that "the social aspects of learning computing may also be important.... [T]ransformations were seen in the context

Class discussion could tease out the need for rules to account for most, if not all, outcomes in relevant cases; the preference for relying on the most factually similar cases to make strong analogies possible; and the need to commit to a synthesized rule that allows for creativity yet may also bring uncertainty. Alternatively, students could engage in self- or peer evaluation of their or a classmate's writing based on written questions geared toward a deeper understanding of rule synthesis in the context of the memorandum or more generally in predictive analysis.[80]

2. *Using Summative Assessments to Gauge Deep Learning*

Summative assessments often take the form of scores or grades on assignments that students do not have an opportunity to revise. For that reason, summative assessments should be geared towards helping students improve on the next writing task (be it within the same course or beyond). For example, students could be encouraged to use the same rubric or checklist for revised assignments on any final drafts.[81] Regardless of the form, any substantive feedback in the form of individualized or class comments can address both students' performance on the particular assignment as well as the extent to which the writing reflects an understanding of the associated threshold concepts and where improvement is needed in future assignments.

Another possibility for assessing student understanding of threshold concepts is to ask them to reflect on their overall learning.[82] For example, at the end of a unit within the course or the course itself, students could be asked to reflect on and describe the evolution of their thinking on any given concept(s) taught in class.[83] Summative questions could also be based on questions students have

---

of team projects, and other sorts of peer to peer interaction."). For a similar exercise that can be used to improve curriculum design, see *supra*, at 134.

80. *See* Concept 2.5, ch. 4, *supra*, at 71 (legal writers synthesize rules for a particular context).

81. *See supra* at 138.

82. These questions could count toward course participation points but should not likely be graded so as not to inhibit authentic reflections or punish students still struggling with certain concepts. The goal is for students to engage with the concepts and reflect on their learning. *See* Atherton & Meulemans, *supra* note 59, at 9.

83. For a similar sample exercise that can be used to improve teaching methods, *see supra* at 135.

answered in their journaling assignments.[84] For example, students could be asked, "What do you think were the three most important concepts taught in this unit (or class)? Which were the most difficult? Which do you understand best? Which do you understand least? What most affected—positively or negatively—your learning? Where would you still like to improve?[85]

Finally, a summative assessment could take the form of asking students to answer several questions designed to indirectly elicit their understanding of certain threshold concepts. For example, assume the goal of the assignment is to assess students' understanding of genre, hierarchy of authority, rule synthesis, analogical reasoning, citation practices, and the creativity inherent in legal writing.

First, students could begin by reading a hypothetical and a packet of relevant legal sources. Second, they could review a sample (or draft their own) analysis of a specific factor or element relevant to the legal issue (e.g., "duty" in negligence or "reliance" in a fraud claim). Third, students would be asked a series of questions assessing how well the sample demonstrates an understanding of the relevant concepts and achieves it intended purpose.

Questions might include: Does the sample demonstrate an understanding of predictive legal analysis? Is the answer well-supported and clear? How well does the rule gather the relevant primary authorities and account for their outcomes? How else could the rule have been written? Does the analysis proceed deductively? Does the writer effectively use analogical reasoning to compare to or distinguish relevant cases? Do the signals and citations reflect the ways in which the writer relied on authority?

Either alternatively or in addition, faculty could share their feedback on several sample answers (student or faculty-written). Students would then be asked to assess their own answers based on the faculty feedback. Finally, students could be asked to reflect on how their reflections might help them improve their learning in the same course or in their legal studies more generally.[86]

---

84. *See supra* at 136.

85. *See, e.g.*, Niedwiecki, *supra* note 60, at 188–89.

86. For a detailed explanation of these sorts of assessment activities, see Meyer, *Pedagogic Representation*, ch. 5, *supra* note 4, at 472–73 (citing Jan H.F. Meyer et al., *An Empirical Exploration of Metacognitive Assessment Activities in a Third-Year Civil Engineering Hydraulics Course*, 40:3 EUROPEAN J. ENG'G EDUC. 309 (2015)).

D. Using Threshold Concepts to Promote Student Well-Being

In addition to improving curricula and hastening learning, threshold concepts theory can promote student well-being. As students enter the liminal state,[87] they may experience a range of emotions, including the desire to learn, nervousness, a sense of vulnerability, and even humility.[88] Crossing the threshold of understanding often requires a "repositioning of self in relation to the subject"[89] and can be accompanied by a sense of loss or imposter syndrome.[90]

For "knowledge [ ] to have a transformative effect it probably should be troublesome, or at least troubling."[91] However, "that does not mean it should be stressful or should provoke the kinds of anxiety, self-doubt and frustration that can lead students to give up."[92] Acknowledging the difficulties students are struggling with helps them feel less alone or unworthy. In particular, we can be more mindful about reinforcing the subjective nature of their choices,[93] reflecting the legal reader's likely response to those choices, and encouraging students to become comfortable with a certain level of uncertainty.[94]

As Cousin explains, we must create a holding environment that supports them as they grapple with this troubling process.[95] We can assure students that they are not alone in their struggle. By sharing early on that certain course material is troublesome for all students, those who fear they are the only ones

---

87. *See* ch. 2, *supra*, at 20.

88. *See* Cousin, *Introduction*, ch. 2, *supra* note 12, at 4; Meyer & Land, *Epistemological Considerations*, ch. 2, *supra* note 11, at 375–76.

89. Land et al., *Implications*, *supra* ch. 1, note 10, at 58; *see also* Meyer & Land, *Epistemological Considerations*, ch. 2, *supra* note 11, at 374.

90. *See* Land et al., *Implications*, ch. 1, *supra* note 10, at 58; *see also* Meyer & Land, *Linkages*, ch. 1, *supra* note 10, at 422 (explaining that the insight gained from crossing the portal of a threshold concept may be experienced as "rob[bing] one of an illusion").

91. Ray Land & Jan H.F. Meyer, *Editors' Preface*, *in* OVERCOMING BARRIERS TO STUDENT UNDERSTANDING: THRESHOLD CONCEPTS AND TROUBLESOME KNOWLEDGE xiv (Jan H.F. Meyer & Ray Land, eds. 2006).

92. *Id.*

93. *See, e.g.*, Concept 2.5, ch. 4, *supra*, at 71 (legal writers synthesize rules for a particular context).

94. *See* Concept 3.5, ch. 4, *supra*, at 105 (legal writers must become comfortable with uncertainty).

95. Cousin, *Introduction*, ch. 1, *supra* note 12, at 4.

will not "suffer in silence."[96] As Joseph Williams explains, the challenge for legal writing teachers is to help students realize that "they are behaving in wholly predictable ways" and "free themselves ... from 'being'" weak or incompetent writers.[97]

Threshold concepts theory can also remind us to resist the temptation to fall back on "lazy classifications of our students," based on their ability to negotiate the liminal space more or less quickly.[98] Instead, we can "cultivate a third ear that listens not for what a student knows (discrete packages of knowledge) but for the terms that shape a student's knowledge, her not knowing, her forgetting, her circles of stuck places and resistances."[99] By tolerating students' uncertainty, we encourage their active engagement and help them build confidence as they develop into independent legal writers.

---

96. *Id.* at 5.

97. Williams, ch. 1, *supra* note 1, at 31.

98. Cousin, *Introduction*, ch. 1, *supra* note 12, at 5.

99. Land et al., *Implications*, ch. 1, *supra* note 10, at 58 (citations omitted).

SIX

Implications for Professional Identity Formation

Our proposed concepts shed light not only on the nature of legal writing expertise but also on the ways in which law students form their professional identities. As Concept 3.7 explains, lawyers shape and communicate their professional identities primarily through writing.[1] To understand our students' struggle to internalize the threshold concepts of legal writing is to recognize the accompanying shift in identity that crossing those thresholds requires.[2] By definition, threshold concepts represent "a shift in learner subjectivity, a transconfiguration of self, of identity; an ontological shift."[3] In this context, "learning to write like a lawyer means acquiring a new discoursal identity."[4]

Threshold concepts theory has been used outside the United States to discern the nature of professional identity in law and other disciplines. As detailed below, we emphasize four themes that can be articulated from this body of work: client-centeredness, the role as professional, the value of reflective practices and lifelong learning, and the need to anticipate and manage uncertainty. These same themes permeate scholarship on professional identity in U.S. legal education, as well as our proposed legal writing concepts. Thus, our concepts serve several purposes: to identify the components of legal writing expertise, to help us understand the extent to which legal writing forms our students' professional identities, and to encourage us to consider how we can better

---

1. *See* Concept 3.7, ch. 4, *supra*, at 114.

2. *See* Rideout & Ramsfield, *View From Within*, ch. 4, *supra* note 264, at 737 (explaining that learning to write like a lawyer involves taking on a new identity, "one inscribed with ways of understanding the world that are constrained by the positions and possibilities available within the discourse of the law").

3. Baillie, *Threshold Capabilities*, ch. 2, *supra* note 16, at 229.

4. Rideout & Ramsfield, *View from Within*, ch. 4, *supra* note 264, at 744.

assist students in crossing the thresholds of both legal writing and professional identity formation.

This chapter begins by examining professional identity formation in terms of how we conceptualize it and how it has been explored and instantiated in legal education. We then examine four themes that have emerged in threshold concepts scholarship on professional identity formation in other disciplines and how professional identity scholars in the United States have explored these same themes in legal education. Using these themes as key thresholds in professional identity formation, we examine how each of these is reflected in the threshold concepts of legal writing we articulate in Chapter Four.

A. The Nature of Professional Identity Formation

While there is admittedly "definitional haze"[5] around professional identity[6] and professional identity formation in legal education,[7] we use the term professional identity to refer to the lawyer's role and sense of self within the professional community. We view professional identity formation as the process by which novices become members of a professional community. Pro-

5. Harmony Decosimo, *A Taxonomy of Professional Identity Formation*, 67 St. Louis U. L.J. 1, 4 (2022).

6. *See* Eli Wald, *Formation Without Identity: Avoiding A Wrong Turn in the Professionalism Movement*, 89 UMKC L. Rev. 685, 691–93 (2021). Distinguishing between professional identity and professional identity formation, Wald explains that professional identity is "a representation of self, achieved in stages over time, during which the characteristics, values, and norms of the [legal] profession are internalized, resulting in an individual thinking, acting, and feeling like a [lawyer]." *Id.* at 692 (citations omitted). Wald notes that professional identity formation "introduce[es] law students to the ethical standards, social roles, values, responsibilities, and fundamental purposes of the profession by helping students begin critically reflecting on the roles they will play in different contexts as lawyers." *Id.*

7. *See, e.g.*, Kellye Y. Testy & Zachariah J. DeMeola, *Leading the Way: The Power of Professional Identity Formation for Lawyers*, 76 Baylor L. Rev. 115, 119–121 (2024). The authors distinguish professionalism, professional responsibility, and professional identity formation. "[P]rofessionalism focuses on the outward conduct the legal profession desires its members to exhibit without also requiring reflection on why such conduct is likely to be consistent with an individual's own value system," while professional responsibility relates to adherence to the model rules of professional conduct. *Id.* at 120–21. Professional identity formation is broader, as it is "necessarily personal and involves self-exploration to achieve the level of selfawareness [sic] necessary to identify and map personal and professional values. It challenges students to engage the fundamentals of who they are, what they want the world to be, and their role in, and responsibility for, creating both." *Id.* at 120.

fessional identity and professional identity formation encompass a lawyer's ethical standards, role perception, personal and professional values, expertise, commitment to upholding the rule of law and acting as an officer of the court, interpersonal skills, and dedication to continuous improvement.[8]

For legal writers, professional identity formation includes mastering substantive legal knowledge, including the ethical rules of the profession. This requires students to traverse what might be referred to as doctrinal threshold concepts, but it also requires them to master disciplinary-specific ways of being and practicing within the professional community, which might be referred to as dispositional threshold concepts.[9] Based on the dispositional transitions explored in other disciplines as well as legal education, we see a strong connection between traversing the threshold concepts of legal writing and professional identity formation in legal education.

---

8. *See, e.g.*, Concept 3.7, ch. 4, *supra*, at 114. David I.C. Thomson has taken the view that professional identity formation primarily encompasses "'the virtues of integrity, consideration, civility, [and] conceptions of the personal meaning that legal work has for practicing attorneys and their sense of responsibility toward the profession.'" David I.C. Thomson, *Symposium Introduction: Interrogating the Hidden Curriculum: Implications for Formation of Professional Identity*, 2 J. L. TEACHING & LEARNING 1, 1 (2025) (citing WILLIAM M. SULLIVAN ET AL., EDUCATING LAWYERS: PREPARATION FOR THE PRACTICE OF LAW 132 (The Carnegie Found. for the Advancement of Teaching, 2007) [hereinafter EDUCATING LAWYERS]).

9. *See e.g.*, Alia Amin, *"A Trend or a Need" Threshold Concepts in Medicine and Surgery; A Qualitative Synthesis*, 18 J. MED. EDUC. 176, 185–188 (2019) (differentiating between discipline-specific threshold concepts that are "fundamental to the subject" such as "thermodynamics or free energy in biochemistry" and "threshold concepts of practicing" which are "more related to ways of practicing than knowing" such as "developing as individual agency, developing social capital, patient centeredness, developing cognitive skills and becoming part of community of practice"); Helen Jones & Lucy Hammond, *Threshold Concepts in Medical Education: A Scoping Review*, 56 MED. EDUC. 983, 989 (exploring the relationship between threshold concepts related to "basic scientific knowledge" and threshold concepts related to "ways of thinking and practicing" in medical education); Virginia M. Tucker & Michelle Holschuh Simmons, *Identity Transformation on Becoming a Teacher: Threshold Concepts and Professional Praxes*, 10 J. TCHR. EDUC. AND EDUCATORS 275, 277 (2021) (using threshold concepts theory as a lens to assess teachers' acquisition of professional dispositions, defined as the "'habits of professional action and moral commitments that underlie an educator's performance'").

B. Professional Identity Formation in Legal Education

In legal education, the foundational examination of professional identity formation occurred in 2007, when the Carnegie Foundation published an extensive study of how lawyers are educated in America. That study, *Educating Lawyers: Preparation for the Profession of Law*,[10] concluded that law schools were not doing enough to help students form their professional identity as lawyers.[11] In particular, *Educating Lawyers* encouraged law schools to engage students in exploring and assuming "the identity, values and dispositions consonant with the fundamental purposes of the legal profession."[12] Since then, law professors, educators, and scholars have sought to flesh out and implement these recommendations.

The formation of professional identity in legal education has been described as the process by which law students and lawyers develop a sense of character that internalizes the norms and values of the legal profession.[13] In 2022, the ABA established Standard 303(b), which now requires law schools to "provide substantial opportunities to students for … the development of a professional identity."[14] Interpretation 303-5 defines professional identity as focusing "on what it means to be a lawyer and the special obligation lawyers have to their clients and society."[15] Accordingly, the interpretation exhorts law schools to provide opportunities for students to "intentional[ly] explor[e] the values, guiding principles, and well-being practices concerned foundational to successful legal practice."[16]

At the same time, Interpretation 303-5 recognizes that professional identity formation requires "reflection and growth over time."[17] As a result, law students

---

10. EDUCATING LAWYERS, *supra* note 8, at 135 (noting that professional identity can be described as answers to questions such as, "Who am I as a member of this profession?," "What am I like, and what do I want to be like in my professional role?," and "What place do ethical-social values have in my core sense of professional identity?").

11. *Id.* at 126–61.

12. *Id.* at 194.

13. *See generally* Holloran Center for Ethical Leadership in the Professions, *What Is a Law Student's Professional Identity and What Is Professional Identity Formation? A Short Introduction*, https://law.stthomas.edu/_media-library/documents/holloran-center/professional-identity-definition1.pdf (2022) [hereinafter Holloran Center, *What Is a Law Student's Professional Identity*].

14. ABA STANDARDS, *supra* ch. 1, note 38, STD. 303(b), at 20.

15. *See id.*, Interpretation 303–5, at 21.

16. *Id.*

17. *Id.*

"should have frequent opportunities for [professional identity] development during each year of law school and in a variety [of ways]."[18] This means engaging students in "ethical-social" development[19] and internalizing the norms associated with "thinking, acting, and feeling" like a lawyer.[20]

Various definitions have also been suggested for what it means to have acquired a professional identity.[21] Daisy Hurst Floyd defines it as "'the way that a lawyer integrates the intellectual, practical, and ethical aspects of being a lawyer and also integrates personal and professional values.'"[22] Neil Hamilton and Louis Bilionis assert that professional identity is acquired by internalizing the following norms of the legal profession:

1. ownership of continuous professional development toward excellence at the major competencies that clients, employers, and the legal system need;
2. a deep responsibility and service orientation to others, especially the client;
3. a client-centered problem solving approach and good judgment that ground each student's responsibility and service to the client; and
4. well-being practices.[23]

---

18. *Id.*

19. Educating Lawyers, *supra* note 8, at 147.

20. Holloran Center, *What Is a Law Student's Professional Identity*, *supra* note 13, at 1 (citing Richard L. Cruess et al., *Reframing Medical Education to Support Professional Identity Formation*, 89 Acad. Med. 1446, 1557 (2014)). For several recent articles addressing the need for large scale reform in legal education to teach professional identity formation as required by ABA Standard 303, see 2 J. L. Teaching & Learning (2025) (entire issue dedicated to symposium held at Denver Law on formation of professional identity).

21. *See* Decosimo, *supra* note 5. Decosimo asserts that, given the myriad definitions surrounding professional identity and professional identity formation, it could be argued that "what it means to form a lawyerly professional identity and to form it well is debatable, and so expansive by some accounts as to be almost entirely in the eye of the beholder." *Id.* at 10. Nonetheless, Decosimo superimposes structure on the theories of professional identity formation by taxonomizing the dominant approaches.

22. Daisy Hurst Floyd, *Practical Wisdom: Reimagining Legal Education*, 10 Univ. St. Thomas L. J. 195, 201 (2012) (citations omitted).

23. Neil W. Hamilton & Louis D. Bilionis, Law Student Professional Development and Formation: Bridging Law School, Student, and Employer Goals 1–2 (2022), https://www.cambridge.org/core/product/identifier/9781108776325/type/book.

Professional identity formation has been described in terms strikingly similar to that of threshold concepts theory. Floyd, for example, focuses on its integrative aspects.[24] Hamilton conceptualizes it as a journey that involves a law student evolving from a community outsider to insider, moving from observer to participant.[25] This journey is marked by "identity transformations" that often involve "anxiety, stress, and risk"[26] and requires that legal education integrate doctrine and skills with a law student's ethical-social development.[27]

As noted, we view professional identity formation expansively, related not only to the ethical and moral obligations of the profession, but also to the ways in which law students cross various thresholds to view themselves as legal writers and fully fledged members of the profession. Thus, there is a relationship between the threshold concepts of legal writing and the professional identity formation of lawyers.

C. Threshold Concepts on Professional Identity Formation in Other Disciplines and Their Relationship to Legal Education

Researchers in other disciplines have used threshold concepts theory to consider how professional identity is formed.[28] Four themes that emerge from

---

24. *See* Floyd, *supra* note 22, at 217 (explaining that a "framework of practical wisdom builds upon an ethical professional identity, one in which the lawyer integrates professional and personal skills and values").

25. *See* Neil Hamilton, *The Major Transitions in Professional Formation and Development from Being A Student to Being A Lawyer Present Opportunities to Benefit the Students and the Law School*, 73 Baylor L. Rev. 139, 141 (2021) (noting that "each law student during law school...will [] have significant transitions where the student is growing, step by step, from being a novice outsider with a stance of an observer ultimately to join a new community of practice as an insider to the profession.") [hereinafter Hamilton, *Major Transitions*].

26. Holloran Center, *What Is a Law Student's Professional Identity*, *supra* note 13, at 1 (citing Cruess et al., *supra* note 20, at 1557).

27. Educating Lawyers, *supra* note 8, at 147.

28. *See, e.g.*, Laura M. Farrell et al., *Thresholds of Becoming: An Exploration of Threshold Concepts as a Means to Support Professional Identity Formation in Competency-Based Curricula*, 29 Advances in Health Sciences Educ.: Theory and Prac. 349, 351 (2024) (proposing "the theory of threshold concepts, a theory that has increasingly been gaining acceptance in medicine—as a means to bridge the gap between assessing compe-

these studies correlate with our proposed threshold concepts of legal writing:[29] patient/client-centeredness,[30] the role as professional,[31] the value of reflective practices and lifelong learning,[32] and anticipating and managing uncertainty.[33]

---

tency development and supporting professional identity formation."); *see also* Amin, *supra* note 9, at 188–89 (exploring threshold concepts related to ways of practicing in medicine and surgery); Jones & Hammond, *supra* note 9, at 984 (noting that the threshold concepts framework "provides a lens for exploring how [medical] curricula can best prepare students for real-world practice and address issues which hinder professional identity formation.")

29. The themes we identify here are set forth in our own terms as different studies employ different terminology. These themes are not the only themes present in this body of work; the four we identify were chosen for their relevance to professional identity formation in legal education.

30. *See e.g.* Amin, *supra* note 9, at 189–90 (describing "adopting patient centered practice" as a component of the larger threshold concept described as "developing social capital"); Jones & Hammond, *supra* note 9, at 987 (identifying "enactment of patient-centredness and the provision of holistic care" as a threshold concept theme that emerged across studies in medical education); Tucker & Simmons, *supra* note 9, at 282 (identifying student-centered instruction as a threshold concept theme that emerged in professional identity formation in student teachers).

31. *See e.g.*, Amin, *supra* note 9, at 189 (identifying "building relationship between individual as professional, professional circle and society" and "'becoming part of community of practice'" as aspects of the "developing social capital" threshold concept in medicine and surgery); *see also* Liz Springfield et al.,, *Threshold Concepts and Authentic Assessment: Learning to Think Like an Occupational Therapist*, 12 PRAC. AND EVIDENCE OF SCHOLARSHIP OF TEACHING AND LEARNING IN HIGHER EDUC. 125, 127 (2017) (positing "identity as an occupational therapist" as a threshold concept for occupational therapy education).

32. *See e.g.*, Amin, *supra* note 9, at 188 (describing being an "active learner" as an aspect of the professional identity threshold concept "developing as individual agency" for undergraduate medical and surgical students); Virginia Randall et al., *Threshold Concepts in Medical Education*, 7 MEDEDPUBLISH 3, 6 (2021) (studying medical students and identifying "[l]earning is lifelong" as a threshold concept); Virginia M. Tucker, *Becoming an Information Architect: The Evolving Librarian's Skillset, Mindset, and Professional Identity*, 37 EDUC. FOR INFO. 485, 491 (2021) (identifying "learning as recursive activity" and "learning as a journey" as "threshold concepts curriculum considerations" in library or information science education).

33. *See, e.g.*, Amin, *supra* note 9, at 188 (identifying "expecting and managing uncertainty" as a component of "developing as individual agency"); Jones & Hammond, *supra* note 9, at 988 (explaining that "[u]ncertainty, for example, was a concept that featured at all stages of training and professional development, linked to both discipline conceptual change and modelling conceptual change"); Monica W. Tracey & Alisa Hutchinson, *Uncertainty, Reflection, and Designer Identity Development*, 42 DESIGN STUD. 86, 87 (2016) [hereinafter Tracey, et. al *Uncertainty, Reflection*] (noting that uncertainty as a threshold concept in design education "holds the potential to open up a new pathway of understanding that may be otherwise elusive and is necessary for forward progress in the discipline.")

The threshold concepts of identity formation have not been widely studied in the United States. Yet as suggested above,[34] the same themes emerge in studies of professional identity formation in U.S. legal education.

1. *Client/Patient-Centeredness*

Patient- or client-centeredness is a common theme in professional identity research. For example, in one survey of threshold concepts in medical education in the United Kingdom, patient/client centeredness appears across several subspecialties.[35] While not couched in terms of threshold concepts theory, a similar theme emerges in the Carnegie Foundation's study of medical education, *Educating Physicians*.[36] This report asserts that "[t]he physician we envision has, first and foremost, a deep sense of commitment and responsibility to patients, colleagues, institutions, society, and self."[37]

Client-centeredness also appears as a theme in professional identity formation in legal education. For example, Hamilton focuses on the importance of emphasizing the client, asserting that "the formation of professional identity entails the student's acceptance and internalization of a responsibility... to others whom the student will serve as a professional including clients, colleagues, and the legal system."[38] Sullivan similarly emphasizes that "the 'chief formative challenge' for higher education in the professions is to help each student... accept[] and internaliz[e] []responsibility to others (particularly the person served)."[39]

34. *See supra* note 29 (noting the similarity in language between threshold concepts theory and theories of professional identity formation in legal education).

35. *See* Amin, *supra* note 9.

36. Molly Cooke et al., Educating Physicians: A Call For Reform of Medical Sch. Residency (2010).

37. *Id.* at 41.

38. Neil Hamilton, *The Next Steps of A Formation-of-Student-Professional Identity Social Movement: Building Bridges Among the Three Key Stakeholders—Faculty and Staff, Students, and Legal Employers and Clients*, 14 U. St. Thomas L.J. 285, 285–86 (2018).

39. Hamilton, *Major Transitions, supra* note 25, at 142 (citing William Sullivan, *Foreword*, in Teaching Medical Professionalism xi, xv (Richard Creuss et al. eds., 2d ed. 2016)).

2. *Role as Professional*

Another threshold concept identified in other disciplines as essential to professional identity formation is internalizing one's role as a professional.[40] Teaching the role of the professional in medical education has been described as a "threshold of practicing," characterized variously as "developing a[n] individual agency" and "becoming part of community of practice."[41]

Similarly, legal ethics scholar Eli Wald has identified developing a "'deep sense of role'" as critical to professional identity formation in legal education.[42] Wald states, "Professional identity entails a lawyer's capacity to 'reflect on [their] roles within social contexts and systems' and to 'self-define as a professional with a moral core of responsibility and service to others.'"[43] Martin Katz describes professional identity as "the way a lawyer understands [their] role relative to all of the stakeholders in the legal system, including clients, courts, opposing parties and counsel, the firm, and even the legal system itself (or society as a whole)."[44]

3. *The Value of Reflective Practices and Lifelong Learning*

The value of learning, reflection, and lifelong learning has been identified as important to professional identity formation across a variety of disciplines.[45] For example, in the fields of medicine and surgery, active or self-directed learning has been noted as a subcategory within the threshold concept of "developing as individual agency."[46] In information science education, "learning as recursive activity" and "learning as a journey" have been identified as "threshold concepts curriculum considerations."[47] Similarly, Margaret Reuter explains that "[i]mplicitly or explicitly,... professional identity in legal education requires metacognition: reflective practice, self-awareness, and internally

40. *See supra* note 31.

41. Amin, *supra* note 9, at 188.

42. Wald, *supra* note 6, at 691 (citations omitted).

43. *Id.* at 691–92 (citations omitted).

44. Katz, ch. 4, *supra* note 262, at 45.

45. *See supra* note 32.

46. Amin, *supra* note 9, at 188.

47. Tucker, *supra* note 32, at 491.

directed learning."[48] More specifically, she cites Hamilton's focus on "pivotal elements of professional identity... [including] ownership of one's professional development."[49] Denise Lacey goes on to state that these reflective practices serve as "a key pedagogy for professional identity formation."[50] Indeed, "[s] elf-reflection and lifelong learning skills are qualities of an effective, responsible lawyer."[51]

4. *Anticipating and Managing Uncertainty*

Finally, uncertainty emerges as a common theme in threshold concept studies of identity formation.[52] For example, in design studies, researchers emphasize that uncertainty "brings a certain measure of imbalance and challenge to the design situation both needed to promote creative thinking, to spur innovative designs, and to grow as a designer" and that it "is essential that design curriculum include the development of the who—the designers' professional identities and their ability to think and creatively solve complex design problems."[53] "Expecting and managing uncertainty" has also been considered one aspect of "developing as individual agency" for medical students.[54]

Similarly, uncertainty emerges in the context of professional identity formation in legal education. For example, Timothy Floyd and Kendall Kerew explain that a

> fully formed professional identity... requires integration... [and that] to fulfill professional obligations and to practice with excellence, a law-

---

48. Margaret Reuter, *Professional Identity in A Time of Uncertainty: Not A Moment Too Soon*, 89 UMKC L. Rev. 487, 489 (2021).

49. *Id.* at 492 (citing Neil Hamilton, *The Gap Between the Foundational Competencies Clients and Legal Employers Need and the Learning Outcomes Law Schools Are Adopting*, 89 UMKC L. Rev. 559 (2021)).

50. Denise Platfoot Lacey, *Do All Roads Lead to Rome? Effectively Using Asynchronous Online Reflective Practice in an Externship Course*, 89 UMKC L. Rev. 609, 613 (2021).

51. *Id.*

52. *See infra* note 33.

53. Monica W. Tracey & Alisa Hutchinson, *Uncertainty, Agency and Motivation in Graduate Design Students*, 29 Thinking Skills and Creativity 196, 202 (2018); *see also* Tracey et al., *Uncertainty, Reflection, supra* note 33, at 87–89 (identifying the value of exploring uncertainty in design education).

54. Amin, *supra* note 9, at 188–89 (noting that uncertainty in medicine is troublesome in part because "it is difficult for trainees to deal with the unexpected, for which they need careful preparation").

> yer must integrate professional knowledge, skills, and values and the ability to access multiple capacities at once in the midst of conditions of inherent uncertainty.[55]

Further, the need for lawyers to operate in conditions of uncertainty in professional identity formation is recognized by scholars who emphasize the importance of developing judgment or practical wisdom.[56]

D. Understanding the Threshold Concepts of Legal Writing Enhances Law Students' Professional Identity Formation

In the first-year legal writing curriculum, students confront for the first time each of the four themes of professional identity formation that will benefit them as legal writers and as practicing lawyers. In the first semester, students are typically assigned a hypothetical that involves the representation of a client. They are asked to predict the outcome of the client's claim or charge, requiring them to research the applicable law and to prioritize client goals. In writing their analysis, students not only engage in creating and recreating the law,[57] they simulate their role as a professional advocate and advisor. The recursive nature of legal writing, with its cycles of revision,[58] also introduces students to the reflective practices and lifelong learning of experienced professionals. Finally, the need for students to make concrete predictions in light of

---

55. Timothy W. Floyd & Kendall L. Kerew, *Marking the Path from Law Student to Lawyer: Using Field Placement Courses to Facilitate the Deliberate Exploration of Professional Identity and Purpose*, 68 MERCER L. REV. 767, 774 (2017).

56. *See, e.g.*, Patrick Emery Longan, Daisy Hurst Floyd & Timothy Floyd, *A Virtue Ethics Approach to Professional Identity: Lessons for the First Year and Beyond*, 89 UMKC L. REV. 645, 650 (2021) (explaining the value of virtue or practical wisdom to adapt to particular circumstances, a skill that is necessary to help "students to chart a course in circumstances where more than one virtue is relevant, where the virtues might conflict, and where there is uncertainty").

57. *See* Concept 1.1, ch. 4, *supra*, at 36 (legal writers create and recreate the law).

58. *See* Concept 3.3, ch. 4, *supra*, at 97 (legal writers understand that writing is a recursive process that takes time).

competing considerations underscores the uncertainty—as well as the creativity—inherent in legal analysis.[59]

Legal writing instruction thus implicates professional identity development as students engage in what is typically their first practical experience of law practice through writing. The pedagogies employed in this context help students see themselves in their role within the professional community. And, by naming the threshold concepts of legal writing, educators can better assist students in developing their professional identities.

1. *How Legal Writing Instruction Informs Professional Identity Formation*

Legal writing pedagogy lends itself to professional identity formation in part because of the authentic experience of law practice implicated by this instruction[60] and because the process and practice of writing is an enactment of identity. As the authors of *Educating Lawyers* observed, the pedagogies of legal writing blend content knowledge and skills, and also reveal the "uncertainties of specific practical contexts."[61] "In its fully developed form, the [legal writing] pedagogy makes this developmental process itself visible to the learners, so that they can become aware of the components of their growing abilities to write—and think—as legal professionals."[62]

Hamilton illustrates the relationship between practical experience students have in law school, including legal writing courses, and professional identity formation.[63] He explains that, as first and second year students reflect on their own professional identity formation, two elements emerge as essential to their

---

59. *See* Concepts 2.1 (legal writers know they engage in a rhetorical practice even though the law tends to deny its rhetorical nature), 3.4 (legal writers are creative), and 3.5 (legal writers must become comfortable with uncertainty), ch. 4, *supra*, at 60, 102, and 105, respectively.

60. Educating Lawyers, *supra* note 8, at 106–08 (describing "legal writing as simulated practice").

61. *Id.* at 110.

62. *Id.* The authors further observe that "the teaching of legal writing can be used to open a window for students onto the full complexity of legal expertise." *Id.* at 111.

63. Hamilton, *Major Transitions, supra* note 25, at 156 (noting "that law schools should provide some curricular support at several significant transitions where students may also experience substantial stress... [including] right after major professionally authentic experiences like the first graded memorandum or an oral argument for lawyering skills").

development: "(1) ongoing solicitation of feedback and self-reflection, and (2) an internalized standard of excellence at lawyering skills."[64]

In this regard, he studied first and second year law students to see how they reflected on their professional identity formation. Hamilton found that they "rate[d] professionally authentic experiences (real-life or mimicking the real-life work of a lawyer) as having the greatest impact on their growth toward later stages of ownership of their own continuous professional development."[65] The third most impactful experience was "receiving [] the first graded memorandum [in a legal writing course] (with nineteen percent responding great impact)."[66]

The legal writing curriculum uniquely positions legal writing faculty to attend to students' professional identity formation. As Kierstead and Abner note, professional identity is formed in large part by "the preparation of documents in the service of clients."[67] Learning to write like a lawyer is thus essential to identity formation because a "considerable proportion of legal work is enacted in the many different types of documents that lawyers prepare.... These documents 'make something happen' in the world: they provoke a response, persuade a judge, transfer money or other property interest, create a relationship, dissolve a relationship, or tell a story."[68] Because the "[t]ransformation of identity or professional identity [] is closely linked to thinking and language,"[69] legal writing is a space in which identity is both developed and performed.

Threshold concepts researchers have also studied the impact of practical experiences on professional development.[70] As the authors of one study on health care students explain, "practical experience always entail[s] the student

64. *Id.* at 144.

65. *Id.* at 154–55.

66. *Id.* at 155. Hamilton notes that forty-two percent of these students reported substantial or overwhelming stress associated with this event, with fifteen percent reporting overwhelming stress. *Id.* at 156.

67. Kierstead & Abner, ch. 4, *supra* note 264, at 329.

68. *Id.* at 330; *see also* Concept 3.7, ch. 4, *supra*, at 114 (legal writers form and enact their identity through writing).

69. Angelica Fredholm et al., *The Practice of Thresholds: Autonomy in Clinical Education Explored Through Variation Theory and the Threshold Concepts Framework*, 25 TEACHING IN HIGHER EDUC. 305, 316 (2019).

70. *See e.g.*, *id.* at 309 (explaining that the study analyzed interviews with medical, nursing, occupational therapy and biomedical analyst students).

as the 'doer', showing that something is happening as the task or act is carried out, [and] the action itself seems to be loaded with power to change thought and identity."[71] Similarly, when medical students are asked to "conquer[ ] a practical act or procedure, an acquisition of a 'procedural discourse' or repertoire takes place [and t]his ownership of the procedural discourse or repertoire seems to enhance student's view of themselves as professionals."[72]

Experts in writing studies also recognize that "writing in new contexts is not only about learning abstract conventions but also about learning how to be within a group with social conventions, norms and expectations."[73] This kind of learning goes on within the legal writing classroom as well. Engaging in legal writing can thus be viewed as "an act of identity and affiliation."[74]

Developing professional identity is a challenging, potentially troublesome experience, particularly for law students who are learning new discourse practices[75] and who are adapting to the "radical epistemological break between common sense and legal thought, and also to the gate-keeping practices of the legal profession."[76] Nonetheless, because [w]riting instruction ... allows the communication process to be stopped for a while to enable students to observe and analyze the discourse being developed," the legal writing classroom helps students to "grow into a more expansive and self-aware professional competence."[77]

---

71. *Id.* at 316.

72. *Id.*

73. Heidi Estrem, *Disciplinary and Professional Identities are Constructed Through Writing*, *in* NAMING WHAT WE KNOW, ch. 1, *supra* note 15, at 56 .

74. *Id.*

75. Kelli Nicola-Richmond, et al., *Threshold Concepts in Higher Education: A Synthesis of the Literature Relating to Measurement of Threshold Crossing*, 37 HIGHER EDUC. RSCH. & DEV. 101, 102 ("grasping the meaning of a threshold concept should involve a shift in the identity of the learner, [and] the integration of new verbal and/or mental language specific to the discipline").

76. Rod Maclean, *First-year Law Students' Construction of Professional Identity Through Writing*, 12 DISCOURSE STUDIES 177, 177–78 (2010).

77. EDUCATING LAWYERS, *supra* note 8, at 110.

2. How Our Proposed Concepts Relate to the Four Themes of Professional Identity Formation

The central role of the client is reflected throughout our proposed concepts of legal writing.[78] For example, in Category One, which pertains to meaning-making in legal writing, understanding the importance of framing an issue from the perspective of the client,[79] recognizing that the parties contribute to the legally significant facts as they are determined,[80] and telling the client's story effectively[81] underscore the centrality of the client in legal writing.

In Category Two, which pertains to the rhetorical conventions to which legal writers must conform, client-centered conventions include the understanding that legal writing often presents itself as neutral when in fact it is influenced by choices that prioritize the client's perspective.[82] These Category Two concepts also capture the fact that legal writers read with a specific purpose in mind, usually to advance their client's cause;[83] gather facts and law in an interdependent and recursive manner for the benefit of the client before they write;[84] and create and shape rules of law to benefit their client's position.[85]

Similarly, in Category Three, which relates to the nature of the legal writer, client-centeredness is inherent in the legal writer's need to make choices about what constitutes a "a good argument,"[86] the restrictions that precedent places

---

78. The word "client" appears in the explanations of all but seven of our concepts.

79. *See* Concept 1.4, ch. 4, *supra*, at 42 (legal writers understand the importance of framing)

80. *See* Concept 1.5, ch. 4, *supra*, at 45 (facts in law are determined by an adjudicator).

81. *See* Concept 1.6, ch. 4, *supra*, at 49 (legal writing involves a blend of rules and storytelling).

82. *See* Concept 2.1, ch. 4, *supra*, at 60 (legal writers know they engage in a rhetorical practice even though the law tends to deny its rhetorical nature).

83. *See* Concept 2.2, ch. 4, *supra*, at 62 (legal writers read actively, efficiently, and effectively).

84. *See* Concept 2.3, ch. 4, *supra*, at 66 (legal writers must gather both fact and law).

85. *See* Concept 2.4, ch. 4, *supra*, at 69 (legal writers have a flexible understanding of sources of authority).

86. *See* Concept 3.1, ch. 4, *supra*, at 91 (legal writers make choices about what constitutes "good" arguments).

on making credible arguments that favor the client,[87] and the time-limits imposed by clients that affect the legal writer's process.[88]

With respect to the legal writer's "role as professional," Concept 3.7 makes explicit the ways in which legal writers enact their professional identity through their writing.[89] Indeed, most of our concepts illustrate how, through the writing process, law students begin to envision themselves as members of the professional community. For example, they understand that it is through writing that they create and recreate the law,[90] construct arguments about the meaning of language,[91] and engage in a rhetorical practice.[92] The legal writer's role and responsibility toward their clients is also reflected in the need to synthesize credible rules of law,[93] use effective analogical reasoning, [94] and make "good arguments" on behalf of clients.[95]

When legal writers realize that legal writing is not right or wrong, they can appreciate the value of engaging in reflective practices and lifelong learning. [96] This realization implicitly reinforces the need for continued study and refinement of legal communication. Further, the knowledge that legal writing is both a reflective and recursive process speaks to lifelong learning.[97] Similarly, the knowledge that legal writing has a tendency to perpetuate dominant power but can be used to disrupt it[98] and that the language of law embodies values and

---

87. *See* Concept 3.2, ch. 4, *supra*, at 94 (precedent both guides and restrains legal writers).

88. *See* Concept 3.3, ch. 4, *supra*, at 97 (legal writers understand that legal writing takes time and is a recursive and reflective process).

89. *See* Concept 3.7, ch. 4, *supra*, at 114 (legal writers form their professional identity through writing).

90. *See* Concept 1.1, ch. 4, *supra*, at 36 (legal writers create and recreate the law).

91. *See* Concept 1.2, ch. 4, *supra*, at 37 (the foundational role of legal writers is to construct arguments about the meaning of language).

92. *See* Concept 2.1, ch. 4, *supra*, at 60 (legal writers know they engage in a rhetorical practice even though the law tends to deny its rhetorical nature).

93. *See* Concept 2.5, ch. 4, *supra*, at 71 (legal writers construct rules of law for specific contexts).

94. *See* Concept 2.7, ch. 4, *supra*, at 77 (legal writers use analogy to make their case for validity).

95. *See* Concepts 3.1, ch. 4, *supra*, at 91 (legal writers make choices about what constitutes "good" arguments).

96. *See* Concept 1.7, ch. 4, *supra*, at 51(legal writing is neither right nor wrong).

97. *See* Concept 3.3, ch. 4, *supra*, at 97 (legal writers understand that legal writing takes time and is a recursive and reflective process).

98. *See* Concept 1.8, ch. 4, *supra*, at 55 (legal writing perpetuates and disrupts power).

norms with which the writer may struggle[99] relate to the nature of legal writing as an ongoing, reflective practice.

Finally, uncertainty is also represented in many of the concepts. Concept 3.5 describes in explicit terms the extent to which legal writers must become accustomed to uncertainty in the practice of law.[100] Uncertainty is also captured in the legal writer's understanding that their role is to construct arguments about the meaning of language,[101] while working with rules that are themselves malleable.[102] More specifically, as students gain practical writing experience, they begin to appreciate the degree of discretion and creativity afforded them in choosing authorities to rely on[103] and synthesizing rules.[104]

In sum, threshold concepts theory enhances our understanding of legal writing expertise and the ways in which law students develop their professional identities through writing. As Rachael Field and Jan Meyer explain, threshold concepts help us "focus on those transformational learning experiences that really matter; those learning episodes that capture the quintessential essence of the liminal process of becoming, self-identifying as, and transforming into, a lawyer."[105] Our hope is that these concepts will both raise our consciousness as teachers and help us better convey to students the troubling yet transformative process of becoming expert legal writers.

---

99. *See* Concept 3.6, ch. 4, *supra*, at 109 (legal writing is identifiable and yet often exclusionary).

100. *See* Concept 3.5, ch. 4, *supra*, at 105 (legal writers must become comfortable with uncertainty).

101. *See* Concept 1.2, ch. 4, *supra*, at 37 (the foundational role of legal writers is to construct arguments about the meaning of language).

102. *See* Concept 1.3, ch. 4, *supra*, at 40 (legal writers understand the malleability of law).

103. *See* Concept 2.4, ch. 4, *supra*, at 69 (legal writers have a flexible understanding of authority).

104. *See* Concept 2.5, ch. 4, *supra*, at 71 (legal writers construct rules of law for specific contexts).

105. Field & Meyer, *Threshold Concepts in Law*, ch. 5, *supra* note 5, at 152.

SEVEN

Food for Thought: Where Do We Go from Here?

Inspired by *Naming What We Know*[1] and *(Re)Considering What We Know*,[2] this book represents the first attempt to define the legal writing discipline using threshold concepts theory. In their work, editors Linda Adler-Kassner and Elizabeth Wardle emphasize that the naming of threshold concepts is always "contingent, contextual, and threshold-for-now."[3] So too, our proposed concepts represent what we know, for now. They derive from our experience as legal practitioners and legal writing professors and are subject to debate and revision.

This project also represents both a scholarly and political effort to further build our discipline. Naming—and defining—the discipline has both internal and external benefits.[4] As writing studies scholar Jennifer Maher explains, "Disciplinary histories serve the important function of legitimizing the identity and work of a discipline."[5] Differentiating between "internal and external orientations of these histories," Maher notes that internally, threshold concepts "serve[ ] to inculcate newcomers and create a shared sense of identity rooted in the innate value of its disciplinary knowledge."[6] Externally, they "aim[ ] to

1. Naming What We Know, ch. 1, *supra* note 15.

2. (Re)Considering What We Know ch. 1, *supra* note 15.

3. *Id.* at 9.

4. Jennifer Helene Maher, *Rhetoric as Persistently "Troublesome Knowledge": Implications for Disciplinarity, in* (Re)Considering What We Know, ch. 1, *supra* note 15, at 94–96.

5. *Id.* at 94.

6. *Id.*

generate legitimation for the discipline and its knowledge beyond the discipline itself."[7]

This chapter begins by addressing first the challenges—both internal and external—in defining the legal writing discipline, and second, our response to the perceived weaknesses in threshold concepts theory itself. The chapter concludes by posing questions specific to our proposed concepts for consideration and comment.

A. Challenges in Defining the Legal Writing Discipline

Legal writing has struggled to achieve legitimacy in part because of "the contested nature of the discipline" itself.[8] With regard to writing studies, Maher observed, "Debates over the status of rhetoric and composition as a discipline reveal that *discipline* is a highly contested term in the field."[9] Maher argues that rhetoric is itself a threshold concept that is not only initially but persistently troublesome because it is viewed as "somehow supplemental" to the curriculum and because language is "a constitutive part of every discipline."[10] This view of rhetoric dates back to Plato, who argued that language is part and parcel of all disciplines, making rhetoric a subject without substance.[11]

Like writing studies, legal writing is often viewed as "somehow supplemental" to traditional legal education.[12] Law school administrators and faculty often place a lesser value on practical skills training, treating legal writing courses as "ancillary to the real law."[13] This limited understanding of legal writing stems in part from outmoded composition theories that assumed "writing was secondary to thinking"[14] and the fact that legal writing programs were not

---

7. *Id.*

8. *See id.* at 94–96.

9. *Id.* at 95 (citations omitted) (emphasis in original).

10. *Id.* at 99.

11. *See, e.g.*, Plato, *Gorgias*, *in* COMPLETE WORKS 449d–450d (John M. Cooper & D.S. Hutchinson eds., Hackett Publ'g Co. 1997) (c. 380 BCE) (arguing that all subjects, including arithmetic and astronomy, influence their audience through speech).

12. *See, e.g.*, Rideout & Ramsfield, *A Revised View*, ch. 4, *supra* note 235, at 40–44 (1994) (noting the traditional view that legal writing is just good writing, incapable of being taught, and remedial in nature).

13. *Id.* at 44.

14. *Id.* at 45.

formally integrated into legal education until the late 1900s. It persists today in the structural hierarchies sanctioned by ABA Standard 405[15] and is reflected in legal writing faculty's lower salaries, lesser status, and fewer governance rights than tenured podium faculty.[16]

An equally important challenge for the legal writing discipline is that it too is squarely rooted in rhetorical theory. As Christopher Rideout has noted, "The first component of the doctrine of legal writing is legal rhetoric—the discursive conventions and rhetorical commitments that are specific to the discourse of the law."[17] As Linda Berger, Linda Edwards, and Terry Pollman further explain,

> The core of [legal writing] study and practice is rhetoric, and in particular, the rhetorical concept that meaning is constructed out of the interaction of reader and writer, text and context.... The study and practice of "law as rhetoric" is a thread that can run through the fabric of a professional life, weaving together the legal writing professor's work in scholarship, teaching, and professional service.[18]

The irony is that rhetoric was initially studied in ancient Greece and Rome for the purpose of improving public speaking in civic matters, including legal argument.[19] But Plato argued not only that rhetoric is a subject without a subject matter,[20] he viewed it as the false art of justice, manipulating truth to

---

15. ABA Standards, ch. 1, *supra* note 38, Std. 405. To date, legal writing faculty are eligible for traditional tenure at roughly thirty percent of law schools. *ALWD/LWI Legal Writing Survey, 2021–2022 Report of the Institutional* Survey, Q. 8.2, at 55 [hereinafter *2021–2022 Survey*].

16. *See, e.g.*, *2021–2022 Survey*, *supra* note 15, Q.12.5, at 145; Q. 8.2, at 55; & Q. 10.2, at 83; *see also* Jo Anne Durako, *Second-Class Citizens in the Pink Ghetto: Gender Bias in Legal Writing*, 50 J. Legal Educ. 562 (2000); Susan P. Liemer & Hollee S. Temple, *Did Your Legal Writing Professor Go to Harvard?: The Credentials of Legal Writing Faculty At Hiring Time*, 46 U. Louisville L. Rev. 383 (2008); Kristen K. Tiscione & Amy Vorenberg, *Podia and Pens: Dismantling the Two-Track System for Legal Research and Writing Faculty*, 31 Colum. J. Gender & L. 47, 48–59 (2015).

17. Rideout & Ramsfield, *On the Doctrine of Legal Writing*, ch. 4, *supra* note 268, at 109.

18. Linda L. Berger, Linda H. Edwards, & Terrill Pollman, *The Past, Presence, and Future of Legal Writing Scholarship: Rhetoric, Voice, and Community*, 16 Legal Writing: J. Legal Writing Inst., 521, 521–22 (2010) (citations omitted).

19. *See, e.g.*, Aristotle, Rhetoric, ch. 4, *supra* note 104, at 1.3, 1358b (explaining that rhetoric comprises political, judicial, and ceremonial speech).

20. *See supra* note 11 and accompanying text.

gain advantage.[21] Although ancient rhetoricians understood that rhetoric is valuable because it operates in a sphere where absolute truth is not possible,[22] Plato's view has influenced centuries of general disdain for the legal writing profession, even within the profession itself.[23]

In our view, identifying the threshold concepts of legal writing is a powerful response to these challenges, further defining and elevating our discipline both internally and externally. Indeed, "this kind of reverse engineering [in naming threshold concepts]" may even be necessary to identify a common vocabulary for the core of our expertise—"those gateways so fundamental, yet still too often alien, to the tacit and problematic knowledge about 'good writing'" in the legal context.[24] As Rideout has explained, "If we want to understand legal writing as a discipline, we can do so by looking at our own disciplinary practices. As legal writing professionals, we are what we do, and in what we do lies the key to those larger answers about the nature of our discipline."[25]

B. Perceived Weaknesses in Threshold Concepts Theory

Although we believe in the benefits of threshold concepts theory, it is not without its critics. The theory has been criticized largely for the instability of its definitional framework. For example, the "portal" conception of a threshold concept has been described as "far too metaphorical to serve scientific purposes."[26] Further, some critics argue that threshold concepts cannot be studied scientifically because their defining characteristics vary within the literature

---

21. *See, e.g.*, *Gorgias*, *supra* note 11, at 464b–d (equating rhetoric and cookery because both are designed to gratify).

22. *See, e.g.*, Aristotle, Rhetoric, ch. 4, *supra* note 104, at 1.1, 1355a (explaining that rhetoric is designed to achieve justice by juxtaposing competing arguments).

23. *See, e.g.*, *Citizens United v. Fed. Election Comm'n*, 558 U.S. 310 (2010) (expressing the view that the government's arguments in defense of the Bipartisan Campaign Reform Act of 2002 were merely rhetoric, intended to distort the reality that Section 441b suppressed political speech on the basis of the speaker's identity).

24. Maher, *supra* note 4, at 98 (citations omitted).

25. J. Christopher Rideout, *Discipline-Building and Disciplinary Values: Thoughts on Legal Writing at Year Twenty-Five of the Legal Writing Institute*, 16 Legal Writing: J. Legal Writing Inst., 477, 479 (2010).

26. Håkan Salwén, *Threshold Concepts, Obstacles or Scientific Dead Ends?* 26 Teaching in Higher Educ. 36, 40 (2021).

and have not been uniformly articulated as essential.[27] Finally, the "hedging language" used in describing the defining characteristics, such as ""likely to be.... probably irreversible... possibl[ly] often (though not necessarily) bounded... potentially (and possibly inherently) troublesome"[28] has been referred to as the "floating signifier problem," leading to an "inconsistent operationalization of the theory."[29]

In response to this "definitional problem," Meyer has argued that "it is [not] desirable, let alone possible, to formulate a definition of 'concept' that will be accepted as complete and valid in all disciplinary contexts."[30] More recently, Meyer noted:

> An extensive literature confirms a wide spectrum of subject experts and professional practitioners who apparently, unfettered by concerns of 'vague' language, have merrily gone about the business of reaching a consensus on the presence, as well as the epistemological and ontological function, of threshold concepts in the subject matter they teach and practise.[31]

In this project, once we found a way to tap into our shared expertise as legal writers and legal writing professors, the inherent flexibility of the defining

---

27. *Id.* at 38 (emphasizing that "[d]efinitions are used for clarificatory purposes. With reference to definitions, scientists can clarify what they are talking or thinking about and thereby make it possible for themselves or others to investigate whether or not there are objects or phenomena of the sort the definitions specify"); *see also* Rod O'Donnell, *A Critique of Threshold Concepts Hypothesis and an Application in Economics*, University of Technology Sydney School of Finance and Economics Working Paper No. 164 (2010). O'Donnell addresses six questions associated with the definitional framework under the heading "Extraordinary Elasticities": "How many characteristics are required?, Can probable characteristics be defining characteristics?, How important is troublesomeness?, Can threshold concepts have all five characteristics simultaneously?, How many learners must undergo the specified experiences?, and How many threshold concepts are there?" *Id.* at 3–5.

28. Megan E. L. Brown, Paul Whybrow & Gabrielle M. Finn, *Do We Need to Close the Door on Threshold Concepts?* 34 Teaching and Learning in Medicine 301, 305 (2022).

29. *Id.*

30. Meyer, *Pedagogic Representation*, *supra* ch. 5, note 4, at 466.

31. Jan H.F. Meyer, *Twaddle, Conformity, and Variation: A Retrospective 'Endnote' for Meyer and Land (2003)*, *in* Threshold Concepts in the Moment 472 (Jason P. Davies, et al., eds., 2024) [hereinafter Meyer, *Twaddle, Conformity, and Variation*].

characteristics was useful, permitting us to include concepts that needed only be "likely bounded"[32] and that arguably apply to all forms of legal writing.

Relatedly, threshold concepts theory has been criticized on the basis of the "agent-relative" nature of student learning.[33] In other words, what proves to be troublesome or transformative for one student might not be troublesome or transformative for another. In legal writing, differences among learners are particularly salient. Students arrive at law school with vastly different levels of familiarity with academic and professional discourse. As a result, their paths through threshold progression are uniquely shaped by their prior education, language background, and personal identity.

With regard to the "agent-relative" problem, threshold concepts theorists have long recognized that "students will vary in their experiences of comprehending a threshold concept because of individual differences."[34] These include differences in "relevant prior knowledge of that concept, its disciplinary context, or an inclination to 'think' in a certain way (a 'habit of mind') that resonates with the epistemic and ontological function of that concept."[35] To that point, "the vagary" of the defining characteristics (the "definitional problem") is intentionally designed to account for those differences. According to Meyer, the flexibility in the definitional framework alerts students to the "presence and location of variability in [their] cognitive and emotional engagement with threshold concepts."[36]

Another criticism of threshold concepts theory relates to its "body of knowledge" problem.[37] Critics argue that naming threshold concepts in a discipline presumes that there is a core set of beliefs and dispositions unique to each discipline.[38] There are troubling implications associated with this presumption, including potential negative impacts on critical and creative thinking,[39] the

---

32. *See* ch. 2, *supra*, at 18–19.

33. *See, e.g.*, O'Donnell, *supra* note 27, at 6 (criticizing the agent-dependent nature of threshold concepts); *see also* Darrell Patrick Rowbottom, *Demystifying Threshold Concepts*, 41 J. PHIL. EDUC. 263, 267 (2007).

34. Meyer, *Pedagogic Representation*, ch. 5, *supra* note 4, at 467.

35. Meyer, *Twaddle, Conformity, and Variation*, *supra* note 31, at 474.

36. *Id.*

37. *See, e.g.*, Brown et al., *supra* note 28, at 306–07.

38. O'Donnell, *supra* note 27, at 9 (criticizing a "key presumption [] that a discipline has an established body of fundamental knowledge that is likely to change").

39. *Id.* (noting that alternative perspectives within a discipline "are exactly what are required for critical reflection on the adequacy of dominant categories."); *see also* Isaac

inevitable siloing that occurs in the context of establishing disciplinary boundaries,[40] and the potential for the entrenchment of power and control within a discipline.[41] As one group of health professions scholars cautions, "so long as [threshold concepts] are identified and implemented by those in positions of authority—researchers and educators—students are subjected to the power of the dominant educational class in deciding what is troublesome and what is not."[42] Moreover, they warn that "such practice may perpetuate dominant social structures and stifle the disciplary [sic] development that comes from student participation and engagement.[43]

Both mindful of and sensitive to the "body of knowledge" problem, we maintain that the process of naming what we know—as a fluid and evolving body of knowledge—is valuable. Although the threshold concepts framework necessarily includes and excludes particular ideas, "this, too, is a fruitful subject for exploration."[44] As Adler-Kassner and Wardle explain:

> While we think it is important to name the rules of the game or ways of thinking and practicing in a discipline so newcomers can get a clearer sense of the landscape, we should at no time use those mapping and naming exercises to suggest there is one coherent narrative of our (or any) discipline—or that what are named as common ways of thinking and practicing are the only important ideas in a given discipline.[45]

In an interdisciplinary field such as ours, "[i]dentifying threshold concepts can be particularly useful" for a discipline which is "not only relatively new

---

Calduch, *Reframing Threshold Concepts as Open Questions*, *in* IN THE MOMENT, *supra* note 31, at 59 (cautioning that "threshold scholars should be aware that the identification, selection, and promotion of certain threshold concepts could exert epistemic violence or epistemicide (understood as the delegitimation of certain possibilities of knowing, of other possibilities of knowing)").

40. O'Donnell, *supra* note 27, at 9.

41. *Id.*

42. Brown, et al. *supra* note 28, at 306.

43. *Id.*

44. Linda Adler-Kassner and Elizabeth Wardle, *Editors' Introduction: Threshold Concepts, Naming What We Know, and Reconsidering our Shared Conceptions*, *in* RE(CONSIDERING WHAT WE KNOW, ch. 1, *supra* note 15, at 9 [hereinafter Adler-Kassner & Wardle, *Editors' Introduction*].

45. *Id.*

to disciplinarity... but also has a history of struggling with what, if anything, constitutes its disciplinarity."[46]

Indeed, we believe there is "risk in *not* naming ideas and *not* pointing to research that has been conducted about writing."[47] Although not the only method for defining a discipline, threshold concepts theory provides a framework for helping "disciplinary insiders investigate, make visible, interrogate, and critique the epistemological foundations of their disciplines, the values and ideologies associated with those foundations, and what ideas are included and excluded in its discourse practices."[48] Thus, it is critical to the development of our discipline to articulate the expertise we share as legal writers in creating and interpreting legal texts.

Threshold concepts theory can also help us better engage our students. Our goal is not to be their sole "interpretive voice,"[49] but to convey the essence of legal writing expertise, underscoring the creative and individual freedom that legal writers enjoy in the malleability and selection of law, the synthesis of rules, and analogical reasoning, to name just a few examples. At the same time, we can highlight the power dynamic inherent in the legal process. As Concept 1.8 explains, legal writers have an ethical obligation to work with the confines of the law, which in turn, may perpetuate the legal status quo. Yet the law can be used not only to perpetuate but also to disrupt sources of power.[50]

We return to the view that our proposed concepts represent neither a canon of legal writing nor the "be all and end all" of what we know as disciplinary experts.[51] As Adler-Kassner and Wardle explain, "There are always more concepts to be named, additional exploration of the boundaries surrounding the realms where these concepts are operative, and discussions to be had about the relevance of the concepts named."[52] To that end, we invite our readers—legal scholars and practitioners alike— to join us in fleshing out the contours of the

---

46. Maher, *supra* note 4, at 97.

47. Adler-Kassner and Wardle, *Editors' Conclusion: Expanding and Examining What we (Think We) Know*, *in* RE(CONSIDERING) WHAT WE KNOW, ch. 1, *supra* note 15, at 329 (emphasis in original).

48. *Id.* at 330 (emphasis in original).

49. Sarah Barradell & Tai Peseta, *Putting Threshold Concepts to Work in Health Sciences: Insights for Curriculum Design from a Critical Synthesis of Teaching and Learning Research*, 22 TEACHING IN HIGHER EDUC. 349, 368 (2017).

50. *See* Concept 1.8, ch. 4, *supra*, at 55.

51. *See* ch. 1, *supra* at 9.

52. Adler-Kassner & Wardle, *Editors' Introduction*, *supra* note 44, at 9.

discipline and in staking our claim as members of a legitimate if admittedly difficult-to-define discipline.

C. Questions for Consideration

To begin, what did we miss? Are there other thresholds that novice legal writers must traverse that we failed to identify? We included certain aspects of several forms of reasoning—deductive, analogical, and narrative—arguably unique enough to the legal writing discipline to be considered bounded. Did we make the right choices? Are other aspects or forms of legal reasoning troubling, transformative, irreversible, and integrative enough to be considered threshold concepts of legal writing?

We also considered including a concept on client-centeredness, a mindset that permeates all legal representation. Indeed, the concept of client-centeredness is central to threshold concepts literature on professional identity formation.[53] In the end, we decided that as a separate concept, client-centeredness rightly belongs in that professional identity formation realm. Further, the notion of client-centeredness or writing on behalf of another undergirds our entire project; the central role the client plays in legal writing is explicit in nearly all of our concepts. In addition, our goal was to include all forms of legal writing, where the notion of client becomes a bit more attenuated (such as in judicial decisions and legal scholarship). In retrospect, should client-centeredness be its own concept?

Are there some of our proposed concepts with which you disagree in terms of our characterizations of the expertise or as rising to the level of a threshold concept? For example, several members of our focus group questioned the validity of Concept 1.1, that "legal writing creates and recreates the law."[54] In their view, to describe legal writers as "creating law" is misleading, particularly in the context of predictive writing, such as memoranda. In those instances, they argued, legal writers cannot truly be said to "create" law. In the end, we decided to retain this concept because it is consistent with our view

---

53. *See, e.g.*, Amin, ch. 6, *supra* note 9, at 189–90 (describing "adopting patient centered practice" as a component of the larger threshold concept described as "developing social capital"); *see also* Tucker & Simmons, ch. 6, *supra* note 9, at 282 (identifying "student-centered instruction" as a threshold concept theme that emerged in professional identity formation in student teachers).

54. *See* ch. 4, *supra* at 36.

of writing as epistemic. As Linda Berger explains, "Writing is a process for creating knowledge, not merely a means for communicating it."[55] As the result of "an active 'putting together' of meaning between reader, writer, and text," knowledge is created.[56] In that sense, whenever legal writers use language to construct the meaning of law, they either create or recreate it.

We also struggled with whether or not to include rule synthesis as a threshold concept. In an early article on threshold concepts, Mel Weresh considered synthesis as a potential threshold concept in legal education.[57] She concluded that "malleability is likely a threshold for case synthesis, which is a threshold to more fully developed legal reasoning."[58] Yet several members of our core group were hesitant to include synthesis for the same reasons we were hesitant to include deductive reasoning, on the theory that the synthesis of ideas is not sufficiently limited to legal writing to merit its inclusion. In the end though, we chose to include both as separate concepts because they are particularly integral to legal writing and likely different enough in the legal writing community to include them. We also thought we could let readers weigh in on this question.

We note that the results of our project were likely constrained by the framing decisions we made at the onset of the project and the organizational structure we chose to organize individual concepts.[59] Although we believe that the essence of legal writing expertise is common across all forms of legal writing[60]—even if not all of our proposed concepts are equally applicable to all forms—we wonder to what extent that view imposed arbitrary limitations on the results. In short, the decisions we made at the onset of the project affected the results, leading us to question whether those decisions obscured other relevant thresholds. If so, what else should we have considered in this disciplinary context?

Further questions surround the implications of our project. These include pedagogical questions, such as how best to implement these concepts to improve our teaching and assessment practices in order to hasten and improve

---

55. Berger, *Applying New Rhetoric*, ch. 4, *supra* note 209, at 156.

56. *Id.* at 157.

57. *See* Weresh, *Malleability*, ch. 2, *supra* note 1, at 713 (noting that 59 out of 84 legal writing professors surveyed believed that case synthesis is a threshold concept).

58. *Id.* at 715.

59. *See generally* ch. 3, *supra*.

60. *See* ch. 1, *supra* at 7.

student learning. Chapter Five considers in general terms how threshold concepts theory might be used to improve our teaching—from stating more explicit learning objectives to using formative and summative assessments to gauge deep learning and spark student reflections. Yet it remains to be seen how these concepts might successfully be implemented in specific terms in specific programs. We are also interested in exploring threshold concepts can improve students' confidence in their writing and develop their sense of self as legal writing professionals.

Finally, we are well that we are in a new frontier with regard to written content in the age of generative artificial intelligence (GAI). Text-to-text platforms such as ChatGPT and platforms specific to legal research and writing (such as Westlaw's Co-Counsel and Lexis's Protege) likely represent a "paradigm shift in legal communication teaching, learning, and practice."[61] Questions abound regarding the extent to which GAI will alter how we think about disciplinary expertise, the creative writing process,[62] and the practice of law.[63] We must consider which legal writing tasks in practice have already been and will likely be replaced by GAI and how that affects the content of our coursework.[64]

As these technologies force us to rethink legal education and legal writing curricula, our proposed threshold concepts may help us identify those legal writing tasks—that implicit expertise—that will continue to require human intervention and contribution. As GAI generates more and more types of legal texts, including memoranda, briefs, complaints, and wills, students will likely spend more time rewriting than drafting.[65] As a result, students will need to

---

61. *See* Kirsten K. Davis, *A New Parlor Is Open: Legal Writing Faculty Must Develop Scholarship on Generative AI and Legal Writing*, 7 Unending Conv. 1, 2 (2024) https://www2.stetson.edu/law-review/article/category/unending-conversation/unending-conversation-spring-2024/.

62. *See, e.g.*, José Antonio Bowen & C. Edward Watson, Teaching with AI: A Practical Guide to a New Era of Human Learning (2024) (exploring the massive impact of AI on teaching, learning, and writing); John Warner, More Than Words: How to Think About Writing in the Age of AI (arguing that writing is both thinking and feeling and that writing activities should challenge students to engage their imagination and experience).

63. *Davis*, *supra* note 61, at 20 (arguing that "skills like critical reading, rhetorical analysis of text, and information literacy will be more important than ever").

64. *See generally* Regalia, *From Briefs to Bytes*, ch. 4, *supra* note 200.

65. *See* Davis, *supra* note 61, at 20 (speculating that "competent legal analysis and argument development might someday ethically *require*, not just permit, the use of a large language model in the prewriting stage").

develop the critical skills necessary to assess whether the generated text is accurate, comprehensive, and well-suited for the intended audience. The greatest challenge may be in determining whether such texts appropriately capture, in creative yet ethical ways, the nuances of the relevant law and its application to a set of facts.[66] Our proposed concepts may just help us isolate the nature of those critical skills.

Food for thought, indeed.

66. Kirsten K. Davis, Professor of Law, Stetson Law, *Breaking the Pedagogical Paradigm: Transformative Approaches to Legal Writing in an AI-Centric Future*, AI & Legal Skills Virtual Conference (June 3, 2025).

Bibliography

A

ADLER-KASSNER & LINDA & ELIZABETH WARDLE, NAMING WHAT WE KNOW (Linda Adler-Kassner & Elizabeth Wardle, eds., 2015).

ADLER-KASSNER, LINDA & ELIZABETH WARDLE, (RE)CONSIDERING WHAT WE KNOW (Linda Adler-Kassner & Elizabeth Wardle eds., 2019).

Akerlind, Gerlese, Jo McKenzie & Mandy Lupton, *A Threshold Concepts Focus To Curriculum Design: Supporting Student Learning Through Application of Variation Theory* (Australian Teaching and Learning Council, 2011).

ALDISERT, RUGGERO, LOGIC FOR LAWYERS: A GUIDE TO CLEAR LEGAL THINKING (3d ed. 2012).

ALTMAN, ANDREW, CRITICAL LEGAL STUDIES: A LIBERAL CRITIQUE (1990).

AM. BAR ASS'N, STANDARDS FOR APPROVAL OF LAW SCHOOLS (2024).

AMERICAN LIBRARY ASS'N, PRESIDENTIAL COMMITTEE ON INFORMATION LITERACY: FINAL REPORT (available at https://www.ala.org/acrl/publications/whitepapers/presidential).

Amin, Alia, *"A Trend or a Need" Threshold Concepts in Medicine and Surgery; A Qualitative Synthesis*, 18 J. MED. EDUC. 176 (2019).

AMSTERDAM, ANTHONY & JEROME BRUNER, MINDING THE LAW (2000).

ARISTOTLE, RHETORIC (c. 333 BCE), *reprinted in* THE RHETORIC OF ARISTOTLE (Lane Cooper, trans., 1932).

Armstrong, Ken, *Death by Deadline*, THE MARSHALL PROJECT, PART ONE (Nov. 15, 2014, 4:30 p.m. EST).

AsymaDesign, LLC v. CBL & Assocs. Mgt. Inc., 103 F.4th 1257 (7th Cir. 2024).

Atherton, Matthew Christopher & Yvonne Nalani Meulemans, *Threshold Concepts Theory as a Pedagogical Tool for Articulating Transformational Learning: An Initial Exploration*, J. TRANSFORMATIVE EDUC. 1 (2020).

Austin, Randy T., *Better Off with the Reasonable Man Dead or the Reasonable Man Did the Darndest Things*, 1992 B.Y.U. L. REV. 479.

B

Baillie, Caroline, John A. Bowden & Jan H.F. Meyer, *Threshold Capabilities: Threshold Concepts and Knowledge Capability Linked Through Variation Theory*, 65 HIGHER EDUC. 227 (2012).

Barnett, Daniel L., *Triage in the Trenches of the Legal Writing Course: The Theory and Methodology of Analytical Critique*, 38 UNIV. TOLEDO L. REV. 651 (2007).

Barradell, Sarah, *The Identification of Threshold Concepts: A Review of Theoretical Complexities and Methodological Challenges*, 65 HIGHER EDUC. 265 (2012).

Barradell, Sarah & Tracy Fortune, *Bounded—The Neglected Threshold Concept Characteristic*, 57 INNOVATIONS IN EDUC. AND TEACHING INT'L 296 (2020).

Barradell, Sarah & Tai Peseta, *Putting Threshold Concepts to Work in Health Sciences: Insights for Curriculum Design from a Critical Synthesis of Teaching and Learning Research*, 22 TEACHING IN HIGHER EDUC. 349 (2017).

Beazley, Mary Beth, *Hiding in Plain Sight: "Conspicuous Type" Standards in Mandated Communication Statutes*, 40 J. LEGIS. 1 (2014).

——. LEGAL WRITING FOR LEGAL READERS (2014).

BEAZLEY, MARY BETH & MONTE SMITH, LEGAL WRITING FOR LEGAL READERS (2014).

Beeler, Kent D., *Graduate Student Adjustment to Academic Life: A Four-Stage Framework*, 28 NASPA J. 163 (1991).

Berger, Linda L., *Applying New Rhetoric to Legal Discourse: The Ebb and Flow of Reader and Writer, Text and Context*, 49 J. LEGAL EDUC. 155 (1999).

——. *How Embedded Knowledge Structures Affect Judicial Decision Making: An Analysis of Metaphor, Narrative, and Imagination in Child Custody Disputes*, 18 S. Cal. Interdisc. L.J. 259 (2009).

Berger, Linda L. & Kathryn M. Stanchi, Legal Persuasion: A Rhetorical Approach To The Science (2018).

Berger, Linda L., Linda H. Edwards, & Terrill Pollman, *The Past, Presence, and Future of Legal Writing Scholarship: Rhetoric, Voice, and Community*, 16 Legal Writing: J. Legal Writing Inst. 521 (2010).

Berenguer, Elizabeth et al., Critical And Comparative Rhetoric: Unmaking Privilege And Power In Law And Legal Advocacy To Achieve, Truth, Justice, And Equity (2023).

Bitzer, Lloyd, *The Rhetorical Situation*, 1 Philosophy & Rhetoric 1 (1968).

Blasi, Gary L., *What Lawyers Know: Lawyering Expertise, Cognitive Science, and the Functions of Theory*, 45 J. Legal Educ. 313 (1995).

The Bluebook: A Uniform System of Citation (22d ed. 2025).

Blumenfeld, Barbara, *Rhetoric, Referential Communication, and the Novice Writer*, 9 Legal Comm. & Rhetoric 207 (2012).

Broadwell, Martin M., *Teaching for Learning*, 20 Gospel Guardian 1 (1969).

Brown, Megan E. L., Paul Whybrow & Gabrielle M. Finn, *Do We Need to Close the Door on Threshold Concepts?* 34 Teaching and Learning In Medicine 301 (2022).

Burton, Steven J., Introduction to Law and Legal Reasoning (2d ed. 1995).

Butterick, Matthew, Typography for Lawyers (2d ed. 2015).

C

Calduch, Isaac, *Reframing Threshold Concepts as Open Questions*, *in* In the Moment (Jason P. Davies et al. eds., 2024).

Campbell, John, *Ex Machina: Technological Disruption and the Future of Artificial Intelligence in Persuasive Legal Writing*, 5 Univ. Bologna L. Rev. 294 (2020).

Caster, Donald R. & Brian C. Howe, *Taking a Mulligan: The Special Challenge of Narrative Creation in the Post-Conviction Process*, 76 Md. L. Rev. 770 (2017).

Chestek, Kenneth D., *The Plot Thickens: The Appellate Brief as Story*, 14 Legal Writing: J. Legal Writing Inst. 127 (2007).

Chew, Alexa Z., *Citation Literacy*, 70 Ark. L. Rev. 869 (2018).

——. *Stylish Legal Citation*, 71 Ark. L. Rev. 823 (2019).

Christensen, Leah M., *The Paradox of Legal Expertise: A Study of Experts and Novices Reading the Law*, 2008 B.Y.U. Educ. & L.J. 53.

Citizens United v. Fed. Election Comm'n, 558 U.S. 310 (2010).

Clark, Jessica & Christy DeSanctis, *Toward A Unified Grading Vocabulary: Using Rubrics in Legal Writing Courses*, 63 J. Legal Educ. 3 (2013).

Clinical Educ. for the Health Professions (D. Nestel et al. eds., 2020).

Colo. R. App. Proc. 32.

Constable, Marianne, Our Word Is Our Bond: How Legal Speech Acts (2014).

Conti, Delia B., Linda L. Berger, Michael J. Cedrone, Mark A. Hannah, Melissa E. Love Koenig & Julie A. Oseid, Law And Rhetoric: A Primer (2023).

Cooke, Molly et al., Educating Physicians: A Call for Reform of Medical Sch. Residency (2010).

Cooper, Jennifer M., *The Science of Legal Synthesis*, 95 St. John's L. Rev. 285 (2021).

Corbett, Edward P.J. & Robert J. Connors, Classical Rhetoric For The Modern Student (4th ed. 1999).

Coughlin, Christine, Joan Malmud Rocklin & Sandy Patrick, A Lawyer Writes: A Practical Guide to Legal Analysis (4th ed. 2024).

Cousin, Glynis, *An Introduction to Threshold Concepts*, 17 Planet 4 (2006).

Cruess, Richard L. et al., *Reframing Medical Education to Support Professional Identity Formation*, 89 Acad. Med. 1446 (2014).

Cullen, Donna, *Threshold Concepts & Troublesome Knowledge in Curriculum Design*, Principles in Patterns Project Report 2 (2010).

Culver, Leslie P., *(Un)wicked Analytical Frameworks and the Cry for Identity*, 21 NEV. L.J. 555 (2021).

Cummins, Daniel E., *A Portrait of the Lawyer as an Artist*, 30 PA. LAW. 26 (2008).

D

DAMASIO, ANTONIO R., DESCARTES' ERROR: EMOTION, REASON, AND THE HUMAN BRAIN (1994).

Davies, Peter & Jean Mangan, *Recognising Threshold Concepts: An Exploration of Different Approaches* (unpublished paper), https://www.researchgate.net/publication/228377119_Recognising_Threshold_Concepts_an_exploration_of_different_approaches (last accessed July 27, 2025).

Davis, Kirsten K., *Building Credibility in the Margins: An Ethos-Based Perspective for Commenting on Student Papers*, 12 LEGAL WRITING: J. LEGAL WRITING INST. 73 (2006).

——. *A New Parlor Is Open: Legal Writing Faculty Must Develop Scholarship on Generative AI and Legal Writing*, 7 UNENDING CONV. 1 (2024).

——. *A Provisional Definition of "Legal Writing Scholarship*, 2 PROCEEDINGS 6 (2021).

Decosimo, Harmony, *A Taxonomy of Professional Identity Formation*, 67 ST. LOUIS U. L.J. 1 (2022).

DeSanctis, Christy, *Narrative Reasoning and Analogy: The Untold Story*, 9 LEGAL COMM. & RHETORIC 149 (2012).

DESANCTIS, CHRISTY & MICHAEL MURRAY, LEGAL WRITING AND ANALYSIS (3d ed. 2021).

Downs, Doug, *"Time Is a Threshold Concept in Writing": Expanding Access to Undergraduate Research by Mentoring for Threshold Concepts and Self-Concept*, 84:6 COLLEGE ENGLISH 613 (2022).

Durako, Jo Anne, *Second-Class Citizens in the Pink Ghetto: Gender Bias in Legal Writing*, 50 J. LEGAL EDUC. 562 (2000).

E

Easterbrook, Frank H., Judge for the U.S. Court of Appeals for the Seventh Circuit, *Challenges in Reading Statutes* (Sept. 28, 2007).

EDWARDS, LINDA H., LEGAL WRITING: PROCESS, ANALYSIS, AND ORGANIZATION (3d ed. 2002).

Elbow, Peter, *Appendix Essay*, WRITING WITHOUT TEACHERS (1973).

Enquist, Anne, *Critiquing and Evaluating Law Students' Writing: Advice from Thirty-Five Experts*, 22 SEATTLE UNIV. L. REV. 1119 (1999).

F

Fajans, Molly and Mary Falk, *Against the Tyranny of Paraphrase: Talking Back to Legal Texts*, 78 CORNELL L. REV. 163 (1993).

Fajer, Marc A., *Authority, Credibility, and Pre-Understanding: A Defense of Outsider Narratives in Legal Scholarship*, 82 GEO. L.J. 1845 (1994).

Farrell, Laura M. et al., *Thresholds of Becoming: An Exploration of Threshold Concepts as a Means to Support Professional Identity Formation in CompetencyBased Curricula*, 29 ADVANCES IN HEALTH SCIENCES EDUC.: THEORY & PRAC. 349 (2024).

FED. R. CIV. P.

Felsenburg, Miriam E. & Laura P. Graham, *Beginning Legal Writers in Their Own Words: Why the First Weeks of Legal Writing Are So Tough and What We Can Do About It*, 16 J. LEGAL WRITING 223 (2010).

FEMINIST JUDGMENTS: FROM THEORY TO PRACTICE (Rosemary Hunter, Clare McGlynn & Erika Rackley eds., 2010).

FEMINIST JUDGMENTS: REWRITTEN OPINIONS OF THE UNITED STATES SUPREME COURT (Kathryn M. Stanchi, Linda L. Berger, & Bridget J. Crawford eds., 2016).

FEY, TINA, BOSSYPANTS (2011).

Fischer, Judith D., *Bareheaded and Barefaced Counsel: Courts React to Unprofessionalism in Lawyers' Papers*, 31 SUFFOLK U. L. REV. 1 (1997).

FLA. R. OF APP. PROC. (2024).

FLETCHER, JENNIFER, TEACHING ARGUMENTS: RHETORICAL COMPREHENSION, CRITIQUE, AND RESPONSE (2015).

Floyd, Daisy Hurst, *Practical Wisdom: Reimagining Legal Education*, 10 UNIV. ST. THOMAS L. J. 195 (2012).

Floyd, Timothy W. & Kendall L. Kerew, *Marking the Path from Law Student to Lawyer: Using Field Placement Courses to Facilitate the Deliberate Exploration of Professional Identity and Purpose*, 68 MERCER L. REV. 767 (2017).

FOUCAULT, MICHEL, THE HISTORY OF SEXUALITY: AN INTRODUCTION (1978).

——. POWER/KNOWLEDGE: SELECTED INTERVIEWS AND OTHER WRITINGS 1972–77 (Colin Gordon ed., Colin Gordon et al. trans., 1980).

Franklin, Kris, *". . . . See Erie.": Critical Study of Legal Authority*, 31 U. ARK. LITTLE ROCK L. REV. 109 (2008).

Fredholm, Angelica et al., *The Practice of Thresholds: Autonomy in Clinical Education Explored Through Variation Theory and the Threshold Concepts Framework*, 25 TEACHING IN HIGHER EDUC. 305 (2019).

G

GARDNER, JAMES A. & CHRISTINE P. BARTHOLOMEW, LEGAL ARGUMENT: THE STRUCTURE OF LEGAL ARGUMENT AND ADVOCACY (3d ed. 2020).

Garner, Bryan A., *The Aesthetics of Your Pages*, *in* GARNER ON LANGUAGE AND WRITING (2009).

——. THE ELEMENTS OF LEGAL STYLE (2d ed. 2002).

——. *Know Thy Reader: Writing For The Legal Audience*, 98 MICH. B.J. 46 (Nov. 2019).

Gilman, Michele, *The Future of Clinical Legal Scholarship*, 26 CLINICAL L. REV. 189 (2019).

Gionfriddo, Jane Kent, *Dangerous! Our Focus Should Be Analysis, Not Formulas Like IRAC*, 10:1 SECOND DRAFT 2 (1995).

——. *The "Reasonable Zone of Right Answers": Analytical Feedback on Student Writing*, 40:3 GONZAGA L. REV. 427 (2004/5).

——. *Thinking Like a Lawyer: The Heuristics of Case Synthesis*, 40 TEX. TECH L. REV. 1 (2007).

Greenhaw, Leigh Hunt, *"To Say What the Law Is": Learning the Practice of Legal Rhetoric*, 29 VAL. U. L. REV. 861 (1995).

H

Hamilton, Neil, *The Gap Between the Foundational Competencies Clients and Legal Employers Need and the Learning Outcomes Law Schools Are Adopting*, 89 UMKC L. Rev. 559 (2021).

——. *The Major Transitions in Professional Formation and Development from Being A Student to Being A Lawyer Present Opportunities to Benefit the Students and the Law School*, 73 Baylor L. Rev. 139 (2021).

——. *The Next Steps of A Formation-of-Student-Professional Identity Social Movement: Building Bridges Among the Three Key Stakeholders—Faculty and Staff, Students, and Legal Employers and Clients*, 14 U. St. Thomas L.J. 285 (2018).

Hamilton, Neil W. & Louis D. Bilionis, Law Student Professional Development and Formation: Bridging Law School, Student, and Employer Goals (2022).

Hand, Learned, *Book Review*, 35 Harv. L. Rev. 479 (1922).

Hedges, Mary, *Embedding Threshold Concepts: The Use of a Practice – Theory—Practice Cycle*, 19 Waikato J. Educ. 83 (2014).

Higdon, Michael J., *The Legal Reader: An Exposé*, 43 N.M. L. Rev. 77 (2013).

Holloran Center for Ethical Leadership in the Professions, What Is a Law Student's Professional Identity and What Is Professional Identity Formation?A Short Introduction (2022), https://law.stthomas.edu/_media-library/documents/holloran-center/professional-identity-definition1.pdf.

Hunter, Dan, *No Wilderness of Single Instances: Inductive Inference in Law*, 48 J. Legal Educ. 365 (1998).

Huxley-Binns, Rebecca, *Tripping over Thresholds: A Reflection on Legal Andragogy*, 50:1 Law Teacher 1 (2016).

I

Improving Student Learning: Diversity And Inclusivity (Chris Rust ed., Oxford Centre for Staff & Learning Dev. 2005).

J

Jewel, Lucy, *Does the Reasonable Man Have Obsessive Compulsive Disorder?* 54 Wake Forest L. Rev. 1049 (2019).

Jones, Helen & Lucy Hammond, *Threshold Concepts in Medical Education: A Scoping Review*, 56 MED. EDUC. 983 (2022).

Jones, Ruth, *Assessment and Legal Education: What Is Assessment, and What the # Does It Have to Do with the Challenges Facing Legal Education?*, 45 MCGEORGE L. REV. 86 (2014).

Joy, Peter A., *Challenges to Legal Education, Clinical Legal Education, and Clinical Scholarship*, 26 CLINICAL L. REV. 237 (2019).

K

KAHNEMAN, DANIEL, THINKING, FAST AND SLOW (2011).

Kahneman, Daniel & Gary Klein, *Conditions for Intuitive Expertise: A Failure to Disagree*, 64 AM. PSYCHOLOGIST 515 (2009).

Kamler, Barbara & Pat Thomson, *The Failure of Dissertation Advice Books: Toward Alternative Pedagogies for Doctoral Writing*, 37 EDUC. RESEARCHER 507 (2008).

Kandel, Eric, *The New Science of Mind and the Future of Knowledge*, 80 NEURON 546 (2013).

Katz, Martin J., *Teaching Professional Identity in Law School*, 42 COLO. LAW. 45 (2013).

KEY DIRECTIONS IN LEGAL EDUCATION: NATIONAL AND INTERNATIONAL PERSPECTIVES (Emma Jones & Fiona Cownie eds., 2020).

Kiernan-Johnson, Derek, *Telling Through Type: Typography and Narrative in Legal Briefs*, 7 J. ALWD 87 (2010).

Kierstead, Shelley & Erika Abner, *Text Work As Identity Work for Legal Writers: How Writing Texts Contribute to the Construction of A Professional Identity*, 9 LEGAL COMM. & RHETORIC 327 (2012).

Kim, Kangmoon & Young-Mee Lee, *Understanding Uncertainty in Medicine: Concepts and Implications in Medical Education*, 30:3 KOREAN J. MED. EDUC. 181 (2018).

KLEIN, GARY A., SOURCES OF POWER: HOW PEOPLE MAKE DECISIONS (1999).

Klinger, Geoffrey D., *Law as Communicative Praxis: Toward a Rhetorical Jurisprudence*, 30 ARGUMENTATION & ADVOC. 236 (1994).

Koehlert-Page, Cathren, *Stranger Than Fiction: How Lawyers Can Accurately and Realistically Tell a True Story by Using Fiction Writers' Techniques that Make Fiction Seem More Realistic than Reality*, 78 LA. L. REV. 907 (2018).

Kraft, Diane, *CREAC in the Real World*, 63 CLEV. ST. L. REV. 567 (2015).

Kruse, Katherine R., *Clinical Scholarship and Scholarship by Clinicians*, 26 CLINICAL L. REV. 307 (2019).

L

Lacey, Denise Platfoot, *Do All Roads Lead to Rome? Effectively Using Asynchronous Online Reflective Practice in an Externship Course*, 89 UMKC L. REV. 609 (2021).

Liemer, Susan P. & Hollee S. Temple, *Did Your Legal Writing Professor Go to Harvard? The Credentials of Legal Writing Faculty At Hiring Time*, 46 U. LOUISVILLE L. REV. 383 (2008).

Liljedahl, Matilda, Per J. Palmgren, & Cormac McGrath, *Threshold Concepts in Health Professions Education Research: A Scoping Review*, 27 ADVANCES IN HEALTH SCIENCES EDUC. 1457 (2022).

Litowitz, Douglas, *Legal Writing: Its Nature, Limits, and Dangers*, 49 MERCER L. REV. 709 (1998).

Longan, Patrick Emery, Daisy Hurst Floyd & Timothy Floyd, *A Virtue Ethics Approach to Professional Identity: Lessons for the First Year and Beyond*, 89 UMKC L. REV. 645 (2021).

M

Maclean, Rod, *First-year Law Students' Construction of Professional Identity Through Writing*, 12 DISCOURSE STUD. 177 (2010).

Margolis, Ellie, *Is the Medium the Message?* 12 LEGAL COMM. & RHETORIC 1 (2015).

McMahon, Susan, *What We Teach When We Teach Legal Analysis*, 107 MINN. L. REV. 2511 (2023).

McMurtry-Chubb, Teri A., *Writing at The Master's Table: Reflections on Theft, Criminality, and Otherness in the Legal Writing Profession*, 2 DREXEL L. REV. 41 (2009).

MERTZ, ELIZABETH, THE LANGUAGE OF LAW SCHOOL: LEARNING TO "THINK LIKE A LAWYER" (2007).

Meyer, Jan H.F., *Threshold Concepts and Pedagogic Representation*, 58 EDUC. + TRAINING 463 (2016).

Meyer, Jan H.F. & Ray Land, *Threshold Concepts and Troublesome Knowledge (2): Epistemological Considerations and a Conceptual Framework for Teaching and Learning*, 49 HIGHER EDUC. 373 (2005).

MEZIROW, J., LEARNING AS TRANSFORMATION: CRITICAL PERSPECTIVES ON A THEORY IN PROGRESS (2000).

MODEL CODE OF JUD. CONDUCT (2025).

MODEL RULES OF PROF. CONDUCT (2025).

Monahan, Marie A., *Towards a Theory of Assimilating Law Students into the Culture of the Legal Profession*, 51 CATH. U. L. REV. 215 (2001).

Montana, Patricia Grande, *Live and Learn: Live Critiquing and Student Learning*, 27:1 PERSP: TEACHING LEGAL RES. & WRITING 22 (2019).

Moström, Jan Erik et al., *Computer Science Student Transformations: Changes and Causes*, 41:3 ACM SIGCSE BULL. 181 (2009).

N

NEUMANN, RICHARD K., LEGAL REASONING AND LEGAL WRITING: STRUCTURE, STRATEGY, & STYLE (2009).

Nicola-Richmond, Kelli et al., *Threshold Concepts in Higher Education: A Synthesis of the Literature Relating to Measurement of Threshold Crossing*, 37 HIGHER EDUC. RSCH. & DEV. 101 (2010).

Niedwicki, Anthony, *Teaching for Lifelong Learning: Improving the Metacognitive Skills of Law Students Through More Effective Formative Assessment Techniques*, 40 CAP. L. REV. 149 (2012).

O

O'Donnell, Rod, *A Critique of Threshold Concepts Hypothesis and an Application in Economics*, (working paper 164 (2010), https://ideas.repec.org/p/uts/wpaper/164.html.

OVERCOMING BARRIERS TO STUDENT UNDERSTANDING: THRESHOLD CONCEPTS AND TROUBLESOME KNOWLEDGE (Jan H.F. Meyer & Ray Land eds., 2006).

P

Paskey, Stephen, *The Law is Made of Stories: Erasing the False Dichotomy Between Stories and Legal Rules*, 11 LEGAL COMM. & RHETORIC 51 (2014).

Pearse, Noel, *An Illustration of Teaching and Assessment Practices of the "Conceptual Framework" as a Threshold Concept*, 20 ELEC. J. BUS. RSCH. METHODS 122 (2022).

Phelps, Teresa Godwin, *The New Legal Rhetoric*, 40 SW. L.J. 1089 (1986).

Phelps, Teresa & Kevin Ashley, *"Alexa, Write a Memo": The Promises and Challenges of AI and Legal Writing*, 26 LEGAL WRITING: J. LEGAL WRITING INST. 329 (2022).

Pierce, George W., *The Legal Profession*, 30 THE TORCH 5 (1957).

Pitsoe, Victor & Moeketsi Letseka, *Foucault's Discourse and Power: Implications for Instructionist Classroom Management*, 3 OPEN J. PHIL. 23 (2013).

PLATO, GORGIAS, *in* COMPLETE WORKS (John M. Cooper & D.S. Hutchinson eds., Hackett Publ'g Co. 1997) (c. 380 BCE).

Pollman, Terrill, *Building a Tower of Babel or Building a Discipline? Talking About Legal Writing*, 85 MARQ. L. REV. 887 (2002).

——. *The Sincerest Form of Flattery: Examples and Model-Based Learning in the Classroom*, 64 J. LEGAL. EDUC. 298 (2014).

Precision Specialty Metals, Inc. v. United States, 315 F.3d 1346 (Fed. Cir. 2003).

Pryal, Katie Rose Guest, *The Genre Discovery Approach: Preparing Law Students to Write Any Legal Document*, 59 WAYNE L. REV. 351 (2013).

——. *Genre Discovery 2.0*, 28 BARRY L. REV. 1 (2023).

Puerto Rico Soccer League NFP, Corp. v. Federación Puertorriqueña De Futbol, No. 23-1203 (RAM), 2025 WL 1080732 (Apr. 10, 2025).

R

Randall, Virginia et al., *Threshold Concepts in Medical Education*, 7 MEDEDPUBLISH 3 (2021).

Rasch, David A. & Meehan Rasch, *Overcoming Writer's Block and Procrastination for Attorneys, Law Students, and Law Professors*, 43 N.M. L. REV. 193 (2013).

Reeves, Jay, *Missed Deadlines Top 2021 Malpractice Claims*, BYTE OF PREVENTION (May 23, 2022).

Regalia, Joe, *From Briefs to Bytes: How Generative AI is Transforming Legal Writing and Practice*, 59 TULSA L. REV. 193 (2024).

Reuter, Margaret, *Professional Identity in A Time of Uncertainty: Not A Moment Too Soon*, 89 UMKC L. REV. 487 (2021).

Rideout, J. Christopher, *Applied Legal Storytelling: An Updated Bibliography*, 18 LEGAL COMM. & RHETORIC 221 (2020).

——. *Discipline-Building and Disciplinary Values: Thoughts on Legal Writing at Year Twenty-Five of the Legal Writing Institute*, 16 LEGAL WRITING: J. LEGAL WRITING INST. 477 (2010).

——. *Knowing What We Already Know: On the Doctrine of Legal Writing*, 1 SAVANNAH L. REV. 103 (2014).

——. *A Twice-Told Tale: Plausibility and Narrative Coherence in Judicial Storytelling*, 10 LEGAL COMM. & RHETORIC 67 (2013).

Rideout, J. Christopher & Jill J. Ramsfield, *Legal Writing: A Revised View*, 69 WASH. L. REV. 35 (1994).

——. *Legal Writing: The View from Within*, 60 MERCER L. REV. 705 (2010).

Robbins, Ruth Anne, *An Introduction to Applied Legal Storytelling and to this Symposium*, 14 LEGAL WRITING: J. LEGAL WRITING INST. 3 (2008).

——. *Painting with Print: Incorporating Concepts of Typographic and Layout Design into the Text of Legal Writing Documents*, 2 J.AWLD 108 (2004).

ROBBINS, RUTH ANNE, STEVEN JOHANSEN & KENNETH CHESTEK, YOUR CLIENT'S STORY: PERSUASIVE LEGAL WRITING (3d ed. 2024).

Robinson, W. L., *Conscious Competency—The Mark of a Competent Instructor*, 53 PERSONNEL JOURNAL—BALTIMORE 538 (1974).

ROCKLIN, JOAN M. ET AL., AN ADVOCATE PERSUADES (2022).

Ross, Julie & Diana Donahoe, *Lighting the Fires of Learning in Law School: Implementing ABA Standard 314 by Incorporating Effective Formative Assessment Techniques Across the Curriculum*, 81 U. PITT. L. REV. 657 (2020).

Rowbottom, Darrell Patrick, *Demystifying Threshold Concepts*, 41 J. PHIL. EDUC. 263 (2007).

Ruschill, Olivia, *Creative, Vulnerable and Bold: Learning the Art of Good Legal Writing*, 91 J. KAN. BAR ASS'N 14 (2022).

S

Salwén, Håkan, *Threshold Concepts, Obstacles or Scientific Dead Ends?* 26 TEACHING IN HIGHER EDUC. 36 (2021).

Saunders, Kurt M., *Law as Rhetoric, Rhetoric as Argument*, 44 J. LEGAL EDUC. 566 (1994).

Scarcella, Mike, *Lawyer's 'Twilight Zone' Font Irks US Appeals Court in Typeface Takedown*, REUTERS (June 4, 2024).

Schiess, Wayne, *Ethical Legal Writing*, 21 REV. LITIG. 527 (2002).

SCHLAG, PIERRE & AMY J. GRIFFIN, HOW TO DO THINGS WITH LEGAL DOCTRINE (2020).

Schnee, Anita, *Legal Reasoning "Obviously,"*, 3 LEGAL WRITING: J. LEGAL WRITING INST. 105 (1997).

Schwartz, Louis B., *With Gun and Camera Through Darkest CLS-Land*, 36 STAN. L. REV. 413 (1990).

Seidelson, David E., *Reasonable Expectations and Subjective Standards in Negligence Law: The Minor, the Mentally Impaired, and the Mentally Incompetent*, 50 GEO. WASH. L. REV. 17 (1981).

Sholtis, Amanda L., *Say What? A How-To Guide On Providing Formative Assessment To Law Students Through Live Critique*, 49 STETSON L. REV. 1 (2019).

SLOAN, AMY, BASIC LEGAL RESEARCH: TOOLS AND STRATEGIES (6th ed. 2015).

SMITH, MICHAEL R., ADVANCED LEGAL WRITING: THEORIES AND STRATEGIES IN PERSUASIVE WRITING (3d ed. 2013).

Sparrow, Sophie M., *Describing the Ball: Improve Teaching by Using Rubrics-Explicit Grading Criteria*, 2004 MICH. ST. L. REV. 1.

Springfield, Liz et al., *Threshold Concepts and Authentic Assessment: Learning to Think Like an Occupational Therapist*, 12 PRAC. & EVIDENCE OF SCHOLARSHIP OF TEACHING & LEARNING IN HIGHER EDUC. 125 (2017).

Steel, Alex, *Succeed, Question, Repeat: Threshold Concepts and Variation Theory in Understanding How Law Students Build Competency*, 53:3 LAW TEACHER 231 (2019).

Steel, Alex et al., *Critical Legal Reading: The Elements, Strategies and Dispositions Needed to Master this Essential Skill*, 26:1 LEGAL EDUC. REVIEW 187 (2017).

Steel, Genevieve Frances, *Constructing the Trident of the Reasonable Person: Enough Is Enough! It's Time for The Reasonable Indian Standard*, 12 ELON L. REV. 62 (2020).

Stephens, Georgina C., Mahbub Sarkar, & Michelle D. Lazarus, *'I Was Uncertain, but I Was Acting on It': A Longitudinal Qualitative Study of Medical Students' Responses to Uncertainty*, MED. EDUC. 1 (2023).

SULLIVAN, WILLIAM M. ET AL., EDUCATING LAWYERS: PREPARATION FOR THE PRACTICE OF LAW (The Carnegie Found. for the Advancement of Teaching, 2007).

T

TEACHING MEDICAL PROFESSIONALISM (Richard Creuss et al. eds., 2d ed. 2016).

Testy, Kellye Y. & Zachariah J. DeMeola, *Leading the Way: The Power of Professional Identity Formation for Lawyers*, 76 BAYLOR L. REV. 115 (2024).

Thomson, David I. C., *Symposium Introduction: Interrogating the Hidden Curriculum: Implications for Formation of Professional Identity*, 2 J. L. TEACHING & LEARNING 1 (2025).

THRESHOLD CONCEPTS & TRANSFORMATIONAL LEARNING (Ray Land, Jan H.F. Meyer & Caroline Baillie eds., 2010).

THRESHOLD CONCEPTS IN THE MOMENT (Jason P. Davies et al. eds., 2024).

Tiaglo, O. V., *Logic of Legal Reasoning*, 2022:2 ANALYTICAL AND COMPARATIVE JURISPRUDENCE 349 (2022).

TINDALE, CHRISTOPHER W., PRINCIPLES OF THEORY AND PRACTICE (2004).

Tiscione, Kristen K. & Amy Vorenberg, *Podia and Pens: Dismantling the Two-Track System for Legal Research and Writing Faculty*, 31 COLUM. J. GENDER & L. 47 (2015).

Tiscione, Kristen K. & Melissa H. Weresh, *Legal [Writing] Scholarship: Why It Counts*, 6:3 UNENDING CONVERSATION LEGAL WRITING SCHOLARSHIP 1 (2023).

TODOROV, TZVETAN, GENRES IN DISCOURSE (Catherine Porter trans., 1990).

Tracey, Monica W. & Alisa Hutchinson, *Uncertainty, Agency and Motivation in Graduate Design Students*, 29 THINKING SKILLS & CREATIVITY 196 (2018).

——. *Uncertainty, Reflection, and Designer Identity Development*, 42 DESIGN STUD. 86 (2016).

Tu, S. Sean, Amy Cyphert & Samuel J. Perl, *Artificial Intelligence: Legal Reasoning, Legal Research and Legal Writing*, 25 MINN. J. L. SCI & TECH. 106 (2024).

Tucker, Virginia M., *Becoming an Information Architect: The Evolving Librarian's Skillset, Mindset, and Professional Identity*, 37 EDUC. FOR INFO. 485 (2021).

Tucker, Virginia M. & Michelle Holschuh Simmons, *Identity Transformation on Becoming a Teacher: Threshold Concepts and Professional Praxes*, 10 J. TCHR. EDUC. AND EDUCATORS 275 (2021).

U

United States v. Hayes, No. 2:24-cr-0280-DJC, 2025 WL 235531 (D.C. Cal. Jan. 17, 2025).

U.S. SUP. CT. RULE 33.

V

Vatz, Richard, *The Myth of the Rhetorical Situation*, 6 PHIL. & RHETORIC 154 (1973).

Venter, Christine M., *Analyze This: Using Taxonomies to "Scaffold" Students' Legal Thinking and Writing Skills*, 57 MERCER L. REV. 621 (2006).

W

Wald, Eli, *Formation Without Identity: Avoiding A Wrong Turn in the Professionalism Movement*, 89 UMKC L. REV. 685 (2021).

Wanderer, Nancy A., *Legal Writing and Creativity: Polar Opposites or Perfect Partners?* 35 ME. BAR J. 80 (2020).

WEEDON, CHRIS, FEMINIST PRACTICE & POSTSTRUCTURALIST THEORY (2d ed. 1996).

Wellford-Slocum, Robin S., *The Law School Student-Faculty Conference: Towards a Transformative Learning Experience*, 45 SOUTH TEX. L. REV. 255 (2004).

Weresh, Melissa H., *Stargate: Malleability as a Threshold Concept in Legal Education*, 63 J. LEGAL EDUC. 689 (2014).

Wetlaufer, Gerald, *Rhetoric and Its Denial in Legal Discourse*, 76 VA. L. REV. 1545 (1990).

WHITE, JAMES BOYD, WHEN WORDS LOSE THEIR MEANING: CONSTITUTIONS AND RECONSTITUTIONS OF LANGUAGE, CHARACTER, AND COMMUNITY (1984).

——. *Law as Rhetoric, Rhetoric as Law: The Arts of Cultural and Communal Life*, 52 UNIV. CHICAGO L. REV. 684 (1985).

——. *Legal Knowledge*, 115 HARV. L. REV. 1396 (2002).

WILLIAMS, CAROLYN V., THE ALWD GUIDE TO LEGAL CITATION (2021).

Williams, Joseph, *On the Maturing of Legal Writers*, 1 LEGAL WRITING: J. LEGAL WRITING INST. 1 (1991).

WILLIAMS, PATRICIA J., THE ALCHEMY OF RACE AND RIGHTS: DIARY OF A LAW PROFESSOR (1991).

Wilson, Anna et al., *Measurement Uncertainty as a Threshold Concept in Physics* (paper presentation at the 16th UniServe Annual Conference, 2010).

Y

Yin, Kenneth & Carmela De Maio, *Transformative, Troublesome and Liminal: Does The Presentation of Legal Reasoning in the Legal Studies Curricula in Higher Education Institutions Satisfy the Characteristics of a Threshold Concept?* 57:1 LAW TEACHER 1 (2023).

APPENDIX

Skills Typically Taught in the Spring Semester of a First-Year Legal Writing Course

Skill	Writing Assignment	Core Concepts	Threshold Concepts
Persuasive versus predictive analysis	Brief or memorandum in support of a motion	The difference between persuasion and predictive analysis, based on purpose, audience, and stance	**Threshold Concept 1.2** (the foundational role of legal writers is to construct arguments about the meaning of language) **Threshold Concept 2.1** (legal writers know they engage in a rhetorical practice even though the law tends to deny its rhetorical nature) **Threshold Concept 2.8** (legal writers recognize and employ different genres of writing based on the writers' goals)
Learning to tell the client's story in statements of fact and in legal argument		The elements of story, as well as inferential and narrative reasoning; the theory of the case	**Threshold Concept 1.5** (facts in law are determined by an adjudicator) **Threshold Concept 1.6** (legal writing involves a blend of rules and storytelling) **Threshold Concept 2.3** (legal writers must gather both fact and law)

continues

continued

Skill	Writing Assignment	Core Concepts	Threshold Concepts
Revisit rule synthesis and framing rules from the client's perspective		Primary versus secondary sources of authority, mandatory and binding authorities, the structure of federal and state courts, the hierarchy of authority, stare decisis, and common law analysis	**Threshold Concept 1.3** (legal writers understand the malleability of law} **Threshold Concept 1.4** (legal writers understand that "framing" is necessary to open the door to legal remedies) **Threshold Concept 2.4** (legal writers have a flexible understanding of sources of authority) **Threshold Concept 2.5** (legal writers construct rules of law for specific contexts) **Threshold Concept 3.2** (precedent both guides and restrains legal writers) **Threshold Concept 3.5** (legal writers must become comfortable with uncertainty) **Threshold Concept 3.7** (legal writers form their professional identity through writing)
Revisit rule application in more complicated contexts using a variety of argument types (text, intent, precedent, policy, and tradition)		Applying a synthesized rule to client facts to predict outcome on a given legal issue in a logical and convincing manner; various ways to structure different types of arguments and counterarguments	**Threshold Concept 2.6** (legal writers use deductive reasoning to reach convincing yet probable conclusions) **Threshold Concept 2.7** (legal writers use analogy to make their case for validity)
Revisit citing rules of law in support of assertions		Perhaps more emphasis on use of signals and explanatory parentheticals	**Threshold Concept 2.8** (legal citations are concise arguments that serve as proxies for proof and professionalism)
Revisit rewriting, revising, and polishing		The various stages of the writing process, the difference between first and final drafts, strategies for all phases of the post-writing process	**Threshold Concept 2.10** (legal writing requires typographic judgment) **Threshold Concept 3.3** (legal writers understand that legal writing takes time and is a recursive and reflective process) **Threshold Concept 3.7** (legal writers form their professional identity through writing)

Index

C

D

E

N

O

P

Q

R